# Successful
## Inclusion Strategies
### for Secondary and Middle
### School Teachers

# Successful
# Inclusion Strategies
## for Secondary and Middle
## School Teachers
### Keys to Help Struggling Learners
### Access the Curriculum

## M.C. GORE

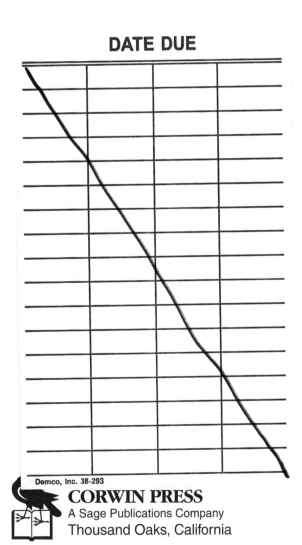

DATE DUE

Demco, Inc. 38-293

**CORWIN PRESS**
A Sage Publications Company
Thousand Oaks, California

*For information:*

Corwin Press
A Sage Publications Company
2455 Teller Road
Thousand Oaks, CA 91320
www.corwinpress.com

Sage Publications Ltd.
6 Bonhill Street
London EC2A 4PU
United Kingdom

Sage Publications India Pvt. Ltd.
B-42, Panchsheel Enclave
Post Box 4109
New Delhi 110 017  India

Printed in the United States of America

**Library of Congress Cataloging-in-Publication Data**

Gore, M. C.
Successful inclusion strategies for secondary and middle school teachers : keys to help struggling learners access the curriculum / by M.C. Gore.
      p.  cm.
Includes bibliographical references and index.
ISBN 0-7619-3972-5 (cloth) — ISBN 0-7619-3973-3 (pbk.)
   1.  Children with disabilities—Education (Secondary)—United States.
2.  Inclusive education—United States.  I. Title.
LC4031.G64 2004
371.95'2--dc21

                                        2003014659

This book is printed on acid-free paper.

   04   05   06   07   7   6   5   4   3   2

| | |
| --- | --- |
| *Acquisitions Editor:* | Robert D. Clouse |
| *Editorial Assistant:* | Jingle Vea |
| *Production Editor:* | Julia Parnell |
| *Copy Editor:* | Eugenia Orlandi |
| *Proofreader* | Colleen Brennan |
| *Typesetter:* | C&M Digitals (P) Ltd. |
| *Indexer:* | Will Ragsdale |
| *Cover Designer:* | Michale Dubowe |
| *Production Artist:* | Lisa Miller |

**Illustrations by Courts Griner**

# Contents

# Preface

In the fifteen years I spent teaching sixth grade through twelfth grade students who had learning problems, I learned many things, among them: middle and secondary school teachers love their disciplines. Their disciplines hold precious gems for them, rare and exquisite. They hunger to share the beauty with their students. When, in the vernacular, students "blow them off" with a sneer, arms folded across the chest, and eyes glazing over, content specialist teachers die a little inside.

I have listened to their laments in the teachers' lounge, not griping about students, but wondering how to reach the reluctant learner. In the thousands of hours I spent with my friend, Dr. Rosemary Grant of Monett, Missouri, the finest high school teacher I have ever known, I came to sense the fire in her breast to make every student love history and humanities as she does. I came to feel her despair when a student seemed apathetic about the things to which she cleaves so dearly: democracy, freedom, rigorous intellectual inquiry, and intellectual integrity.

As a special education teacher, I desperately wanted to help. We knew how to work with students with special needs in the special education classroom in those years, but we did not know much about good inclusion strategies then. We now have powerful research to guide us in including the learner with special needs in the general education classroom. But as Mastropieri and Scruggs (1994) wrote, "It is commonly agreed by educators that findings from experimental research are of little value unless it is shown how such findings can be adapted and implemented in actual classroom practice . . . " How true. That is why I deigned to write this book: to help practitioners access what the research tells us about teaching students with disabilities in middle school and secondary school classrooms.

Many inclusion books for elementary teachers are on the market, but those books do not satisfy the needs of middle and secondary school teachers. I wanted that overlooked population to have a quick resource of research-supported strategies or those showing great promise that they could keep on the desk and reach for when needed. I wanted it to be a book of strategies that I or my students had field tested and found teacher-friendly. That was the sort of book I had ached for when I was still in public schools. The practitioners who reviewed the initial draft of this book for Corwin Press indicated that this, too, was the sort of book they wanted. I am greatly encouraged.

From this point onward, I will write in the first person plural representing, in addition to myself, the thoughts and feelings of the many special education teacher-researchers whose work led us to the findings I report, my students who have used and enjoyed these strategies in their fieldwork, and their teacher friends who have embraced the strategies as well.

May this book provide the keys that you need to help all of your students unlock the doors to learning, so you can invite them in, introduce them to the jewels of your discipline, and help them develop the tools they need to turn rough gems into beautiful rings and tiaras.

# Acknowledgments

Thank you to all of my wonderful students, especially my undergraduates Sharon Devereaux, Jessica Dunn, Amy Jarvis, Kourtney Jones, and Margory Smith; you keep me inspired by your fresh, young enthusiasm for every inclusion strategy you learn. You are making the journey from raw diamonds into a one million dollar tiara, and I love being along for the ride.

Thank you, too, to my graduate students, diamond tiaras all, who try out new strategies and change the world one youngster at a time.

Thank you to my darling Don, who always greets me with a smile and a hug, and who lives alone whenever I work on a book. I love you best of the world's six billion people.

Thank you to Wee Mum and Pop Lancaster, for your unfailing belief in me.

Thank you to my beloved colleagues in the Midwestern State University Gordon T. and Helen West College of Education. I love the life we share together and the future we believe we can help create for all children.

Thank you, too, to my dear friend Elizabeth Lewandowski, who always knows the right time to call or show up with a pot of soup.

**Corwin Press would like to acknowledge the contributions of the following reviewers:**

Joe Bellanti
Director of Special Education
Shelby County Schools
Bartlett, TN

Dr. Robin Barton
Secondary Transition Specialist
Virginia Department of Education
Richmond, VA

Laura Cumbee
Teacher
South Central Middle School
Emerson, GA

Joyce Dresser
SPED Teacher
West Tisburry School
West Tisburry, MA

Rober Krajewski
Professor
Department of Foundations of Educational Policy & Practice
University of Wisconsin – Lacrosse
Lacrosse, WI

Gayle Y. Thieman
Portland State University Graduate School of Education
Department of Educational Policy, Foundations, and Administrative Studies
Portland, OR

# About the Author

**Dr. M. C. (Millie) Gore** is Chair of the Special Education Department of the Gordon T. and Helen West College of Education at Midwestern State University in Wichita Falls, Texas. She is the author or coauthor of several books, including the Corwin Press title (with Dr. John F. Dowd), *Taming the Time Stealers: Tricks of the Trade from Organized Teachers.*

Dr. Gore received undergraduate and master's degrees from Eastern New Mexico University and a doctorate from the University of Arkansas.

She and her husband Don are parents to Belle, a blind Shetland sheepdog, and to Winnie, an emotionally fragile Australian shepherd mix.

To Harold O. Gore, Esquire—father, gentle counselor, and friend—who has spent
a lifetime working for the inclusion of people who are oppressed,
and to Ruth Martin Gore—mother, sparkling jewel, and friend—who includes everyone by
inviting people who are lonely, sick, or afraid to come into her home and be loved.


In memory of
beloved aunt, Doris Gore Blair, rare and special soul;
Dr. Ronnie Finley, champion of children;
and Little Man, my constant companion for 17 years, waiting
faithfully for me by Heaven's Gate.

# 1

# The Locks That Bar Access to Learning

**W**e are high school and middle school teachers. We love our disciplines passionately. The Big Ideas of our disciplines are our diamonds, rubies, emeralds, and sapphires; they catch the light and fling it in one thousand directions. The tools that help us fashion the jewels are the fire over which we soften the gold that encases them, the jeweler's loupe, the gauges, and the cutting tools. Those are our scientific methods, our deconstructions, our primary documents, and our stacks of reference books.

We want to share the wealth, and we laugh out loud when students wow at the colors and the shapes and the way the light dances off the facets of our jewels.

But some of our students, often those who have learning problems, appear apathetic about entering our stronghold and immersing themselves in the mounds of gems; they shrug their shoulders, roll their eyes, and yawn. Sometimes our tempers flare at their cavalier dismissal. Sometimes we tell ourselves that they do not deserve our treasures.

What we teachers do not see are the invisible locks that bar those students' entrance into our treasure rooms. Not one lock, but many, one after the other, bar their way. When they were younger, these students were as eager as their peers to get their hands on the jewels to sort, cut, polish, and make jewelry of their own, but years of battling the locks reduced them to a fatalism apparent in their mantra of "who cares?"

We did not realize that they did not have any keys to the locks on the doors. Only in the last thirty years have we begun to know more about the keys that would help them open the locks. The keys do work for our students with learning problems. They work, and they work well. All we have to do is learn which keys fit which locks and then use them to help all of our students access the treasure. This book is designed to help.

**Figure 1.1**

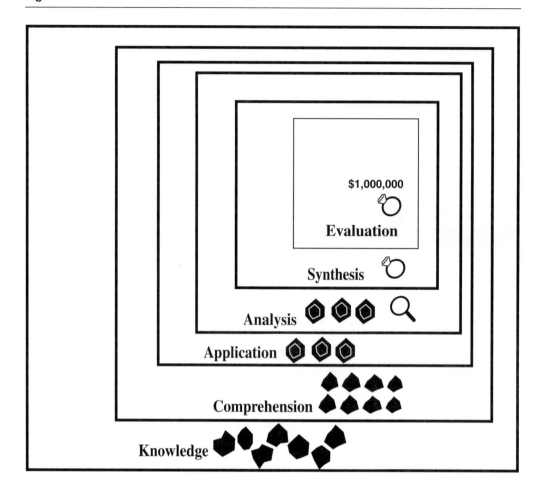

The metaphor of the jewel and the stronghold works well for this purpose. The rooms are the levels of learning in Bloom's Taxonomy. The rooms are Knowledge, Comprehension, Application, Analysis, Synthesis, and Evaluation. In the first room, Knowledge, we collect the rough, uncut stones; in the second room, Comprehension, we study and sort the stones. The third room is Application, and here we cut and polish the gems. The first of the Higher-Order Thinking Skills rooms is Analysis, and here we study each stone to determine how best to use it. We decide whether it should be a solitaire in a ring or one of a dozen stones in a heart-shaped necklace.

The doors to each of those rooms are Acquisition, Proficiency and Fluency, Maintenance, Generalization, and Adaptation (Smith, 1981), and our students must go through all the doors to enter each room.

Theoretically, our students must Acquire, become Proficient and Fluent, Maintain, Generalize/Transfer, and Adapt Knowledge before they are completely ready to move on to the next level of learning.

Currently, in pedagogical circles, discounting the importance of Knowledge level learning is de rigueur. We think that is unwise and that the phenomenon comes from a lack of deep understanding of Bloom and colleagues' (1956) Taxonomy of Cognitive Objectives. When we ask friends exactly what the taxonomy means by Knowledge, they are unable to tell us.

**Figure 1.2**

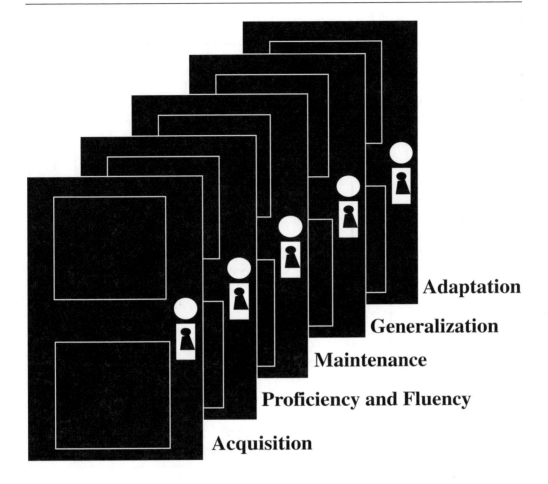

Adaptation

Generalization

Maintenance

Proficiency and Fluency

Acquisition

According to the taxonomy, Knowledge consists of a discipline's terminology; specifics; ways and means of dealing with those specifics (conventions, trends and sequences, classifications and categories, criteria, and methodology); and universals and abstractions (principles and generalizations, theories and structures). Knowledge is significant, and we think Knowledge is a prerequisite to higher levels of thinking.

Bloom and his colleagues (1956) defined Comprehension as being able to translate the data, interpolate it, or extrapolate from it. We cannot translate, interpolate, or extrapolate until we have the requisite knowledge, so we argue that our students must have full access to the first room before we can enter the doors into the second room. Knowledge is mastery of the classification that 3, 7, and 9 are odd numbers. Comprehension is interpolating that 5 and extrapolating that 1, 11, and 223 are odd numbers. Comprehension is also telling someone else that an odd number is one indivisible by 2.

Like Knowledge, Comprehension has five doors. We must Acquire Comprehension, become Proficient and Fluent at Comprehending, Maintain our Comprehension, Generalize/Transfer, and Adapt it. That is requisite to further manipulation of the data.

**Figure 1.3**

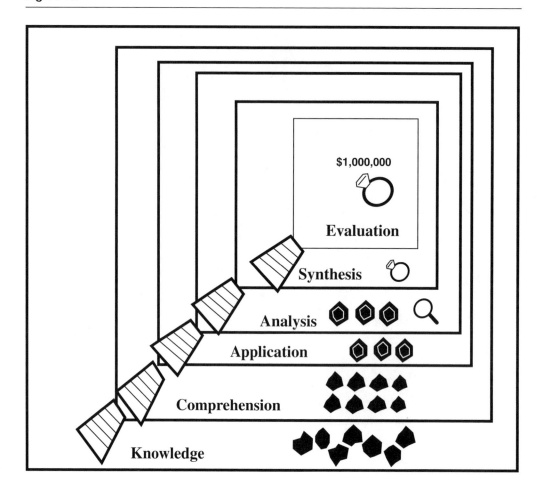

So it is with Application. We cannot authoritatively Apply a concept or skill until we have mastery of its Knowledge and Comprehension. Without knowing that an odd number is indivisible by 2 and without being able to extrapolate that 23 is an odd number, we cannot apply the knowledge and decide whether we can have our students work in pairs when the class has 23 students enrolled.

When we reach the Higher-Order Thinking Skills of Analysis, Synthesis, and Evaluation, we find that each of them has five doors, too. We have to Acquire the skills needed to Analyze, become Proficient and Fluent at them, Maintain the skill, Generalize/Transfer and use it when appropriate, and Adapt it when necessary. The same sequence applies to Synthesis and Evaluation.

Although the doors are metaphorically and theoretically opened one at a time, in practice, students usually open multiple doors at once; for example, Knowledge and Comprehension often come hand in hand.

Locating the rooms and their doors is the first step. Next is understanding the locks, and we describe them next. In Chapter 2, we will discuss three master keys, and in subsequent chapters, we will describe specific keys for accessing specific rooms.

**Figure 1.4**

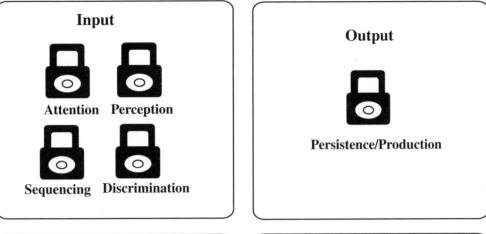

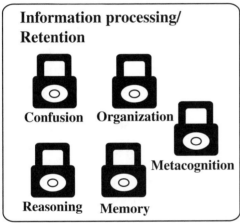

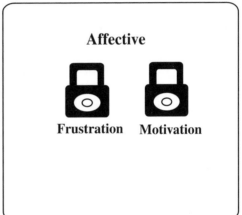

## THE LOCKS ON THE DOORS  ■

Rather than discussing each type of disability category separately, we will use noncategorical but useful terms, such as *students with disabilities* or *students with learning problems*. Unless we note otherwise, the information refers to this generic group.

For simplicity, we have organized the learning problems into categories drawn from the work of cognitive psychologists (Flavell, 1999) with the addition of an Affective category: Input Locks, Information Processing/Retention Locks, Affective Locks, and Output Locks. The Input Locks are Attention Problems, Perception Problems, Discrimination Problems, and Sequencing Problems. The Information Processing/Retention Locks are Confusion, Organization Problems, Reasoning Problems, Memory Problems, and Metacognition Problems. The Affective Locks are Frustration and Motivation Problems, and they are a direct result of the Input Locks and Information Processing/Retention Locks. The Output Lock is Persistence/Production; it a result of the Affective Locks. We will discuss the Input Locks first because they contribute to the Information Processing/Retention Locks and the Affective Locks.

## The Input Locks

The Input Locks are problems with Attention, Perception, Discrimination, and Sequencing. They all involve difficulty in getting information from the outside world into the processing centers in the brain.

🔒 Attention Problems

Using neuropsychological evidence, Sturm and Zimmermann (cited in Schweitzer, Zimmermann, & Koch, 2000) developed a two-level taxonomy of attention. The upper level consists of two categories of attention: intensity and selectivity. Intensity has three subclassifications: alertness, sustained attention, and vigilance. Selectivity has three subclassifications: selective attention or focus, visual/special selective attention or change of visual focus, and divided attention.

The types of attention that are most important to the teaching and learning process are sustained attention and the selective attention that refers to focus. Klorman (1991) noted that selective attention refers to intentional focusing on relevant information while ignoring irrelevant information. She also noted that sustained attention refers to processes that are involved in maintaining attention over an extended period of time. If problems in sustained attention occur, they happen when an individual has been engaged in selective attention over a period of time.

Unfortunately, many students with learning problems exhibit both sustained attention and selective attention problems. For example, students with attention deficit disorder have poorer comprehension on longer reading passages as compared to shorter reading passages. They also exhibit lower reading comprehension on longer passages than do their peers without attention problems. In addition, students with attention problems tend to be deficient in mathematics achievement, and their mathematics deficits appear to become more pronounced with age (Cherkes-Julkowski & Stolzenberg, 1991; Marshall & Hynd, 1997; Schweitzer et al., 2000).

Fortunately, we have instructional keys that can help students unlock the locks caused by attentional problems. By using research-supported strategies, we can help them attend (selective attention) and remain (sustained attention) engaged.

🔒 Perception Problems

Visual and auditory perception deficits are hallmarks of learning disabilities (see Johnson & Myklebust, 1967), and their study has been voluminous. Our students with visual or auditory perception problems generally have good visual or auditory acuity; that is, they can see the letters on the eye chart or hear the tone on the audiometer. The problem is that the image or sound has a difficult time getting to the right place in the brain so that the brain can make sense of it; it may travel down the wrong neural path and end up in some place in the brain that cannot make sense of it or else wander around before it finally finds the right place. Unfortunately, the perceptual training programs that characterized treatment of learning disabilities in the early days of the field do not help students' academic performance (Rosen, 1968).

Researchers continue to investigate visual and auditory perceptual problems. Recently, Boden and Brodeur (1999) found that reading disabled adolescents are not only slower at processing visual information when it is in the form of the written word, but they are also slower at processing all visual stimuli. Others have noted that students with severe reading disability can be identified by their deficiency in rapid naming ability when they are presented items visually. Their eyes can see the object, but their brains cannot make sense quickly of what their eyes are seeing. As processing demands increase, the visual perceptual performance of students with disabilities slows disproportionately, while the performance of nondisabled students remains strong.

But visual perceptual problems are not the only kind of perceptual problem that students with disabilities may experience. Kruger, Kruger, Hugo, and Campbell (2001) found that the majority of the learning disabled children whom they examined had both visual and auditory perceptual disabilities. Not only could visual input not be efficiently perceived, but neither could auditory input.

The perceptual problems create difficulties for our students outside as well as inside of the classroom. Most and Greenbank (2000) found that eighth graders with learning disabilities in visual and auditory perception were less able than their peers to discriminate the emotions of others whether the stimulus was auditory, visual, or combined. Perceptual difficulties are persistent and remain throughout an individual's life.

While we cannot fix their perceptual deficits, we can use teaching strategies that will help our students with disabilities compensate for their difficulties. The strategies are easy to use, and they are effective at helping students with learning problems succeed.

## 🔒 Discrimination Problems

Discrimination in this context refers to the ability to differentiate something from something else. Errors in discrimination result in overgeneralization and undergeneralization, incorrectly identifying something as a member of a class when it is not and conversely failing to identify something as a member of a class when it is. Discrimination ranges from a young child discriminating between a dog and a cat to a high school student discriminating between essential and nonessential information in writing a critical essay.

In 1970, writing in the *Journal of Learning Disabilities*, Kidd noted that the discriminatory repertoire is the basis of all learning; understanding an object or a concept consists of class inclusion and class differentiation. First, we must be able to determine to what class a thing belongs — such as a lemon belongs to the class of citrus fruit, and then we must be able to differentiate the thing from other members of that class — such as a lemon is yellow, sour, and more oblong, while an tangerine is orange, sweet, and more round. Such discrimination is difficult for students with learning problems.

In addition, Richards, Samuels, Ternure, and Ysseldyke (1990) discovered that students with learning disabilities are more likely to notice salient information than the critical information they are directed to observe; they have difficulty discriminating between the critical data we want them to learn and the irrelevant. They focus on the wrong information, thereby studying for the test and failing and telling us, "I studied the wrong stuff."

Auditory discrimination problems affect many of our students. Watson (1991) examined the relationship of auditory discrimination to intelligence in college students. She found moderate correlations between auditory discrimination and intelligence scores. Subsequently, others have found that young disabled readers may not be able to maintain phonemic information in their short-term memories long enough to discriminate among sounds and that learning impaired children have poorer auditory discrimination on a two-tone discrimination task than do typical children.

Visual discrimination difficulties also affect many of our students. Learning disabled children are less able than typical peers at discriminating between orthographically legitimate and illegitimate pairs of letters, and some children with mental retardation have difficulty with visual discrimination (Kavale, 1982).

Difficulty with discrimination extends to our students' problem-solving and reasoning ability. For example, McLeskey (1977) found that students with disabilities have difficulty discriminating between when a response is appropriate and when it is not. Whereas McLeskey's nondisabled students tried a complex variety of responses in solving a novel problem, his students with disabilities could not discriminate between situations in which a problem-solving strategy was appropriate and when it was not. Other researchers have found that learning disabled adolescents performed worse on discriminant learning tasks requiring them to code, recode, and recall information than did their nondisabled peers.

Discrimination problems extend outside the classrooms to our students' personal lives. Moffatt and others (1995) documented the difficulty of persons with mental retardation in discriminating among emotions and expressing empathy — the greater the degree of mental retardation, the greater the difficulty with discrimination. As noted earlier, eighth graders with learning disabilities were less able than their peers to discriminate the emotions of others.

The research consistently demonstrates that the discrimination tasks in which we engage so cavalierly every day are challenging to our students with learning problems. Fortunately, we can use good inclusion strategies to help them.

### 🔒 Sequencing Problems

The difficulty in sequencing that characterizes students with learning disabilities has been documented since the early days of learning disabilities research. Cohen, Spruill, and Herns (1982) found sequencing to be one of the six most problematic areas for students with auditory learning disabilities. (The others were attention, word retrieval, identification of antonyms, passive relationships, and memory.)

Even gifted children, who have learning disabilities, often experience difficulty with sequencing. Schiff, Kaufman, and Kaufman (1981) studied gifted children with learning disabilities. They found that the children whom they studied had excellent verbal skills and many talents, but they were deficient in sequencing, as well as motor control and emotional development.

The sequencing problems of students with learning disabilities do not retreat with high school graduation, but continue to persist. For example, Blabock (1982) found that learning disabled college students with auditory impairments experienced persistent problems in sequencing.

A number of strategies in this book are designed to help us help our students to ensure that they can properly sequence ordered material in our disciplines. With our encouragement, they may be able to generalize/transfer the strategies to other classes and to their lives outside of school.

## The Information Processing/Retention Locks

Once the information from the external environment enters the brain of our student with disabilities, the student must then process and retain that information. Several locks bar our student from processing and remembering that information. Those locks include Confusion, Organization Problems, Reasoning Problems, Memory Problems, and Metacognition Problems.

🔒 Confusion

Since the early days of learning disability research, confusion has been documented as a learning problem that is characteristic of children with learning disabilities. Such findings continue to be confirmed and expanded across time. For example, Barkin, Gardner, Kass and Polo (1981) documented left-right confusion; others have documented confusion in sequencing, sound-ground and figure-ground confusion, linguistic confusion, and cognitive confusion. In contrast to nondisabled peers, even after becoming acquainted with a task, learning disabled students continue to be confused about how to execute it.

In 1998, Scott and Nelson reported on disabled students' confusion in generalizing social responding, and others have identified their confusion about adult roles. Guyton (1968) even argued that their confused emotions can result in compounding learning disabled students' cognitive confusion.

The jury is in; our students with learning problems are confused much of the time. But we have the ability to help prevent much of their confusion if we use appropriate teaching strategies.

🔒 Organization Problems

Difficulty with organizational skills has long been documented in the learning and emotional disability literature (Zera & Lucian, 2001). The National Information Center for Children and Youth with Disabilities (NICHCY) explained that many learning disabled students have difficulty organizing bits of information to consolidate into concepts, often learning multiple facts that they cannot draw upon to answer related questions. NICHCY noted that the entire context of their lives may reflect this disorganization.

**Figure 1.5**

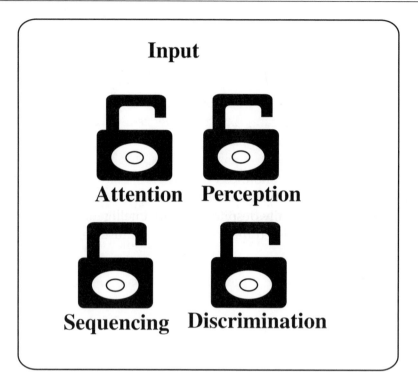

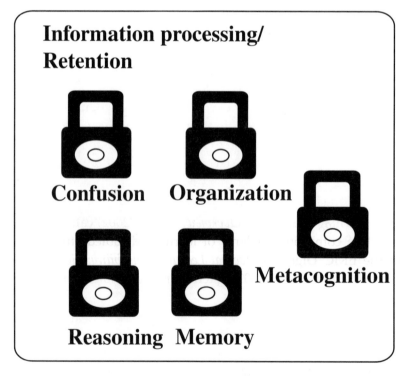

Teachers, parents, and adolescent students with disabilities themselves report that their poor organizational skills create problems with completing work, locating materials, and using time wisely. Adolescents with disabilities and their parents and teachers identify poor organizational skills as one of the three most problematic areas, the other two being communication and social skills. Such difficulty does not lessen with age; adults with learning disabilities report poor organizational skills as an important impediment to their success (Malcolm, Palatajko, & Simons, 1990).

Many of the strategies in this book are designed to help students organize information into meaningful wholes. Not only can we use the strategies to their advantage, but our nondisabled students will benefit as well.

### 🔒 Reasoning Problems

Many students with learning problems have trouble with reasoning skills. In fact, the problem is so pronounced that in 1993, Stanovich proposed a new category of learning disability: *dysrationalia*. Stanovich defined dysrationalia as the inability to think rationally despite adequate intelligence. Although leaders in the field promptly dismissed the concept with amusement (Sternberg, 1993; 1994), Stanovich's notion of it as a separate learning disability points out the extent to which poor reasoning skills characterize the thinking of some of our students with learning disabilities.

Stone and colleagues (1984) found that students having different subcategories of learning disabilities, such as low verbal disabilities, low performance disabilities, and those low in both verbal and performance, differed in their abilities to reason. Children with learning disabilities demonstrate less coordinated thought structures than their nondisabled peers and are less likely to employ second-order logical structures than are their peers. They also display operational logic structures significantly less often than do their peers on mathematics tasks.

The problems persist. College students with learning disabilities have difficulty in learning to use logic and require instruction in thinking skills (Utzinger, 1982).

### 🔒 Memory Problems

Mnemonic problems are generally present in students with learning disabilities (McNamara, 1999). In fact, Boudah and Weiss (2002), writing in the ERIC Digest *Learning Disabilities Overview: Update 2002*, called memory problems one of five common problems of learning disabled students. Likewise, writing in the ERIC Digest *Nonverbal Learning Disability: How to Recognize It and Minimize Its Effects*, Foss (2001) listed memory problems as one of the four difficulties she identified.

The fact that students can have learning disabilities in reading and in mathematics and that memory difficulties are one of the hallmarks of learning disabilities makes memory difficulties in those areas prima facie. But memory problems affect students' performance across the curriculum. Teachers in social studies and sciences have noted the need for memory strategies for students with disabilities in those areas, too (Scholes, 1998; Ward-Lonergan, Liles, Anderson, 1998).

But memory is important in every area of life, not only in academics. McNamara (1999) argued that their memory problems contribute to the social relationship problems of students with learning difficulties. Being unable to remember social conventions, particularly when required to think on their feet, creates relationship difficulties for our students. Forgetting appointments, dates, and promises all cause social difficulties, sometimes rupturing relationships.

Like the other characteristics of students with learning problems, mnemonic difficulties do not end with graduation. Adults with learning disabilities continue to experience problems with mnemonic functions, too (Jordan, 2000). Like the memory problems of our students, those of adults can be devastating.

### 🔒 Metacognition Problems

Metacognition, as discussed by A. I. Brown and J. H. Flavell in their extensive work on the subject, particularly in the area of reading comprehension, refers to thinking about thinking and controlling thinking; also related are metamemory (thinking about and controlling remembering,) meta-attention (thinking about and controlling attention), and metacomprehension (thinking about and controlling comprehension).

A number of authors have noted that students with learning disabilities tend to be passive learners who are unaware of their own learning processes (Wang, 1987); they fail to monitor their own learning. This results in mnemonic difficulties, transfer and generalization problems, reading comprehension problems, and a host of other difficulties (Brown & Palincsar, 1982; Wong, 1985).

Wang, Haertel & Walberg (1993/1994) used a knowledge base of 11,000 statistical findings to identify the magnitude of 28 categories of influences on student learning. Only classroom management was more influential than the teaching of metacognitive strategies on how students learn.

Lloyd and others (1981) improved students' mathematics skill transfer through metacognitive instruction, and others have taught middle school students a metacognitive strategy for improving composition skills and found that prewriting planning, composition, and revision improved and that the students' attitudes toward writing also improved.

Metacognitive training in social skills improves the social adjustment of incarcerated boys with learning problems and reduces the anger behavior and aggressive acts of elementary, middle school, and high school boys with anger management problems (Larson & Gerber, 1987; Smith, 1992).

In the context of our classrooms, we can use metacognitive strategies that will increase students' achievement in our discipline. That is good news. But the better news is that when we teach students to use metacognitive strategies, we are making a critical difference in their lives both inside and outside of the classroom.

## The Affective Locks

Frustration and Motivation Problems are the Affective Locks that bar our students' entry into the vault. Frustration and Motivation Problems are the direct result of Input and Information Processing/Retention Problems. Only by helping students unlock the previous locks can we help them unlock these barriers. But the phenomenon is cyclical in nature. Once we help them unlock

**Figure 1.6**

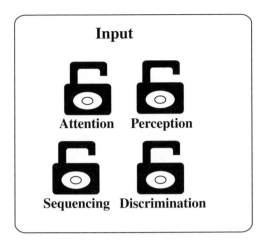

Input

Attention    Perception

Sequencing    Discrimination

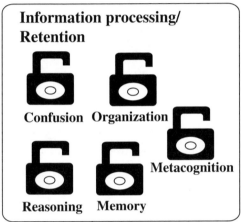

Information processing/
Retention

Confusion    Organization

Metacognition

Reasoning    Memory

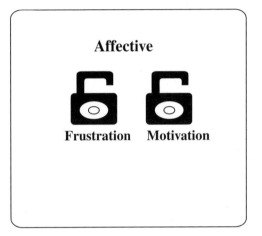

Affective

Frustration    Motivation

these locks, our students will be better able to unlock the previous locks and, at the same time, the Persistence/Production Problems Lock.

🔒 Frustration

Writing in an ERIC Digest, Bergert (2000) noted that frustration is an early warning sign of learning disabilities; the frustration difficulties are evident in both academic and in social arenas.

As early as 1968, Beckman identified low frustration tolerance as a behavioral characteristic of children with learning disabilities. Toro and others (1990) found that the poor social problem-solving skills of children with learning disabilities were complicated by their low frustration tolerance, and Murray and Whittenberger (1983) cautioned that frustration with learning problems contributed to the problems of many aggressive, severely behavior disordered children.

The frustration continues when the students come to us in middle and high school. As early as 1978, Kronick noted that frustration characterizes the life experiences of adolescents with learning disabilities both inside and outside of the classroom. But the problem of frustration does not end when high school does. Mays and Imel (1982), writing in an ERIC Fact Sheet, noted that low frustration tolerance is one of nine observable characteristics of adults with learning disabilities, and Lancaster, Mellard, and Hoffman (2001) reported that college students with learning disabilities reported frustration as one of their six major difficulties. (The other difficulties were concentration, distraction, test anxiety, remembering, and mathematics.) Even high ability students with learning disabilities who have gone on to achieve have noted their frustration with certain academic areas.

Having learning problems frustrates our students who cope with them day in and day out, every day of their lives. Thank goodness we can help prevent much of their frustration when we use good inclusive practices.

### 🔒  Motivation Problems

The Input and Information Processing/Retention locks prevent our students from being able to learn our disciplines, but they do teach them one thing: helplessness. In fact, the Motivation Problems Lock could easily be called the Learned Helplessness (Seligman, 1975) Lock, because Learned Helplessness causes our students' low achievement motivation.

Low academic achievement motivation is a characteristic common to our students with disabilities. In general, students with learning problems tend to be extrinsically — rather than intrinsically — motivated when it comes to schoolwork, and of the various types of learning problems that students experience, our adolescents with learning disabilities demonstrate lower achievement motivation toward schoolwork than do their emotionally disordered peers (Fulk, Brigham, & Lohman, 1998; Okolo & Bahr, 1995; Renick, 1985).

But some students with learning disabilities are highly academically motivated. Those students who are highly academically motivated are intrinsically, rather than extrinsically, motivated to excel in school (Dev, 1996).

Not being academically motivated does not mean that a student is not motivated in nonacademic areas. In areas in which they experience success, students with learning problems are highly motivated (Adelman & Taylor, 1990). We have all seen students work for hours on a project when allowed to choose the topic and medium, and we have certainly seen them work for hours at a complicated video game.

Learned helplessness appears to be at the root of low achievement motivation in students with disabilities (Valas, 2001). After repeated failures, students learn that they cannot succeed in school. This attribution becomes so deeply embedded that they may passively or actively refuse to try to achieve in schoolwork. Once established, learned helplessness tends to persist, but fortunately, we can help combat learned helplessness by making assignments more approachable. Success breeds motivation.

## The Output Lock

The Output Lock refers to Production Problems. However, we include the Persistence Lock with the Output Lock because combining them has a logical appeal. Our students' problems with persistence are most observable when we have required them to produce some product.

**Figure 1.7**

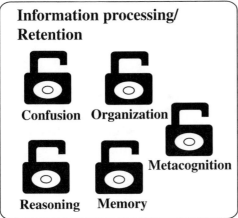

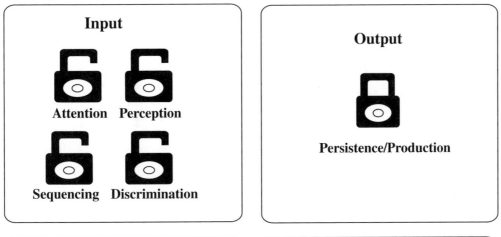

**🔒** Persistence/Production Problems

Our students with disabilities often experience difficulty persisting in and completing schoolwork. For example, learning disabled students have difficulty completing assignments and homework. Their teachers rate them as less persistent than their nondisabled students and as deficient in quantity and quality of story production as compared to their nondisabled peers. In addition, while most students enjoy doing projects, learning disabled students have difficulty completing them (Salend & Gajria, 1995; Graves, Semmel & Gerber, 1994).

Adolescents and young adults with disabilities have difficulties completing their education; they comprise one of the three categories of students most likely to drop out of high school (the others being foreign-born students and those who were retained in one or more grades). Marder and DiAmico (1992), reporting for the National Longitudinal Transition Study of Special Education Students, revealed that fewer students with disabilities complete school and fewer of those who drop out complete GED degrees as compared to their nondisabled peers. College students with disabilities are less likely to have completed their degree in five years than are their peers without disabilities, and numerous studies have noted that adults and adolescents with mild mental

**Figure 1.8**

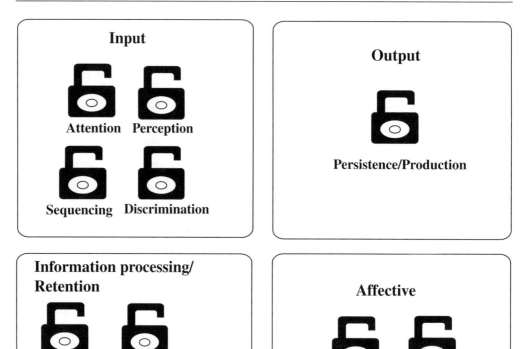

handicaps have difficulty with work completion (Hurst & Smerdon, 2000a, 2000b; McMillan, Kaufman, & Klein, 1997).

From elementary school through adulthood, our students struggle with persisting and completing what they need to do. While we cannot help in every arena, we can use supportive teaching strategies that will help them complete assignments in our classrooms.

## The Sum Total of the Locks

Metaphorically, we do not think that multiple locks represent an additive relationship, such as 3 Input Locks + 3 Processing Locks = 6 Locks; we do not even think that the relationship is multiplicative. Instead, we think that the relationship of multiple locks on a student's learning is exponential: 3 Input Locks interacting with 3 Processing Locks = $3^3$ Locks or 27. As with many other things, a synergy takes place among the locks, and the total damage that they do to our students is greater than the sum of its parts.

The news is serious: the learning problem locks are invidious. Reading about them could discourage us. But that is counterproductive. What we must do is learn the keys to help our students open the locks. Then we can invite them into the stronghold and even into the vault and offer them a handful of jewels.

# 2

# Keys to the Effectiveness of the Inclusion Strategies

**T**he locks on the doors to our students' learning can seem overwhelming to them and to us. The good news is that by using three Master Keys to effective instruction for students with disabilities and the individual keys that are guided by those Master Keys, we can help our students unlock the doors to learning.

The three master keys to effective instruction for students with disabilities are (1) explicitness, (2) structure, and (3) repetition.

In "Instructing Adolescents With Learning Disabilities: A Component and Composite Analysis," published in *Learning Disabilities Research and Practice*, Swanson and Hoskyn (2001) noted the importance of explicitness in all phases of instruction for secondary students with learning problems. Their factor analysis of many studies showed that a factor called organization/explicit was the single most powerful factor of the strategies used in intervention programs for secondary learning disabled students; the explicit part of the factor referred to explicit modeling and explicit practice, with explicit practice being the single most important instructional component related to high effect sizes. The organization/explicit factor includes all three keys: organization refers to structure, and explicitness and practice are prima facie.

But the education community today is extremely concerned with higher-order thinking. So Swanson (2001) conducted a meta-analysis of 58 studies of the factors in interventions that led to higher-order processing, and his findings supported those of Swanson and Hoskyn (2001). He found that extended explicit practice and structure — in this case, the structure of advanced organizers — were the most critical factors in increasing the higher-order thinking skills of adolescents with learning disabilities.

**Figure 2.1**

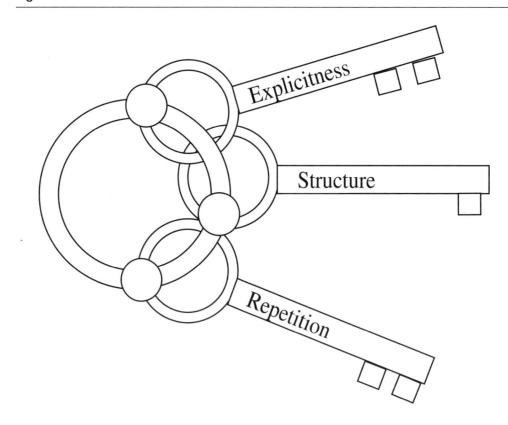

In addition, in their mega-analysis of effective strategies in teaching students with learning problems, Kavale and Forness (1999) found Direct Instruction, a strategy that is a structured approach to explicit instruction that includes repetition through explicit practice with explicit feedback and review, to be one of the most effective strategies, having an effect size of .84; the only strategies more effective were mnemonic strategies (ES 1.62), reading comprehension strategies (ES ranging from 1.13 to .98 depending on the particular strategy), and behavior modification (.93), all of which are structured approaches that include explicitness and repetition to a greater or lesser degree.

Swanson's (1999) study, presented at the National Summit on Research in Learning Disabilities, was an earlier analysis of the 58 studies he reviewed again in 2001; at that time, his analysis focused on instructional models instead of components of instruction within those models. This earlier analysis affirmed that Direct Instruction and strategy instruction were the two most effective strategies in teaching students with learning disabilities; both are structured approaches that include explicitness and repetition.

As compared to their nondisabled counterparts, students with mild disabilities tend to experience difficulty learning important information incidentally and inductively (Di Gennaro & Picciarelli, 1992; Hollingsworth & Woodward, 1993; Kavale & Forness, 1999; Mastropieri, Scruggs, & Butcher, 1997; Oetting & Rice, 1995; Rice & Buhr, 1992; Rice & Oetting, 1994), due to difficulty discriminating the relevant from the irrelevant dimensions of the task (Zeaman & House, 1961). Thus, they may incidentally learn irrelevant information, for example, knowing the name of Harry Truman's dog, but not knowing who Harry Truman was.

Because discriminating between important and unimportant information tends to be difficult for them, students with learning problems benefit from direct instruction (Kavale & Forness, 1999) with its explicit focus on what is important. As part of that direct instruction, they need concrete hands-on experiences and multisensory, multirepresentational instruction (Clark & Paivio, 1991; Gellevij, Van Der Meij, De Jong, & Pieters, 2002; Moseley & Brenner, 1997).

In addition, because they tend to have difficulty encoding information into their memory systems and therefore lack basic skills and cognitions that must be in place before they can attempt higher-order thinking, students with learning problems require repetition in instruction and spaced practice and frequent review. Each time a neural trace is activated, that arm of the neuron becomes stronger and easier to access the next time. An analogy for this is how we sometimes get into our cars to go to the store only to discover that we went the wrong way and headed for the office because that is where we usually go.

The brains of students with learning problems are not as efficient in making those neural traces stronger, so they need to activate the traces more frequently in order to strengthen the connections. Thus, repetition through multisensory, multirepresentational input and practice and frequent review are necessary.

## DUAL CODING THEORY AND ■ TRI-CODING OF INFORMATION

Hebb's Law (1949) theorized that neurons that fire together simultaneously have a high likelihood to fire together again when stimulated. Siegel (1999), cited in Wolfe (2001, p. 76) paraphrased Hebb's Law: "Neurons that fire together, survive together, and wire together."

Wolfe (2001) explained that Information Processing Theory posits that memory starts with sensory input from the five senses. She cited Kotulak (1996), who wrote,

> The brain gobbles up its external environment in bites and chunks through its sensory system: vision, hearing, smell, touch, and taste. Then the digested world is reassembled in the form of trillions of connections between brain cells that are constantly growing or dying or becoming stronger or weaker, depending upon the richness of the banquet. (p. 4)

While the brain dumps 99% of the sensory input (Gazzaniga, 1998), the 1% that it stores in long-term memory is sensory data. Wolfe (2001) cited research that showed the storage of that sensory data actually increases the size and weight of the brain due to larger number of synapses per neuron, large cortical neurons and synapses, and heavier branching of dendrites.

Although all sensory input is important, visual input is particularly powerful. Our eyes contain 70% of our sensory receptors, and we take in more sensory information visually than by any other means.

Paivio's (1991) Dual Coding Theory refers to teaching visually and auditorily at the same time and posits that the more neural paths that a memory involves, the more likely it is to be permanently recorded and to be successfully accessed at a later date. Simpson (1997) extended Dual Coding Theory to what he called Tri-Coding of Information by adding the kinesthetic pathway to the visual and auditory pathways.

Maria Montessori, a pioneer in the education of poor children and children with disabilities, hailed the use of multiple sensory channels input as early as the middle of the nineteenth century. Grace Fernald, one of the twentieth century pioneers of special education, developed a method she called VAKT for visual, auditory, kinesthetic, and tactile teaching. Although more generally referred to as multisensory teaching than tri-coding of information, a number of researchers have produced research support for activities that employ tri-coding activities that employ visual, auditory, and kinesthetic channels. Sparks and Ganschow (1993) and other researchers have found positive effects when using multisensory teaching with high school at-risk foreign language learners, junior high special education social studies students, and mathematics students with learning problems. In addition, multiple studies have showed structured multisensory instruction to be effective in teaching reading to learning disabled delinquents and college students with learning disabilities.

Kubina and Cooper (2000) argued that the use of multiple learning channels within the same lesson adds variety to instruction and practice. They also added that varied instruction via multisensory teacher input and student output allows learners to experience different ways of learning; when teachers alternate the modalities that they have students use as output, the novelty increases student motivation and attention to task and therefore reduces students' failure.

Multicoding helps with attention problems because it involves more than passively listening. It helps with comprehension because the multiple representations increase the likelihood of the student connecting with the material in a way he or she learns best. It also helps with retention because it increases the places in the brain where the information is stored.

Loosely related to multisensory instruction is instruction that employs multiple representations. The National Council of Teachers of Mathematics (www.nctm.org) endorses the use of multiple representations in mathematics teaching. Herbel-Eisenmann (2002) found that multiple representations increased students' acquisition of mathematical vocabulary, and others have found that multiple representations increased junior high students' algebraic thinking significantly over students taught with traditional techniques. Using multiple representations in science, Wu, Krajcik, and Soloway (2001) found that students' understanding of chemical representation increased dramatically, and others have found positive effects in increasing high school students' conceptualization of the molecular structure.

When we use the Master Keys of explicitness, structure, and repetition and we employ those keys through multisensory and multirepresentational means,

**Figure 2.2**

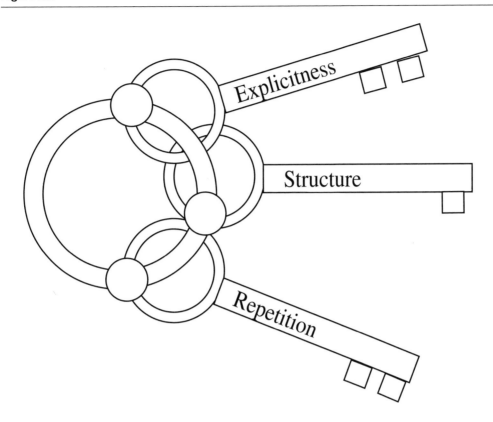

we will be able to help our students with disabilities unlock the doors that block their way to the jewels in our stronghold. Those Master Keys provide the basis for the 70 individual keys in this book.

Not only are the keys effective, but we teachers enjoy using them, and our students enjoy our lessons when we do.

# 3

# Teaching the Concepts and Vocabulary of Our Disciplines

## In This Chapter

*Mastery of the vocabulary concepts of a discipline provides the basic building blocks for comprehension and all higher-order thinking skills in that discipline. Teaching the vocabulary concepts is the most elemental, basic place to start, and in order to assure that our students with special needs learn that vocabulary, we must explicitly teach it. In this chapter, we will discuss several ways to add multisensory dimensions and structure to teaching new vocabulary by using simple keys to unlock the doors barred by problems of confusion, discrimination to acquire comprehension, memory, attention, and motivation.*

Words are concepts, and Greenwood (2002) wrote that knowing the vocabulary, the words of a discipline, is the key to reading comprehension in that discipline. Hennings (2000) wrote that vocabulary is a key factor not only in reading, but also in listening comprehension, especially in secondary and postsecondary education. She warned that students who have limited vocabularies in our disciplines have problems understanding what they read in their textbooks and what they hear in our classes because words are building blocks, and students with limited word knowledge have " 'too few building blocks' with which to construct meanings" (p. 269). We encounter the same problem when we pick up an advanced-level text in an area completely outside of our own realm of study, such as engineering or nutrition. We lack the building blocks, the concepts, with which to construct meaning.

Graves and Penn (1986) identified three levels at which a word is known: unknown, acquainted, and established; Greenwood (2002) described a word at the acquainted level as one in which the user has heard the word and recognizes it, but is "fuzzy" about its meaning. He stated that our goal as content area teachers is to help students move words from the acquainted level to the established level (and of course, from unknown to established), at which they become automatic.

The task of understanding a word exists, in part, in determining to what class of concepts that word belongs and how it is differentiated from other words in that class. One of our crucial jobs as content area teachers is helping students have a rich established vocabulary in our disciplines. So how shall we do it?

Writing in the *Handbook of Reading Research* (Vol. 2) about teaching general education students, Beck and McKeown (1991) wrote,

> The following four statements about the effects of vocabulary instruction on word learning can be made with a high level of confidence: First, all instructional methods produce better word learning than no instruction. Second, no one method has been shown to be consistently superior. Third, there is advantage from methods that use a variety of techniques. Fourth, there is advantage from repeated exposures to the words to be learned. The simple version of these findings is that people tend to learn what they are taught, and more attention to what is being taught is useful. (p. 805)

In "Guidelines for Evaluating Vocabulary Instruction," published in the *Journal of Reading,* Carr and Wixson (1986) identified four guidelines for evaluating vocabulary instruction:

- Instruction should help students relate new vocabulary to their background knowledge.
- Instruction should help students develop elaborated word knowledge.
- Instruction should provide for active student involvement in learning new vocabulary.
- Instruction should develop students' strategies for acquiring new vocabulary independently.

The strategies in this chapter meet Carr and Wixson's guidelines and use the keys to teaching students with special learning needs.

When we want to focus special needs students' attention on the vocabulary we want them to learn, we need to use explicit instruction, and multisensory methods help us increase explicitness because they help students see, hear, feel, and move to experience a word.

A wide variety of strategies allows us to provide multisensory instruction and increase cognitive structure for special needs students in our classes. These

12 multisensory strategies are keys that will help us unlock many of the doors that have barred our special needs students' access to our disciplines:

- Key 1: Taxonomic Tree
- Key 2: Semantic Feature Analysis Matrix
- Key 3: Compare and Contrast Vocabulary Matrix
- Key 4: Typology
- Key 5: Word Analysis Diagram
- Key 6: Semantic Web
- Key 7: Quick Sketching a Definition
- Key 8: Total Physical Response and Vocabulary Drama
- Key 9: Linguistic Link Lists and Word Towers
- Key 10: Keyword Mnemonic Strategy
- Key 11: Vocabulary Word Card Ring
- Key 12: Vocabulary Concept Dictionary

The first six keys we use are types of Graphic organizers. (GOs) are one class of teaching devices. Horton, Lovitt, and Slocum (1988) explained that teaching devices help teachers increase the explicitness of their instruction, elaborate on critical content, and increase students' active learning. Fisher, Schumaker, and Deshler (1995) explained that teachers use teaching devices to increase student understanding and application, memory storage, and subsequent retrieval. Egan (1999) found that GOs have been reported to be effective teaching devices at all levels of learning and that their use in education is widespread.

Fisher et al. (1995) reviewed the literature for validated inclusive practices. They found that GOs were one of the only two teaching devices that met their criteria to be declared validated practices that "benefit most, if not all, students in a class, that allow the integrity of the curriculum to be maintained, and that are practical in terms of time and implementation" (p. 1). GOs provide visual input and a visual structure that helps students organize, comprehend, analyze, and retain information. When students draw the GO instead of receiving it as a teacher's handout, they also receive kinesthetic elements to their learning, thus providing multiple neural pathways from which to process and in which to store the information.

Boyle and Yeager (1997) explained that GOs are learning frameworks. They stated that just as a house needs a framework, learning needs frameworks, too. Learning frameworks are called cognitive frameworks. They wrote,

Cognitive frameworks support student learning by presenting component information in an organized manner and by linking related information together. More specifically, during academic activities cognitive frameworks aid students by highlighting the important points, visually displaying the relationships between ideas, and serving as guides for studying after the lesson. (p. 27)

Horton, Lovitt, and Bergerud (1990) agreed that GOs work by helping students consolidate what they may perceive as a set of unrelated facts rather than an interrelated set of facts and concepts. They develop relational knowledge necessary to conduct deep processing of new concepts, serve as a vehicle for higher-order thinking, and assist in retrieval of information. They help students see information as an integrated whole.

GOs can be categorized as expert-made, student-made, or co-constructed. The best method for student understanding and retention appears to be co-constructed. Expert maps are best when first introducing mapping to students; a benefit of expert maps is that teacher time is saved and students receive a preview of the material. Chang, Sung, and Chen (2002) explained that drawbacks to continuing the use of expert maps include the passive nature of student learning: no autonomous learning takes place. Not only do the students not actively engage with the text, but they miss the crucial benefits of multicoding through the kinesthetic experience of drawing the map.

The two main problems with student-generated maps are time constraint and cognitive overload. Having students construct their own GOs is time consuming, and time is always a concern for teachers. The more important problem, however, is cognitive overload; even college students find generating maps on their own to be difficult.

One solution is for the teacher and students to co-construct the organizer, with the teacher working on the chalkboard or overhead projector and the students working at their seats. As the teacher and students engage in discourse, the teacher scaffolds the students' thinking so that they discover how to best construct the device. The other solution is map correction. In this strategy, the teacher provides the map with approximately 40% of the information incorrect. The students must then correct the map. This approach provides the best of both the expert-made and student-generated organizers: students have the expert map as a framework, but must then think critically about the map (Chang et al., 2002).

Horton et al. (1990) found support for GOs when they compared the use of teacher-directed GOs to self-study with 180 seventh and tenth grade students. Of those students, eight had learning disabilities. When the learning disabled students used self-study on a reading passage (read the material and took notes) for 45 minutes, they scored 19% on a test. When they completed a teacher-prepared blank GO while reading material of similar difficulty for 45 minutes, they scored 71%. The nondisabled students also improved from 56% with self-study to 89% with the GO.

With GOs, students become active instead of passive learners and benefit from the kinesthetic involvement as well as the auditory and visual. This is supported by Horton et al.'s (1990) second experiment. Whereas in the first experiment (see preceding paragraph), the teacher directed the GO construction, in the second experiment, the students directed their own construction of a GO in comparison with a self-study condition. In the student-constructed GO condition, the mean score of the students with learning disabilities was 71% on a quiz; their mean score on the self-study condition quiz was 19%. Likewise, the students who did not have learning problems benefited from constructing their own GOs; they averaged 89% on the self-directed GO condition quiz and 56% on the self-study condition quiz.

Moore and Readence (1984) found that GOs are especially effective in teaching technical vocabulary. Because the technical vocabulary of mathematics is the most difficult vocabulary for students to understand, GOs are especially important keys to learning in mathematics.

We used GOs with a group of high school students with learning problems who were struggling with freshman government. The terms were difficult for them to understand because they viewed each term as an isolated fact. When we used a GO to help them view the terms in relationship to each other, Bryce, the most reluctant learner in the group, said, "Now I get it! It makes sense!"

A number of GOs help students learn the vocabulary of our disciplines. Words are concepts, so all tools useful in teaching concepts are actually teaching words. Vocabulary teaching is concept teaching, and a number of GOs excel at concept teaching.

Because GOs are grounded in schema theory (Dye, 2002), they help students connect new vocabulary to concept networks that they already have. In learning a new word, students start with what they know. They then engage in two processes: (1) determining class inclusion and (2) determining class differentiation of the concept. In other words, students must first determine to what class of concepts the new word belongs and then determine how the word differs from other members of that class. GOs help students connect the new information to what they already know and then make the inclusion/differentiation determinations in learning the new vocabulary.

A Taxonomic Tree is one visual tool we use to teach vocabulary through showing the concept class in which the term is included and the classes from which it is differentiated. Other tools are Semantic Feature Analysis Matrix, Compare and Contrast Matrix, Typology, Word Analysis Diagram, Semantic Web, and Vocabulary Dictionary Matrix.

## ⌘ Key 1 is a Taxonomic Tree

Egan (1999) noted that GOs are used to structure information, and the Taxonomic Tree structures information so that a concept is clearly situated in context for learners. In a Taxonomic Tree, the row superseding a new word represents the class to which the word belongs, the superordinate concept. The words on the same row as the new word represent the classes from which the word is differentiated, the coordinate concepts. The words directly beneath the new word are the subclasses of that word, the subordinate concepts. This tool takes thought that is amorphous to the student with mild disabilities and makes the organization of that thought visible and clear (Tarquin & Walker, 1997). We find that we understand our own disciplines much more clearly when we construct Taxonomic Trees because making thought visible helps teachers as well as students.

The Taxonomic Tree helps students open the Acquisition and Fluency and Proficiency doors that block access to Knowledge and Comprehension because

- 🔑 Auditory Perception is enhanced by the visual and kinesthetic dimensions.
- 🔑 Discrimination is sharpened because the coordinate concepts are clearly delineated.
- 🔑 Memory is enhanced because of the depth of processing.
- 🔑 Organization is provided because of the strategy's inherent organization.
- 🔑 Attention is assured because the student is actively involved.
- 🔑 Frustration is decreased because the concept is presented in a highly explicit manner.

Here is an example from a ninth grade science unit that we taught on diseases. Each day as we introduced new categories, we added to the taxonomy. When the older sister of one of our students saw the tree, she told our student,

"I wish my teacher, Mr. Jones (name changed), had done that with us when I had to take that class. It makes a whole lot more sense this way. Your teacher should teach him how to do it."

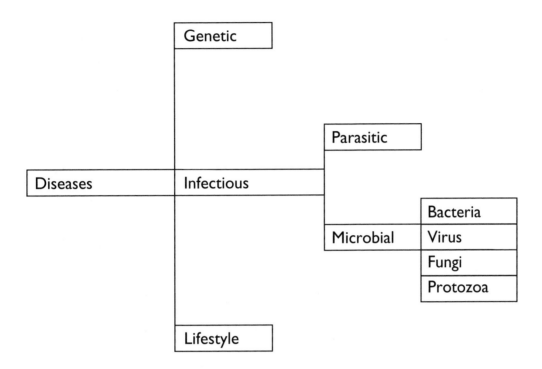

## ⌛ Key 2 is a Semantic Feature Analysis Matrix

The Semantic Feature Analysis (SFA) Matrix lets us help students see the relationships, the fine shades of meaning, between and among similar words (Pittelman, Heimlich, Berglund, & French, 1991). The SFA was designed to be used in the following way: (1) The teacher writes a list of words on the board that are in a common category. (2) The teacher asks the students to list characteristics of one of the words, and the teacher writes these characteristics across the top of the board to make a matrix. The students then complete the matrix with pluses or minuses; if the characteristic is not completely present or absent, the students use a rating scale of 1 to 10. (3) After the students have finished, the class discusses the matrix and adds more items.

Brunn (2002) said that GOs further students' understanding of difficult concepts, and understanding the fine distinctions that differentiate a concept from a similar concept is a difficult task for novices in a subject. The SFA Matrix is designed to help students open the door that makes discrimination difficult, highlighting those fine distinctions between such coordinate concepts. We are all very familiar with apples; in almost every first grade class in America, apples comprise an autumn thematic unit that covers an entire month. In addition, most of us have eaten thousands of apples over the years; but if called on to explain the difference between a Fuji apple and a Braeburn apple, most of us would be hard-pressed. With a SFA Matrix, we could learn those distinctions.

Bos, Anders, Filip and Jaffe (1989) examined the effects of SFA Matrix in an experiment with 50 high school students with learning disabilities. Half of the students were in the SFA group, and the other half of the students were in the Dictionary Method group. The SFA group was taught ten search and seizure terms related to the Right to Privacy and the Fourth Amendment. The terms included: search and seizure, unreasonable search and seizure, and exclusionary rule. The Dictionary Method group was instructed to use the dictionary to look up the terms and write the definitions. All students then read a passage on the topic and were tested on the definition of the terms and the application of the concepts in scenario form. The SFA group significantly outperformed the Dictionary Method group, and at a six-month follow-up, the SFA group continued to significantly outperform their peers.

The intellectual work involved in using the SFA Matrix is challenging, but having that kind of mastery over concepts is empowering. This is a key to accessing the door to increasing student motivation. High school students with disabilities sometimes tell us that they actually help their friends without disabilities study if they have a class in which their teacher does not use these tools.

🎵 Perception is enhanced by using all three sensory dimensions.

🎵 Discrimination is acute because the very fine differences between coordinate concepts are clearly explicated.

🎵 Memory is enhanced because of the depth of processing.

🎵 Organization is provided because of the strategy's matrix organization.

🎵 Attention is enhanced because the student is actively involved.

🎵 Frustration is decreased because the subtle shades of meaning between and among the concepts are highlighted.

Here is an example we used in an English class.

### Semantic Feature Analysis for Clauses

| | Expresses a Complete Thought | Is Used as a Sentence | Contains a Verb and Its Subject |
|---|---|---|---|
| Independent Clause | + | + | + |
| Dependent Clause | − | − | + |
| Phrase | − | − | − |

## ☙ Key 3 is a Compare and Contrast Vocabulary Matrix

This great tool is an offshoot of the SFA Matrix. Langan-Fox, Waycott, and Albert (2000) heralded the fact that GOs can help students grasp concepts much more quickly than most other methods of instruction, and the Compare and Contrast (C&C) Vocabulary Matrix is a tool that maximizes speed of understanding. The C&C, while not allowing for the razor-edge distinctions afforded by the SFA Matrix, provides sufficient understanding for all but the most critical shades of meaning in coordinate concepts, and for most of the concepts we teach, the C&C works well.

In the C&C, instead of placing the critical attributes at the top of the columns of the matrix, the students write more general attribute categories. They then write each concept's characteristics in the squares of the matrix (see Figure 3.3). In general, students tend to prefer using the C&C Vocabulary Matrix to the SFA Matrix strategy because it does not demand such rigorous thinking. We use C&C Vocabulary Matrices approximately ten times more often than we use the SFA Matrix. Occasionally, we start with the C&C, and if students have difficulty distinguishing the fine differences between coordinate concepts, we add a SFA Matrix to clarify.

Alvermann (1981) explored whether tenth grade social studies students increased their understanding of key vocabulary terms encountered in an expository passage with and without a C&C matrix. She found that both the poor and the strong readers benefited from the C&C organizer; it was a key to increasing comprehension as well as helping students to acquire the new knowledge and organize it in their schema.

The C&C Vocabulary Matrix works because

- ♪ Auditory Perception is ensured by using all three senses.
- ♪ Discrimination is enhanced because differences in the confusing coordinate concepts are delineated.
- ♪ Memory is strengthened because of the depth of processing.
- ♪ Organization is enhanced because of the strategy's inherent organization.
- ♪ Attention is focused because the student is actively involved.
- ♪ Frustration is decreased because the similarities and differences between the coordinate concepts are made explicit.

When students with disabilities use this key, their problems in discriminating among concepts are mediated, and the confusion prevented. For example, in the Earth science example below, the matrix we created helped students understand the critical vocabulary terms related to tectonic plate boundaries: convergent, divergent, and transform.

## Tectonic Plate Boundaries

| Boundary Type | Type of Movement | Location | Lithospheric Consequences | Resulting Geographic Features |
|---|---|---|---|---|
| **Divergent** | Plates spread apart | Generally along oceanic ridge crests; can occur on continent | Lithosphere produced | Seafloor spreading; fractures; rifts or rift valleys |
| **Convergent** | Plates collide | Ocean/continent, continent/continent; ocean/ocean | Lithosphere consumed | Lithosphere subducted into mantle; oceanic/continental: deep ocean trench, volcanic arcs; oceanic/oceanic: volcanoes & island arcs (e.g. Alaskan Peninsula, Japan); continental/ continental: no subduction, produces mountains: Alps, Appalachians |
| **Transform** | Plates slide past each other | Generally in ocean | Lithosphere neither produced nor destroyed | Transform faults, generally in oceanic floor |

## ⊶ Key 4 is a Typology

Many people know the word *typology* and have the idea that it discriminates between types of something, but do not know exactly what it is. Many of us confuse *taxonomy* with typology or incorrectly use the terms interchangeably. They are very different tools with very different uses. The taxonomy gives us the big picture: an overview of a concept's class membership, the members of its class that differ from it, and its subclasses. In contrast, a typology shows us how a concept differs from three coordinate concepts along two dimensions. A two-by-two matrix is used in which each of two dimensions is listed along the side and the top of the matrix. Within the intersection of each dimension falls the name of each concept being taught.

Using a taxonomy to give the big picture that situates the words we are targeting, and following that with a typology to clearly differentiate among those words in relation to each other, is a powerful strategy.

We have found that, in general, the distinctions between words taught in a typology are more easily remembered than those taught in other ways. This is a good key to open the door that causes discrimination problems. With only two critical attributes on which to focus and only four terms to consider, the student's cognitive energy invested in the multicoding of seeing the words in relationship to each other while listening to an explanation of the terms, followed by constructing a matrix in his or her own notebook, results in an impressive degree of comprehension, retention, and retrieval. The comprehension is increased because trouble discriminating among the critical attributes is mediated and confusion about which term to use when is reduced.

We have found that memory retrieval is especially high when students with disabilities are explicitly taught to draw the typology whenever they need to access the information from their memory banks. Students without disabilities may do this automatically, but those who have learning problems may need the explicit instruction. With this key, motivation is increased because feelings of competence are generated, success is ensured, and expectation of future success is created.

The Typology is an effective key because

- ♪ Perception is enhanced by using all three senses.
- ♪ Discrimination is ensured because only four concepts are presented, only two dimensions are addressed, and the differences among them clearly explained.
- ♪ Memory is enhanced because only two dimensions and four concepts are addressed and thoroughly processed.
- ♪ Organization is enhanced because of the strategy's inherent binary organization.
- ♪ Attention is ensured because the student is actively involved.
- ♪ Frustration is decreased because two dimensions that differentiate among only four coordinate concepts are made explicit.

Here is an example used with secondary students showing the dimensions that characterize the concept air mass. Note that the dimensions are critical attributes.

### Typology of Air Masses

| Air mass originates . . . | in high latitudes | in low latitudes |
|---|---|---|
| Over land | Continental Polar | Continental Tropical |
| Over water | Maritime Polar | Maritime Tropical |

## ⌘ Key 5 is a Word Analysis Diagram

The Word Analysis Diagram examines one word in great detail. This strategy is an extension of the Frayer Model of Concept Attainment (Frayer, Frederick, & Klausmeier, 1969). In that model, essential and nonessential attributes, examples and nonexamples, and superordinate, subordinate, and coordinate concepts are listed.

In an important study, Peters (1974) compared the Frayer model to a text-book method of teaching social studies vocabulary concepts to 360 ninth grade students. He found that both the good and poor readers in the Frayer group significantly increased their achievement and that the Frayer group outperformed the textbook method group.

Monroe and Pendergrass (1997) compared the Frayer model to the definition-only model in teaching mathematics vocabulary. The definition-only model involved having students write the definition of the new word after an oral review of the word. The Frayer group outperformed the control group after two weeks of instruction, and led Monroe and Pendergrass to declare that the model is an effective model of teaching mathematics vocabulary.

In the Word Analysis Diagram, we modify the Frayer method in two ways. First, we use Graves' (1985) modification that adds a definition of the word, and then we include its origin, root word and affixes, and synonyms and antonyms. But we also place the entire structure in a graphic form.

Including the word origin is more important than many teachers realize. Hennings (2000) noted that a critical problem in reading and listening comprehension is students' lack of understanding of the history of the English language and the origins of words. Simply knowing that the many of our scientific words come from Greek and that *ology* means "the study of" is useful and empowering. After having taught a student with an IQ below 70 that *geo* means "Earth" and *graph* means "write" or "draw," we were pleased weeks later to hear her pass this information on to a nondisabled student in a meaningful context. Her peer was impressed, and her self-concept as a competent member of a learning community was boosted.

The Word Analysis Diagram is best reserved for use on crucial concepts that require extended discussion and deep processing. The strategy is effective because

- ♪ Perception is ensured by using all three senses.
- ♪ Discrimination is strengthened because differences in the confusing coordinate concepts are delineated.
- ♪ Memory is enhanced because of the depth of processing.
- ♪ Attention is enhanced because the student is actively involved.

A good use of the diagram in social studies is in introducing each of the five Big Ideas in geography: location, place, relationships within places, movement, and regions. The figure below represents how we used a Word Analysis Diagram to introduce the concept place. When we finished, the students with disabilities (and without) had a solid understanding of place.

## Word Analysis Diagram

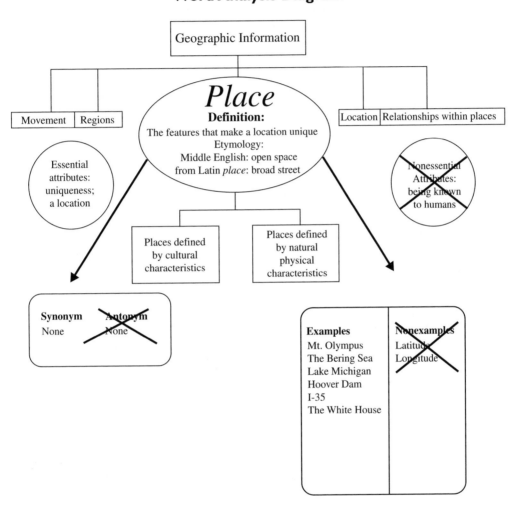

## ⟿ Key 6 is a Semantic Web

A Semantic Web (Freedman & Reynolds, 1980), sometimes called a Semantic Map (Harste, 1980), a Word Web (Kerber, 1980), or a Concept Map (Rowell, 1975), is a complex representation of the multiple facets of a word.

The Semantic Web can include word origins, definitions, superordinate, coordinate, and subordinate concepts, attributes, examples, causes, effects, emotions evoked by the term, and so forth. A word related in any way to the core concept is fair game in a Semantic Web.

Carr and Wixson (1986) noted that we must relate new vocabulary to students' background knowledge, and semantic mapping is an effective tool for stimulating that schemata.

Polloway, Patton, and Serna (2001) explained that a Semantic Map is created when the teacher writes a stimulus word on the board and has students brainstorm to generate words related to the stimulus. Then with the teacher's help, the students group related words, drawing connecting lines to show the relationships among them and the stimulus word. Semantic mapping is also useful after the new learning takes place to demonstrate how the new learning fits into the old learning.

Darch and Eaves (1986) explained that Semantic Mapping involves the "use of lines, arrows, and spatial arrangements to describe text content, structure, and key conceptual relationships" (p. 310). They recommend using keywords and, when possible, pairing those keywords with simple drawings; they warn against the use of complete sentences and too much detail.

Guastello (2000) investigated the effects of concept mapping on the science concept comprehension of inner-city seventh graders who were low achieving. With 64 students in both the experimental and control group, Guastello taught a unit on the circulatory system that lasted for eight days. The groups were introduced to the unit and then read and discussed the chapter together in class. At the end of the unit, the group who was taught each day with the concept mapping increased their performance by six standard deviations over the control group.

A Semantic Web is an effective key to unlocking Acquisition and Fluency and Proficiency to word/concept Knowledge and Comprehension because

- 🎵 Perception is assured by the use of all three senses.
- 🎵 Memory is enhanced because of the depth of processing.
- 🎵 Attention is focused because the student is actively involved.
- 🎵 Motivation is enhanced because the students have serious fun with the activity.

Because GOs are especially effective in teaching technical vocabulary and the technical vocabulary of mathematics is the most difficult for students to understand, we have chosen an example from a secondary geometry class that illustrates the students' understanding of the term *congruent triangle* in the middle of a unit of study.

## Semantic Web

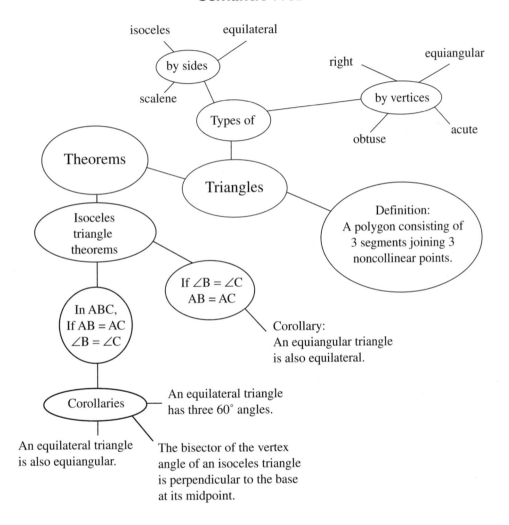

## ☞ Key 7 is Quick Sketching a Definition

In Quick Sketching a Definition, students take a new word and sketch a picture that represents the word to them. They then can share their sketches and rationales with a small group of other students. By drawing and explaining their drawings to each other, the students are using their kinesthetic sense. By seeing their sketches and the sketches of other students, students are using their vision. By hearing the other students' explanations, students are using their auditory sense. By experiencing their own and each other's drawings, the word also becomes multirepresentational and thus stored in multiple places in the students' brains, resulting in a greater likelihood that the word will be remembered and retrieved when needed.

The multiple representations also increase students' comprehension by extending their conceptualization of the word. Students may construct a drawing, thinking that he or she understands the word, but when seeing the drawings of other group members, he or she may discover that he or she had misunderstood the concept. One student with disabilities discovered by this method that unanimous consent did not mean that no one knew who was consenting. She had confused anonymous with unanimous. The misunderstanding would have gone uncorrected if we had not used the Quick Sketching strategy.

The National Council of Teachers of Mathematics endorses the use of multiple representations. Multiple representations increase junior high students' algebraic thinking significantly over students taught with traditional techniques and students' acquisition of the concept of a derivative. Using multiple representations in science has resulted in positive effects in increasing high school students' conceptualization of the molecular structure of water, and students' understanding of chemical representation increased dramatically (Kendall & Stacey, 2000; Wu et al., 2001).

Bull and Wittrock (1973) compared a sketching technique for enhancing understanding and memory of vocabulary words to rote memorization. The retention of the words by the sketching group was much higher than the retention of the control group. One of the recommendations from the Teachers' Curriculum Institute's (1999) *History Alive* curriculum is to stop periodically during lectures to have students sketch a scene to assist them in remembering the concept discussed. Wolfe (2001) recounted the experience of a freshman English teacher who had her students choose partners and create two-minute or three-minute presentations on vocabulary words to teach the rest of the class. Many of the students used sketches to represent their words; the students were delighted with their experiences.

Quick Sketching a Definition is effective in ensuring Acquisition and Proficiency and Fluency in Knowledge and Comprehension because

- ♪ Perception is ensured by using all three senses.
- ♪ Memory is assured because of the depth of processing.
- ♪ Attention is enhanced because the student is actively involved.
- ♪ Motivation is enhanced because the class is often filled with laughter.

Here is an example from a science class when we were teaching the definition of entropy.

# Entropy

## ☛ Key 8 is Total Physical Response and Vocabulary Drama

In addition to the kinesthetic act of creating the graphic organizers and quick sketching definitions, we use Total Physical Response (TPR). It adds a dynamic kinesthetic dimension to our vocabulary instruction, and our junior high and high school students have fun doing it after they get over their initial hesitance.

TPR was first described by Asher in 1969 in the *Journal of Special Education* as a tool for teaching children with disabilities. Then in 1981, Asher published a book on the method as a strategy for teaching foreign languages. We first learned about TPR from a high school Spanish teacher. Lots of noise, laughing, and the sound of desks being moved about in his class led us to ask what good things were happening in there. The high school students in his classes all talked about how much they learned from him. One day we asked him what was the source of the laughter and noise. He invited us to come watch him teach with TPR: he provided the students with a new word and then demonstrated a motor movement that symbolized the word. Then, the students all stood up and performed the movement. For example, he used the Spanish word for airplane, and the students all acted like airplanes flying around the room, a key to great motivation and memory retention.

Wolfe and Jones (1982) taught one group of high school foreign language students using TPR for 20 minutes per day and taught the control group using their traditional method. The TPR group not only scored substantially higher on their unit test, but they also expressed more enjoyment in the unit as compared to their control counterparts.

Closely related to TPR is what we call Vocabulary Drama. Duffelmeyer (1980) found that college students who acted out skits developed around vocabulary words mastered the words significantly more thoroughly than when they used traditional instruction.

TPR is a key to unlocking Acquisition and Proficiency and Fluency in Knowledge and Comprehension because

- ☞ Perception is assured by incorporating all three senses.
- ☞ Memory is assured because of the depth of processing.
- ☞ Attention is focused because the student is actively involved.
- ☞ Motivation is assured because the activity is such fun.

In chemistry, our students were confused about the meaning of single and double replacement reactions. We had Maria, a female student, and Aaron and Jared, two male students, come to the front of the room. We told the class that Jared and Maria went on a date; they then moved together and held hands. Next we said, "But along came Aaron. Maria took one look at Aaron and said 'good-bye' to Jared and left him for Aaron!" Maria dropped Jared's hand and moved over to stand by Aaron, taking his hand. After seeing the demonstration, our students acted out the reaction in groups. They never forgot the meaning of single replacement reaction.

Then, to teach double replacement reaction, we used two females and two males to demonstrate and explained that on a double date that the students decided to switch partners. The two couples acted it out, and the students never missed the definition of either single or double replacement reactions again.

## Double Replacement Reaction

## ☞ Key 9 is Linguistic Link Lists and Word Towers

Linguistic Link Lists and Word Towers are part of Hennings' (2000) "Contextually Relevant Word Study." Writing in the *Journal of Adolescent & Adult Literacy,* Hennings explained an important problem that many struggling students encounter in schools: they grow up in families in which few Greco-Latin (G-L) words are used. She cited Corson (1983) in noting that most of the English affixes and bases are G-L, and that G-L words comprise almost 100% of the academic vocabulary within the sciences and the humanities. Corson (1983) referred to G-L facility as a "lexical bar" which is easily jumped by students from homes in which G-L words are frequently used, but formidable for students without such a home language. We urge all secondary teachers to access Hennings' article, "Contextually Relevant Word Study: Adolescent Vocabulary Development Across the Curriculum" in the November 2000 issue of the *Journal of Adolescent and Adult Literacy,* pp. 268-279. Here, we present only the visual strategies from Principles 1 and 2.

Hennings' method begins with Principle 1: Highlight Greek and Latin roots, or bases, as students meet them across the curriculum. On a class bulletin board that remains up throughout the year, a student records a new target word on the Linguistic Link List, recording the base in upper case red letters and the affix in black lowercase and noting the meaning of each. We have provided an example that we used in a mathematics class. The students were astonished and amused to learn that *triangle* means "three ankles" in Latin and that *pentagon* means "five knees" in Greek.

Then, Principle 2 states: Associate new terms derived from a root with more generally known ones that contain the same root and use visual means to highlight shared elements. The lists that result from these are called Verb Towers, and they are posted on the Linguistic Link List boards as well as in students' notebooks.

Hennings' strategy is successful with students who have learning problems in Acquisition and Proficiency and Fluency of Knowledge and Comprehension because

- ♂ Perception is increased by using all three senses.
- ♂ Discrimination is acute because differences in subtle word meanings are highlighted and explained.
- ♂ Memory is enhanced because of the depth of processing.
- ♂ Attention is ensured because the student is actively involved.

In addition, the strategy is a key to Application and Generalization/Transfer of the word Comprehension because

- Discrimination is enhanced allowing the student to understand in which contexts to use the G-L root and affix.
- Motivation is ensured because mastery of G-L root and affix is powerful and immediately useful in many contexts outside the content area class.

Here is a Noun Tower, our adaptation of Hennings' Verb Tower.

## Word Tower

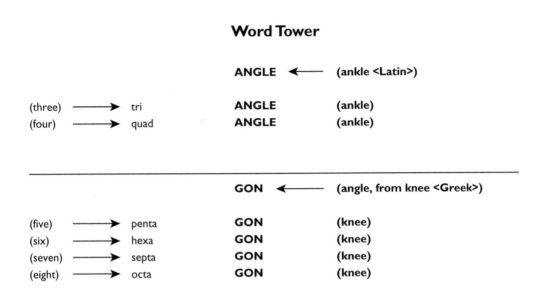

|  |  | **ANGLE** ← | (ankle <Latin>) |
| (three) → | tri | **ANGLE** | (ankle) |
| (four) → | quad | **ANGLE** | (ankle) |

|  |  | **GON** ← | (angle, from knee <Greek>) |
| (five) → | penta | **GON** | (knee) |
| (six) → | hexa | **GON** | (knee) |
| (seven) → | septa | **GON** | (knee) |
| (eight) → | octa | **GON** | (knee) |

## Linguistic Link List

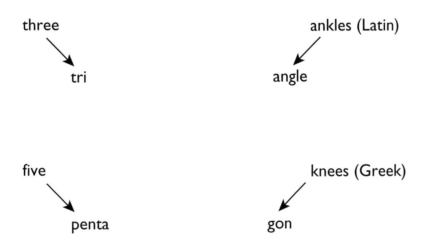

## ⚷ Key 10 is a Keyword Mnemonic Strategy

When Forness, Kavale, Blum, and Lloyd (1997) conducted their mega-analysis of meta-analyses of what works in special education, mnemonic strategies came out in first place. The effect size of mnemonic strategies was far ahead of the strategy in second place. Mnemonic strategies are the single most effective way to raise the achievement level of our students with special needs.

A number of mnemonic strategies are successful, but we have chosen to focus on the Keyword Mnemonic Strategy. The Keyword Mnemonic Strategy was developed by Atkinson (1975) and was simplified by Levin (1988) as recording, relating, and retrieving. In recording, the student changes the word to a well-known, similar-sounding word. This word is the keyword. Then, the student practices saying the target word and the keyword together. Next, in the relating stage, the student visualizes and draws a picture that symbolizes the keyword. Finally, in the retrieving stage, the student hears the target word, thinks of the keyword, and visualizes the picture and retrieves the meaning of the target word.

Mastropieri, Scruggs, and Mushinski (1990) investigated the use of Keyword mnemonics with 23 learning disabled adolescents. The students were assigned either to the Keyword condition or to a rehearsal condition. The students were taught eight difficult concrete vocabulary words and eight difficult abstract vocabulary words, such as *chiton* and *vituperation*. When the students were tested on both production recall and on comprehension, the Keyword students significantly outperformed the rehearsal condition students; on the production test, the Keyword students remembered about five abstract and six concrete words as compared to one abstract and two concrete words remembered by the rehearsal group. On the comprehension test, the Keyword group scored correctly on about seven concrete and six abstract concepts as compared to scores of four concrete and four abstract concepts by the rehearsal group.

Mastropieri and Scruggs (1991) described their investigations of the effect of the keyword strategy on learning disabled junior high school students' memory for and comprehension of abstract words. Using keyword strategy, they taught such incredibly difficult words as *catafalque* and *saprophytic* to one group of students; the second group used a rehearsal-based strategy. The comprehension task required the participants to identify the word in a new context. The keyword group not only outperformed the rehearsal group for memory, but they also demonstrated superior comprehension. The researchers concluded that even with these difficult words that they could teach anything to anyone using this method.

Students with mild disabilities have serious difficulties with memory. The Keyword Mnemonic Strategy is successful in increasing students' Acquisition, Proficiency and Fluency, and Maintenance of Knowledge and Comprehension because

- 🎵 Memory is ensured because of the depth of multisensory processing.
- 🎵 Attention is captured because the student is actively involved.
- 🎵 Motivation is enhanced because the strategy is serious fun.

Here is an example that we used to teach our students how to remember the difference between meiosis and mitosis. Our students never got them confused after we used this strategy.

### Keyword Mnemonic Strategy

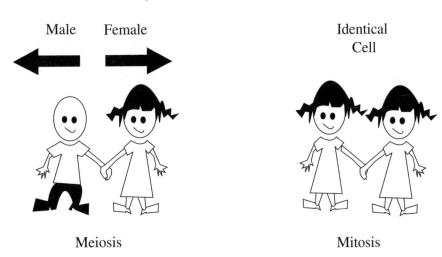

Male   Female

Identical Cell

Meiosis

Mitosis

"Me and old Sis are not identical twins. We go separate ways."

"The Mighty Sisters are identical twins. They stay together."

## ⌒ Key 11 is a Vocabulary Word Card Ring

When our students with special needs confront an important new vocabulary word in a content area, they add it to their Vocabulary Word Card Ring. Using index cards to learn vocabulary words and concepts comes recommended by a number of researchers for use across a number of disciplines and created in a variety of ways (Carr & Wixson, 1986; Dreyer, 1974; Ellis, 1992; Foil & Alber, 2002; Greenwood, 2002; Kagan, 1992; Mosher, 1999).

We use the strategy by having the word written on the front of the card and then the definition, a sketch, a Keyword Mnemonic, a semantic map, a Linguistic Link, or anything else that the student may wish written on the back. For many years, although no one individual's name emerges from the literature, special education teachers have used such cards and provided their students with metal binder rings. We then have the students punch a hole in the upper left-hand or right-hand corner of each card, place them all on the ring, and carry them around in a pocket or purse for review during odd moments. When a card is well-mastered, we remove it from the ring and file it.

After we have taught the strategy in special education pedagogy classes, we have even had our college juniors and seniors tell us that this simple strategy has revolutionized their study skills. We commonly see our students flipping through their cards while sitting in hallways waiting for classes to start or sitting in the student union in a group studying them together. The strategy is not very flashy or fun, but it is a good key to memory retention and retrieval because spaced practice and judicious review are major keys to accessing learning for all students, but especially for special needs students (e.g., see *Vocabulary Acquisition: Curricular and Instructional Implications for Diverse Learners*, Technical Report No. 14 from the National Center to Improve the Tools of Educators and the National Council of Teachers of Mathematics Standards).

A Vocabulary Word Card Ring helps students with Acquisition and Proficiency and Fluency and Maintenance of word Knowledge and Comprehension because

- Memory is enhanced because of repetition and judicious review.
- Motivation is enhanced because students often pull out the handy ring cards and use them with friends when studying for quizzes or exams.

### Vocabulary Word Card Ring

Tessellation

## ⚷ Key 12 is a Vocabulary Concept Dictionary

A Vocabulary Concept Dictionary is a dynamic document that grows with each new word introduced; it is a crucial key to organization and memory for students with disabilities. Because poor memory retrieval is a problem, the dictionary makes mechanical retrieval easy when the elusive memory is not accessible. This results in independence for the student with disabilities, and the ability to work as independently as possible is recognized as an important goal for all special needs students (Eaton & Hansen, 1978; Porter & Brophy, 1988; Pressley & Harris, 1990; Wang, 1987). Eaton and Hansen (1978) stated,

> Students who can successfully manage their own social and academic behaviors learn critical life skills. They learn to accept responsibility for their own actions and for their own learning. Students who can manage their own learning experience the thrill of knowing they can succeed at some very difficult tasks. They can replace their image of failure with one of self-confidence. In actuality, self-management is the real goal of schooling. (p. 215)

We have the students include whatever information they wish in their content area dictionaries, whether a sketch, Keyword Mnemonic, examples and nonexamples, coordinate concepts, a semantic map, or anything else that a student identifies as being most helpful.

This strategy helps create independence by helping students maintain use of the word in order to apply it because it is an:

- Organizational strategy that will allow them to use the word when memory does fail.

Here are several examples from some of our students taking Algebra I.

**Mathematics Vocabulary Dictionary Matrix**

| Word | Definition | Super-ordinate | Sub-ordinate | Co-ordinate | Examples |
|------|-----------|----------------|--------------|-------------|----------|
| Mean | Average; sum of numbers in the set divided by number of numbers | Measure of Central Tendency | | Median, Mode | $3+2+8+5+8 = 26 \div 5 = $ **5.2** |
| Median | Middle number of a set when arranged in numerical order | Measure of Central Tendency | | Mean, Mode | 2, 3, **5**, 8, 8 |
| Mode | Number that occurs most often in a set | Measure of Central Tendency | | Mean, Median | 2, 3, 5, **8, 8** |
| Triangle | Polygon with three sides and three angles | Polygon | Scalene, Equilateral, Isosceles, Right, Equiangular, Obtuse, Acute | Square, Octagon, etc. | |
| Obtuse Triangle | A triangle with one angle greater than 90° | Triangle | | Acute Triangle, Right Triangle, Equiangular Triangle | |

# 4

# Teaching Devices for Increasing Student Learning From Lectures

## In This Chapter

*In this chapter, we will add new keys to our key ring that will help make us more powerful teachers. For only small adaptations to the ways we typically teach, we can teach to all of our students, not simply the average and bright students. When all of our students are educated citizens, we all win.*

*The different strategies in this chapter serve a variety of needs, and each has a place where it fits best in our curricula. Many lessons we teach can be enhanced by using several of the strategies in one lesson and thereby allowing us to accommodate more needs. When more students are finding that we are meeting their needs, they become more highly motivated to learn. The success cycle escalates, and everybody wins.*

**W**e wish that teachers never felt like they had to lecture, but it is a fact that many do rely heavily on lecturing (Brophy, 1988; Good & Brophy, 1984). In fact, Hawkins and Brady (1994) asserted that despite the fact that many instructional options are available to us, lecturing is the most frequently used instructional technique in secondary schools. Thirty years ago, 70% of class time was spent in lectures, and although we have made progress, Putnam, Deshler, and Schumaker (1993) found that we still lecture half the time in junior high and high schools. They interviewed 120 teachers in three states and found that the teachers spent half their time lecturing, with tenth grade teachers lecturing slightly more frequently than seventh grade. Of course, one goal of secondary teachers is to prepare students for success in college, and 80% of college class time is spent listening to lectures.

Hawkins and Brady (1994) noted that lecturing is a cost effective method of instruction but cautioned that many students with learning problems do not learn well from traditional lectures; they need accommodations.

When Suritsky (1992) asked learning disabled college students what their instructors could to help them learn better from lectures, they identified five strategies: giving the students lecture handouts or outlines, slowing down the rate of delivery, explicitly identifying the most important lecture points, using overhead transparencies regularly, and making the tests reflect the lecture content.

The keys presented here will help unlock the doors to Acquisition and Knowledge.

- Key 13: Simply Slowing Down
- Key 14: Pause Procedure
- Key 15: Cueing the Most Important Points
- Key 16: Explicitly Teaching the Big Ideas
- Key 17: Giving a Preview, Overview, or Advance Organizer
- Key 18: Soliciting Concrete Examples From Students' Lives
- Key 19: Providing More Examples Than You Think They Need
- Key 20: Providing Plenty of Concrete Nonexamples in Concept Teaching
- Key 21: Teaching Concepts Through a Concrete, Semiconcrete, Abstract (CSA) or Concrete-Representational-Abstract (CRA) Series of Examples
- Key 22: Role Playing Difficult Content
- Key 23: Incorporating Humor

## ☛ Key 13 is Simply Slowing Down

Hughes and Shuritsky (1993) asked college students with learning disabilities what they most needed lecturers to do in order to help them learn more effectively. The students' biggest complaint was that their instructors lectured too quickly. In addition, different types of content require different speeds of delivery, with more difficult content requiring a slower lecture speed.

A lecture is fast if the rate of speed is 120 or more words per minute. Students with learning problems cannot make sense of what the instructor is saying and write quickly enough to process what is being said and keep up with notes. Nine morphemes per statement is the maximum that people understand without loss of meaning. Some listeners can only process five morphemes per statement; yet Moran (1980) found that teachers average ten morphemes per statement. If the average listener has difficulty understanding the teacher, the task is much more difficult for students with disabilities.

A lecture has high information density if it contains many ideas, also called information units (Hughes & Suritsky, 1993). Writing in an *ERIC Digest*, Potts (1993) recommended that information density be kept low, with no more than 50% of the material in a lecture being new to the students.

We think it is a good idea to record ourselves occasionally when we lecture and then calculate both the speed and the information density of our lectures and adjust accordingly. Just because we think we have taught it, does not mean the students learned it. In the final analysis, what counts is what was learned.

Simply Slowing Down is an effective inclusion strategy helping students acquire knowledge and comprehension because

- ♪ Frustration is decreased when students can keep up with their notes.
- ♪ Motivation is enhanced when students see that they are keeping up with their notes.
- ♪ Perception is increased when students have time to process auditory information.

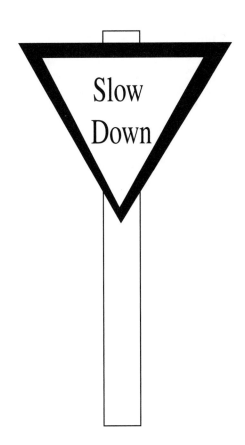

## ⊶ Key 14 is the Pause Procedure

If a lecture is both fast and dense, the special needs students are overwhelmed. In addition to slowing down the rate of presentation, we can use the Pause Procedure (Rowe, 1976, 1980, 1983) to let students retrieve information they missed due to attention problems and also to increase their attention. This is an important strategy for our students with attention deficit disorders.

During the Pause Procedure, students catch up on their notes and ask their group members or neighbors to clarify statements about which they are unclear. Kiewra (1985) reviewed the literature on the Pause Procedure and recommended what he called segmenting lectures; this refers to lecturing for six or seven minutes and then pausing three or four minutes while the students take notes and consult with each other.

DiVesta and Smith (1979) interspersed pauses in conjunction with group discussion and found higher scores on both immediate and delayed free recall tests. Hughes, Hendrickson, and Hudson (1986) studied the Pause Procedure with 16 low-achieving and high-achieving middle school science students. During the pauses, student triads discussed the lecture, shared their notes, and clarified nebulous concepts. The experiment revealed that seven of the eight low-achieving students and seven of the eight high-achieving students improved factual recall during the pause condition.

Hawkins, Brady, and Hamilton (1991) investigated the effects of instructional pauses on the academic achievement of six students with learning problems. All six students improved under the pause condition as compared to the traditional lecture, and their performance under instructional pause conditions improved over time.

Ruhl, Hughes, and Gajar (1990) also found support for the lecture pause in increasing the learning of college students with learning disabilities. They investigated the efficacy of the Pause Procedure with 15 college students with learning disabilities and 15 nondisabled students. Two-minute pauses were interspersed in logical places throughout a videotaped lecture, and as a result, objective test measures improved.

The Pause Procedure is an effective inclusion strategy because

𝄐 Frustration is decreased when students can keep up with their notes.
𝄐 Motivation is increased when students can see that they are keeping up with the other students and the teacher.
𝄐 Perception is increased when students can check with each other to complete their notes and correct as necessary during pauses.

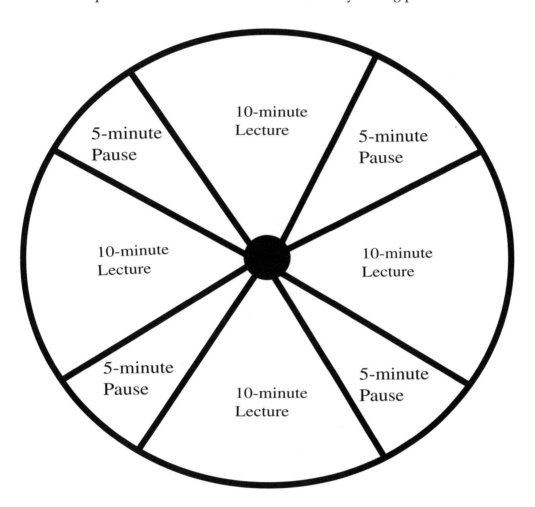

## ⛌ Key 15 is Cueing the Most Important Points

Because we know that students with learning problems have difficulty discriminating between critical and nonessential information, we need to make the main points explicit by cueing them. We do this by explicitly teaching our students with disabilities a set of cues and teaching them to make notes of that cued information (Titsworth, 2001).

In a study of college students with and without learning disabilities, Hughes and Suritsky (1994) found that the total number of uncued information units recorded by the students was 56% for the nondisabled students and 36% for the learning disabled students. When the information was cued, the nondisabled students recorded an average of 77% of the information, and the learning disabled students recorded an average of 44% of the information, a definite improvement but not sufficient in itself.

We must explicitly teach our cueing system to our students because students are often unaware of an instructor's cues. Researchers have found that written cues are more effective than verbal cues, so we should be certain to cue by writing essential information on the board or overhead (Fahmy & Bilton, 1990a, 1990b; Scerbo, Warm, & Dember, 1992).

We develop and explicitly teach a cueing system at the beginning of the school year. For example, some cues we use and teach are

- Writing the essential points on the board in bullet style.
- Stating, "This is a critical detail. Be sure to write this in your notes," and then writing it on the board or overhead.
- Stating, "You will see this on a test. Count on it," and then writing it on the board or overhead.

Many researchers recommend repetition (Annis & Annis, 1987; Belfiore, Skinner, & Ferkis, 1995; Blankenship, 1982; Byrne, 1981; Cahnmann, 2000; Cook, 1994; Maley, 1993; Powell & Thomson, 1996; Sanza, 1982; Wing, 1980) in widely diverse arenas. We use choral responding and reiteration to cue in several ways, such as the following.

- Stating the point three times, as in
  - "Denotation is the dictionary definition of a word; connotation is a feeling or association suggested by the word."
  - "Denotation is the dictionary definition of a word; connotation is a feeling or association suggested by the word."
  - "Denotation is the dictionary definition of a word; connotation is a feeling or association suggested by the word."

Sometimes when we use this technique, we speak in a stage whisper as though we were sharing a very important secret. Sometimes we start in a stage whisper and end by throwing our arms up and shouting.

In addition to repetition, we use choral responding. Researchers have recommended choral responding for mastery and for checking for understanding with all students, but they have strongly recommended the strategy with special needs students in both academic and vocational classes (Heward, Gardner, & Barbetta, 1996; Kagan, 1992). We have used it extensively with special needs high school students and found it not only effective, but fun for the students. College students also enjoy it.

We use it like this:

- Stating a fact and having the students repeat it back as a group, as in stating, "Connecting two sentences by using a comma without a conjunction is an error called a comma splice," and having the students repeat it back three times. We then give them time to write it.

- Stating a fact, then asking the students in a question form to repeat the fact back three times. For example,
  - "An issue is a subject about which people disagree. What is an issue?"
  - "An issue is a subject about which people disagree. What is an issue?"
  - "An issue is a subject about which people disagree. What is an issue?"

Note that when we use choral responding that we need to teach a visual cue to show the students when to respond. This is one way to cue:

(1) We hold our hand up by our throat with palm facing us while we ask the question.

(2) We pause while looking at the students.

(3) Then we say, "Class?" while extending the hand, palm upward to them. This signals them to respond as a group.

Other cue words we teach are those organizing words such as *first*, *next*, and *finally*; *alternatively*, *in contrast*, and *on the other hand*; *if*, *therefore*, and *because*. Not only should we verbally teach our students the code words we select, but making a chart and posting it in our room is imperative. Not only will it help us in the early stages of our students' learning the new words because we can point to a word as we say it in our lecture, but it will remind us of the agreed-upon words when we forget for a moment as we are lecturing.

Explicitly teaching lecture cues is an effective strategy because

- Motivation is increased when students see that they are able to write down what the teacher thinks is important.
- Discrimination between critical information and less important information is ensured when the teacher explicitly cues the critical information.
- Frustration is decreased when students are certain that they recorded the critical information.
- Attention is activated when the student sees or hears the cue.

| **Lecture Cues** |
| :---: |
| I say it three times. |
| I hold up one finger as I say it. |
| I write it on the board or overhead. |
| I have you do a "drum roll" before I say it. |
| I say, "Write this down." |
| I have you say it back to me. |

| **Lecture Cue Words** |
| :---: |
| <u>Sequence</u> |
| First, Second, Next, Then, After, Finally |
| <u>Contrast</u> |
| Alternatively, In Contrast, But, On the Other Hand |
| <u>Causality</u> |
| If, Because, Therefore |

## ⌐ Key 16 is Explicitly Teaching the Big Ideas

A number of researchers have argued that explicitly teaching the Big Ideas of a discipline is crucial for students with disabilities (Carnine, 1994; Coyne, Kame'enui, & Simmons, 2001; Grossen, 2002; Grossen et al., 2002; Kame'enui & Carnine, 1998; NCITE, 1998). Grossen and her colleagues (2002), writing for the U.S. Office of Special Education Programs, wrote that Big Ideas are one of the six principles of accommodation for students with learning problems:

> Big Ideas, concepts and principles that facilitate the most efficient and broad acquisition of knowledge across a range of examples are presented. Big ideas make it possible for students to learn the most and learn it as efficiently as possible, because "small" ideas can often be best understood in relationship to larger, "umbrella concepts." (p. 71)

Every subject has its Big Ideas that are identified by the learned societies of that discipline. During the first week of school, we explicitly explain to the students that every discipline has its Big Ideas around which the study of that discipline revolves. Then, we explicitly teach the Big Ideas of our discipline. Each day when we are ready to begin our lesson, we explicitly identify the Big Idea(s) that we will be addressing that day.

The American Association for the Advancement of Science does not use the words *Big Ideas* in its document, *Science for All Americans* from its Project 2061, but rather uses the term *Common Themes.* Those themes are generally called Big Ideas by practitioners.

Teaching the Big Ideas is good for all learners, but especially for students with special needs because

- Motivation is ensured when we continuously return to a small number of known ideas.
- Attention is captured when the new information is tied to something we know well.
- Discrimination is enhanced when we make the most important ideas explicit.
- Memory is strengthened when we have fewer, but more important, things to remember and when well-known schemata are elaborated.

| Systems | Models | Constancy & Change | | Evolution | Scale |
|---|---|---|---|---|---|
| | Physical | Stability & Equilibrium | Trends | Possibilities | |
| | Conceptual | Conservation | Cycles | Rates | |
| | Mathematical | Symmetry | Chaos | Interactions | |

## ☛ Key 17 involves Giving a Preview, Overview, or Advance Organizer

A number of researchers (Jordan, 1993; Lapp, Fisher, & Flood, 1999; Martin & Blanc, 1994; Whitman, 1982) have recommended previewing/overviewing content before beginning a lesson. Before we begin to lecture, we preview by giving a three to five sentence summary of what the students will learn. If we can provide an overhead of the preview/overview, it is so much better. But at least we have the students write down the preview/overview in their notes.

Ausubel (1968) developed the advance organizer. Although he argued that an advance organizer is very different from an overview, he stated that what the student already knows is the greatest predictor of how much he will learn from a lesson. He said that in contrast to an overview, which simply states key ideas, an advance organizer is a bridge between what the student already knows and what he is going to learn. However, the teachers we know use the term *advance organizer* for almost any activity that engages the student before a lesson and helps him prepare to learn the new material, and the majority of the research on advance organizers uses the term in the same way.

A number of researchers have found a wide variety of advance organizers to be effective interventions with students who have disabilities. For example, Lenz and Alley (1983) investigated the use of advance organizers with learning disabled (LD) secondary students. Their advance organizers involved highlighting the important information in a lesson. Their participants were 46 LD and 51 non-LD students. When the students' teachers used advance organizers before beginning their lessons, the LD students in the experimental group significantly outperformed the LD students who were not provided advance organizers. In addition, the LD students in the advance organizer group identified more important information about the lesson, as compared to the control LD group, who identified more unimportant information. In the advance organizer condition, the gap between LD and non-LD students was significantly narrowed.

Previews/overviews/advance organizers are good inclusion strategies because:

- Organization of thought is promoted.
- Confusion is avoided because students either get the big picture or connect the new learning to a concept with which they are familiar.

Below is an example of a preview/overview of a lesson on giving a persuasive speech.

---

Today we are going to learn about adapting your persuasive essay to use it as a persuasive speech.

Specifically, we are going to:
1. learn about catching and keeping the attention of our audience;
2. think about our audience's counterarguments; and
3. adjust the tone of our speech to fit our audience.

---

## ⊷ Key 18 involves Soliciting Concrete Examples From Students' Lives during the lesson

Gersten, Baker, and Marks (1998) recommended soliciting concrete examples of new concepts from the lives of English language learners with learning problems. Their recommendation was based on a review of the literature and on professional focus groups of practicing teachers.

When we were teaching our students the concept of Cycles of Change in science, we asked them to relate examples of Cycles of Change in their own lives. With nudging from us, one student identified such cycles as the school year starting, Thanksgiving holiday, Christmas holiday, spring break, and the end of school. Another student identified wearing hot, warm, cool, and cold weather clothes. Another identified being born, growing up, growing old, and dying. The cycles they identified from their own experience created a neural network for Cycles of Change, and they could connect the new information we gave them to the network they had created. We turned this information into graphic information on a table and further strengthened the connection.

When we were teaching about migration and asked volunteers to share their reasons for moving from one place to another, we were surprised with the candor with which they talked about how their lives demonstrated the usual causes of migration: economic problems and human rights problems. The students volunteered such economic problems as a parent being laid off and no longer able to afford the upscale apartment, or the birth of a new baby that put a financial strain on the family, or the unexpected cancer of a sibling that caused a mother to quit work to stay with the child. The human rights violations were reflected by problems with neighbors, unreasonable landlords, or abuse by housemates. We never had a student miss a test question on the causes of migration and were consistently impressed with their essay responses on the topic.

When we taught about propaganda techniques in a language arts class, we asked the students to give us examples of the various types of propaganda that they had encountered. All of our students, especially those with special needs, understood the concept much more clearly when we contextualized it in this way than when it was contextualized in other ways.

Soliciting Concrete Examples From Students' Lives is a powerful inclusion strategy because

- Motivation is stronger when students see how a concept applies to themselves.
- Attention is secured when motivation is stronger.
- Confusion is avoided when students have a concrete example in their schema to which to attach the new learning.
- Memory is activated when students deep process to find their own examples and when they develop multiple representations from hearing other students' examples.

## ⌥ Key 19 is Providing More Examples Than You Think They Need

Jones and Wilson (1997) wrote,

Students learn from examples. An important part of the business of education is selecting and organizing examples to use in instruction such that students will be able to solve problems they encounter outside of instruction.... First, the number of instructional examples and the organization of practice activities are frequently insufficient for students to achieve mastery (Silbert, Carnine, & Stein, 1990).... A second deficiency is an inadequate sampling of the range of examples that define a given concept. If some instances of a concept are underrepresented in instruction or simply not included in instruction, students with LD will predictably fail to learn that concept adequately.... The adequacy of a selection of examples depends on several factors, including (a) possible variations of the concept, (b) the likelihood that irrelevant or misleading variables will be erroneously associated with the concept, (c) the complexity of the concept being taught, and (d) the variety of potential applications of the concept. (p. 151)

Yoho (1985) compared teaching social studies concepts using critical attributes as opposed to using best examples and then having students contrast the best examples to other examples. He found that overall his students understood his concepts far better and retained the concepts longer when he used the best example technique as compared to the critical attributes technique. In addition, his male students who were poor readers performed far better with this strategy than with the critical attributes strategy; so in addition to soliciting examples from students' lives, we provide many more examples for them than we think they could possibly need.

Providing many more examples than we think students need promotes the learning of students with special needs because

- ♪ Motivation is heightened if at least one of the examples is related to the students' lives.
- ♪ Attention is stronger if motivation is heightened.
- ♪ Confusion is decreased when students have multiple representations provided by the multiple examples.
- ♪ Memory is enhanced if students find an example among those given that already exists in their schema.

---

**Examples of Transfer in Propaganda**

```
Beautiful people all buy our product!
Rich people all want our product!
Important people love our product!
Movie stars all use our product!
A beautiful woman with a car to sell the car
A happy family at the holidays to sell a
product
A slender, fit person with an exercise
machine to sell it
```

## ⛌ Key 20 is Providing Plenty of Concrete Nonexamples in Concept Teaching

We all use examples when we teach new concepts, and when we teach a new concept, our nondisabled learners may understand the abstraction with few examples. Our special needs learners, however, will probably not understand without both numerous examples and nonexamples. The nonexamples should be those that are frequently confused with examples. They highlight the critical attributes of the concept we are teaching.

Researchers have stressed the importance of nonexamples in physics concept learning, in learning the geometric concept of semiregular polyhedra, and in language learning of students with disabilities (Arons, 1984; Cohen & Carpenter, 1980; Cole, 1979).

Swanson (1972) examined the effects of positive and negative examples on students' learning of environmental concepts. He found that presenting examples and nonexamples in a rational teaching set promoted correct classification of newly encountered items and that omitting nonexamples resulted in students' overgeneralization of the concepts.

McMurray (1974) investigated the use of nonexamples with 64 middle school students with mild mental retardation who were learning geometric shapes. Presenting a wide variety of examples and nonexamples with matched pairs led to the students' best mastering the geometric concepts without overgeneralization.

Concrete nonexamples help students learn new concepts because

- Discrimination between the target concept and similar concepts is made more acute because the nonexamples help point out the critical attributes, and in addition, discrimination is increased when multiple non-representations are provided.
- Memory is supported when examples are contrasted with nonexamples.

---

**Non-Examples of Transfer in Propaganda**

```
Hurry! Gigantic Sale This Weekend
We only Have 150 Left!
First Month's Membership Free!
We provide a solid product at a fair price
It's a wonderful product!
You'll be glad you did!
Catchy Jingles or Slogans
For Service You Can Trust
Looks Great! Feels Great!
```

---

## ⚷ Key 21 is Teaching Concepts Through a Concrete, Semiconcrete, Abstract (CSA) or Concrete Representational-Abstract (CRA) Series of Examples

A number of researchers have recommended teaching new concepts by starting with concrete examples, moving through semiconcrete or representational examples, and only then on to abstractions (CSA or CRA) in teaching students with disabilities. For example, in their review of the literature on teaching algebra to learning disabled adolescents, Maccini, McNaughton, and Ruhl (1999) found empirical support for beginning with concrete examples before advancing to semiconcrete or representational examples and then finally to abstract examples.

Morin and Miller (1998) used a CRA sequence to teach multiplication facts and word problems to three middle school students with mild mental retardation. Pretests and posttests revealed excellent progress for all three students. Student 1 scored 50% on the pretest and 90% on the posttest, Student 2 scored 70% on the pretest and 90% on the posttest, and Student 3 scored 20% on the pretest and 90% on the posttest.

Cass, Cates, Jackson, and Smith (2000) used concrete manipulatives to teach three learning disabled secondary students problem-solving skills involving calculating perimeter and area. Initially unable to solve perimeter and area problems, the students received 15 to 20 minutes of instruction on a geoboard for five to seven days. They reached performance criterion (80%) at that time, and three weekly maintenance checks indicated that they could solve all problems correctly with the geoboard. When they returned from Christmas vacation, the students were instructed to solve four perimeter and four area problems without the use of the geoboard, using only pencil and paper. All three students solved all eight problems correctly.

CSA/CRA help support the learning of students with learning problems because

- ♪ Motivation is increased when students see that they can succeed by working with the concrete examples.
- ♪ Attention is stronger when motivation is strong.
- ♪ Perception is increased by starting with the concrete examples.
- ♪ Memory is activated when the abstract learning is attached to the concrete representations.
- ♪ Confusion is avoided by working with the concrete examples first.

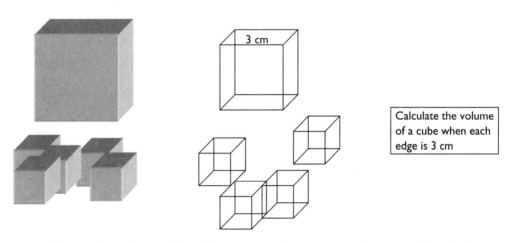

Calculate the volume of a cube when each edge is 3 cm

Phase 1: Concrete (Realia)          Phase 2: Semiconcrete (Representational)          Phase 3: Abstract

## ⚭ Key 22 involves Role Playing Difficult Content

Role playing or simulations are an excellent way to enhance and strengthen didactic instruction. Role play is especially valuable in teaching difficult content. For example, chemistry can be confusing for students who do not have special needs, and it is certainly confusing for the students with special needs who choose to enroll. When Bob, one of our high school students with special needs, encountered chemistry, we had to think of a way to help him understand single replacement reactions and double replacement reactions. We decided to have him, another boy (Ted), and a girl (Mary) act out the process. We explained how he (Bob) and Mary had gone on a date. We had them join hands and walk over to stand by Ted. We then explained that the girl decided that she liked Ted better than she liked Bob. She dropped Bob's hand and took Ted's hand. Using that strategy, he understood single replacement reaction.

Next, we explained that double replacement reaction was like two couples going on a double date. We had a different boy and two different girls act this one out with Bob. (We didn't use the previous students, because we thought it might cause Bob to be confused between single and double replacement reactions.) This time, we had each couple hold hands. Then we told them that each girl decided she liked the other boy better than she liked her own date. Each girl dropped the hand of the boy who was her date and took the hand of the other boy. They then realigned to stand side-by-side with their new date. By this simple, quick strategy, all four of the students had a much clearer understanding of single and double replacement reactions.

A number of science education researchers have successfully used role playing to teach difficult content. Resnick and Wilensky (1998) argued that role playing is a powerful tool in teaching both science and math, especially in the new science of complexity, which is the study of complex systems. Tyas and Cabot (1999) used role play to help students understand the energy changes involved in an exothermic reaction by modeling how bond-breaking takes in energy, activates energy, causes a rise in temperature, and gives out energy. Batts (1999) successfully used role play to help secondary students understand the abstract concept of color subtraction, Johnson (1999) used role play to teach how the kidney functions with good results, and Stencel and Barkoff (1993) used it to teach students about protein synthesis.

Role Playing Difficult Content is a powerful strategy because

- 🎵 Motivation is enhanced when students are physically involved and also when students are having fun.
- 🎵 Attention is heightened when motivation is enhanced.
- 🎵 Perception is stronger when the visual and kinesthetic senses are engaged.
- 🎵 Discrimination is more acute when contrasting concepts are role played.
- 🎵 Confusion is lessened when students have a physical experience of the concept.
- 🎵 Frustration is avoided when confusion is minimized.
- 🎵 Memory is activated when students deep process the information.

Here is how one of our classes looked when we were teaching the concepts of *perpendicular* and *parallel*.

Parallel

Perpendicular

## ⌀┐ Key 23 is Incorporating Humor

Most of us enjoy a lecture more if humor is incorporated. Fun is motivating, and motivating uninterested learners is one of our challenges as middle school and high school teachers. Humor has been found to be a motivator for those most difficult-to-motivate students: students with behavior disabilities.

McDermott, Rothenberg, and Johnson (1999) interviewed six middle and secondary students in high poverty urban schools. They asked the students whom they interviewed to identify the characteristics that exemplified their most outstanding teachers. The use of humor was one of the characteristics identified. High school seniors and college freshmen who were in remedial classes also identified humor as crucial. When 60 British teachers of students with behavioral disorders were asked the most important personal characteristic that a teacher must have in order to work successfully with behavior disordered students, they identified the teacher's use of humor (Blake & Garner, 2000).

In *School Science Review,* Hawkey (1998) noted that humor not only increases student motivation, but can also increase learning, and Myrah and Erlauer (1999) noted that humor is a brain-based strategy. For example, Desberg and colleagues (1981) found that lectures that incorporate humor related to the subject allowed students to remember information longer. Among university students, humor related to the lecture topic that served as a form of repetition of the target information resulted in increased academic performance as opposed to the nonhumorous lecture. Humor unrelated to the content and therefore not a form of repetition did not increase performance. Nonhumorous repetition, like the humorous repetition, did increase performance. Therefore, repetition, whether or not humorous, increased performance; however, the students reported that they enjoyed the humorous presentation more than the nonhumorous presentation. Therefore, Desberg and colleagues recommend humorous repetition.

In his review of the literature, James (2001) found that when teachers filled their classes with relevant humor, students perceived them as interesting, high in support, and affirming. He noted that using relevant humor three to four times per hour for a semester in college statistics and psychology classes significantly increased students' final examination scores over those of control groups using no planned humor.

Schiff (2000) successfully incorporated humor into a Shakespeare class by having students create answering machine messages for the characters and that characters could leave as messages on each others' machines. He explained that this strategy gave students the opportunity to interpret the humor and irony in Shakespeare's work.

Humor is a teacher's friend when working with students who have learning problems because

- ♪ Motivation is captured by funny things.
- ♪ Attention is captured when motivation is captured.
- ♪ Memory is captured when attention is captured.

---

### The Top Ten List

*The Top Ten Things You Need to Know About*
*Graphing Systems of Equations*

(1) A system is **_Consistent_** if it has at least one ordered pair that satisfies both equations.

(2) A system is **_Inconsistent_** if it has no ordered pair that satisfies both equations.

(3) A system is **_Independent_** if it has exactly one solution.

(4) A system is **_Dependent_** if it has an infinite number of solutions.

(5) A set of equations with the same variables is a **_System of Equations_**.

(6) **_Graph an equation_** if you want to estimate the solution.

(7) **_Substitute_** if one of the variables has a coefficient of 1 or −1.

(8) **_Add_** if one of the variables has opposite coefficients in the two equations.

(9) **_Subtract_** if one of the variables has the same coefficient in the two equations.

(10) Your teacher is a **_diva_**!

# 5

# Increasing Learning by Using Notetaking Strategies

## In This Chapter

*Notetaking Strategies are keys to help students with disabilities access the Knowledge and Comprehension domains. In general, notetaking strategies help students by providing (1) an encoding function that causes them to process information deeply and (2) an external storage function that provides access to information that is not yet stored in long-term memory.*

*Notetaking is surprisingly complex. Students must sustain their attention, comprehend what the teacher is saying, discriminate between critical and irrelevant information, paraphrase the information into a note format, organize it in a coherent way, and record it readably and quickly. It is no wonder that so many students with learning problems find notetaking a perplexing activity.*

*We can take great pleasure in the fact that students with disabilities can be taught to take notes more effectively. Because good notetaking strategies impose structure, they are by nature good techniques for working with students with special needs. If our students are to learn to take notes, we have to teach them explicitly how to conduct the notetaking strategies we want them to use. We need to ensure that they receive substantial practice in the strategies we select, and we need to use good lecturing devices to ensure that they know what information should go in their notes.*

Students in secondary school and in college must be able to learn from lectures because lecture is a major method of instruction in those settings. For example, Putnam et al. (1993) interviewed 120 teachers of whom half taught seventh grade students and half taught tenth grade students. The teachers taught in eight school districts in three states. The teachers reported spending approximately half their class periods lecturing, with tenth grade teachers lecturing slightly more than seventh grade teachers.

Because lecture is so prevalent, teaching secondary students to learn from lectures is important. Notetaking is the primary strategy used to learn the content from lectures; so it is important to teach secondary students to apply that strategy effectively. Preparing students who are going to college makes learning how to take notes even more important because Anderson and Armbruster (1986) found that college students spend 80% of class time listening to lectures.

Craik and Lockhart (1972) used a level of processing theory, and Ladas (1980) used an information processing model of memory to try to explain why notetaking is important: the first attributes notetaking's effects to encoding (a process) and the second attributes notetaking's effects to external storage (a product).

DiVesta and Gray (1972) noted that as an encoding function, notetaking activates the student's attention and assists in the transfer of information to long-term memory. They explained that the student actively processes the information; he or she cognitively processes it by coding, integrating, and transforming the lecture content into meaningful notes. By these processes, the information becomes part of the student's schema.

They explained that notetaking provided for external storage by preserving the content of the lecture. This preservation provides for later revision of the material and review of the material as desired. The revision and review allows the student to organize and consolidate the materials more efficiently and elaborate upon them as needed. Carrier, Williams, and Dalgaard (1988) claimed that notetaking provides a permanent, portable documentation of the lecture information and is the vehicle by which students gain the lecture content.

A number of researchers have found that students with Learning Disabilities have difficulty taking notes. This is not surprising because notetaking is complex, and sustaining attention, comprehending, discriminating between critical and irrelevant information, paraphrasing the information into a note format, organizing it in a coherent way, and recording it readably and quickly (Hughes & Suritsky, 1993) are all essential to the process.

Suritsky (1992) wanted to know what kinds of problems students with learning disabilities had with notetaking, so he interviewed 31 college students with learning disabilities. He found that the students' most difficult notetaking problem was writing fast enough. Students also reported difficulty with sustaining attention, discriminating between essential and nonessential information, and interpreting their notes when using them to study later.

Because notetaking is so difficult for students with disabilities, many of the interventions for students in secondary schools and colleges are accommodations rather than remediation. The accommodations, which certainly are appropriate in many instances, include having faculty provide copies of their lecture notes, allowing students to tape their lectures, or providing notetakers. However, Suritsky and Hughes (1991) have argued that this is a Band-Aid approach because it omits the encoding process. Instead, they contended that students with Learning Disabilities should be taught how to take notes effectively and that the accommodations teachers make should allow them to do so.

In this chapter, we will address the following keys to help students with learning problems open the doors of Acquisition and Proficiency and Fluency to enter the rooms of Knowledge and Comprehension in our disciplines:

- Key 24: Guided Notes
- Key 25: Strategic Notes
- Key 26: AWARE Strategy
- Key 27: Brick and Mortar Notes
- Key 28: Three-Column Personalized Notes
- Key 29: Newspaper Notes
- Key 30: Power Notes

## ⊶ Key 24 is Guided Notes

Developed by Lazarus (1988, 1991), Guided Notes are a skeleton outline of the main ideas and related concepts of a presentation with spaces for students to insert supporting information. The guide may include key vocabulary, related issues, and contrasting views. Guides may include less information for more skilled students or more information for less skilled students. While lecturing, the teacher uses a completed Guided Notes overhead transparency so the students can see as well as hear and write the important notes.

Lazarus (1996) explained that the teacher starts with her existing notes and highlights the skeleton information needed on the students' copies. She then asks a paraprofessional, secretary, or volunteer to word process this information, and she saves this as the student copy of the notes under a name such as "Teapot Dome Guided Notes Student Version."

Then, using a different color highlighter, the teacher highlights the information to be filled in the blanks on the overhead transparency and ultimately by the students in their study guide. The teacher gives this to the typist, and the typist opens the previous word-processed document, adds the new information, and saves it under a different name such as "Teapot Dome Guided Notes Overhead Transparency Version." Lazarus (1996) explained that teachers who have tried this strategy consider the time involved reasonable, considering the multiple times the notes will be used.

Lazarus (1996) reported results of using Guided Notes with Review in a secondary science class; two students in the class had disabilities. The first student with disabilities scored between 10% and 25% without Guided Notes on the first five daily quizzes, between 60% and 70% on the first week of Guided Notes without Review, and between 75% and 90% during the second week of Guided Notes with Review.

The second student with disabilities scored between 20% and 35% on the quizzes during the baseline (No Guided Notes) condition, between 55% and 70% during the Guided Notes without Review week, and between 80% and 95% during the week of Guided Notes with Review. The students without disabilities increased in performance also, from approximately 75% on the baseline, to approximately 80% on the Guided Notes without Review, to approximately 90% on the Guided Notes with Review.

Lazarus (1991) also assessed the effectiveness of Guided Notes with and without daily Review in two eleventh grade history classes totaling 45 nondisabled and 5 disabled students. Baseline chapter test scores for the disabled students ranged from 25% to 40%. Under the Guided Note without Review condition, the disabled students' test scores ranged from 59% to 65%, a respectable gain, and if raising a failing grade to a passing grade, it is socially significant. However, when the Guided Notes was paired with daily Review of the notes (ten minutes at the end of the class period), their average scores ranged from 84% to 96%, a highly socially significant change. The Guided Notes provided explicitness and structure, and the daily Review provided repetition, the three keys to helping students with special needs succeed.

Kline (1986) taught ten learning disabled secondary students to use Guided Notes. During a traditional lecture notetaking condition that was augmented by the teacher's overhead transparency of critical information, the students' average grade was in the D range on quizzes. Under the guided notes condition, the students' average grade was in the A range. In addition, the students said that they liked taking the guided notes because it helped them keep focused on the material.

Guided Notes, especially if paired with daily Review, helps students access Knowledge and Comprehension because

- Attention is increased because the students are actively engaged.
- Perception is increased because three modalities are involved.
- Discrimination between essential and nonessential information is increased because the teacher has guided the notetaking process.
- Confusion is decreased because the student is guided through the note-taking process with three modalities involved.
- Memory is increased if used with the daily Review.

Here is an example of a student's Guided Notes Outline for Literature.

| Use this form to take your notes during the class. |
|---|
| **The Plot: A Chain of Related Events** |
| **Conflict** |
| **Complications** |
| **Suspense** |
| **Climax** |
| **Resolution** |

## ⊶ Key 25 is Strategic Notes

Boyle (1996) developed Strategic Notes with students in regular education; he later extended the research to include students with mild disabilities. Strategic notetaking is predicated upon the assumption that students can use metacognitive skills to become more strategic at notetaking.

Students are given generic, as opposed to Lazarus' lecture-specific guides, with written cues to help them develop metacognitive skills during lectures. Boyle (1996) found that by using metacognitive skills, such as activating prior knowledge and organizing information, students engaged in the lecture and improved their comprehension.

The first section of the strategic notetaking guide directs students to identify the lecture topic and connect it to what they know about the topic. Next, the students are directed to cluster together between three and seven main points with details as the instructor lectures. At the bottom of each page, students summarize the information on that page.

The steps of clustering groups of new main points and summarizing them are repeated as necessary. Finally, as a review, the students write five main points presented in the lecture and describe each point. This step is intended to serve as a quick review of the lecture. Boyle (1996) noted that the typical 50-minute lecture will generate five to eight Strategic Notes pages.

Boyle and Weishaar (2001) investigated the effects of Strategic Notetaking on the recall and comprehension of 26 high school students of whom 22 had learning disabilities and 4 had mild mental retardation. The students were members of a special education class in either science or English. Half of the students were in the control group, and the other half of the students were in the experimental group.

The experimental group students were exposed to a videotaped lecture and taught to take Strategic Notes. Then both groups were exposed to a second lecture, with the experimental group using the new strategy; the control group took notes as they usually did.

The experimental group wrote seven times more notes during the lesson than did the control group. The experimental group also performed five times better than the control group on long-term recall of vocabulary terms and almost six times better on long-term number of words from the original notes remembered. The experimental group scored better than the control group in comprehension by about one third.

The use of Strategic Notes is a key that helps unlock the barriers to Acquisition and Proficiency and Fluency of Knowledge and Comprehension because

- Attention is enhanced because the students are actively engaged.
- Memory is enhanced because students are required to activate prior knowledge and organize information and summarize it.
- Comprehension is enhanced because of activating prior knowledge and organizing and summarizing strategies.

Here is how we used this strategy with a literature class.

---

**Strategic Notes**

What is the topic?

What do I already know about the topic?

Idea Cluster 1 (From 3–7 Ideas)

Idea Cluster 2 (From 3–7 Ideas)

Summary

---

## ⊶ Key 26 is the AWARE Strategy

The AWARE Strategy was developed by Hughes and Suritsky (1993). In AWARE, the A stands for "Arrange to Take Notes." This means to arrive early, sit near the front with a good view of the teacher and the chalkboard/whiteboard, and write the date on the paper. W stands for "Write Quickly Using Shorthand" abbreviations whenever possible. We teach our students to use a variety of general abbreviations such as "w/" for "with," "&" for "and," and "—" (a dash) for "the." Hughes and Suritsky also have us teach general abbreviation rules, such as the three or four letters of long words or word phrases such as "ant" for "antecedent," "ex pow" for "executive powers," or "conv" for "convection." They also have us teach students initials for terms that will be frequently used during the lecture, such as CS for "cell specialization." During this step, Hughes and Suritsky also tell us to teach our students a simple organizational strategy: using major headings for main ideas and indenting supporting details.

The second A in AWARE stands for "Attend to Cues" and focuses on recognizing and writing down information that the teacher cues. Cued information is that which we explicitly tell the student is important by such means as saying, "Make sure that you write this down." In addition, Hughes and Suritsky say to teach students to star or checkmark cued information to help them when reviewing their notes.

The last two steps, "Review Notes" and "Edit," are conducted simultaneously. The review step means to read over the notes as soon as possible; the edit step means to add missing information, include details, and clarify or elaborate.

Hughes and Suritsky taught this strategy to learning disabled college students and found that the majority took more organized and complete notes as a result.

The AWARE strategy should help students improve their Acquisition and Proficiency and Fluency in Knowledge and Comprehension because

- Attention is elevated by sitting near the teacher instead of at the back of the room.
- Frustration is lowered because the abbreviation strategies help students write more quickly.
- Memory is elevated because reviewing and editing notes provides repetition and deeper processing.

---

**Methods v Characterization**

*Comes alive
*Reader ID w/

Creat Char
Imag phys app
Pers

*Characterization mst impt
*Show don't tell = indir, pref
Desc app
Show n act
Let char talk
Show thots & feels
Show others reacts t char

Change
*Dyn v stat

---

## ⚷  Key 27 is Brick and Mortar Notes

One of the two important functions of notes is to provide a permanent record of information that can be reviewed at a later time (Carrier et al., 1988; Di Vesta & Gray, 1972). Brick and Mortar Notes facilitate review by allowing the student to see a question without seeing its answer. This allows the student to try to answer each question before reading the answer on the paper. This helps the student to process the information more deeply.

The metaphor of bricks and mortar promotes the idea that the concepts are related to each other in the same way that all the bricks and mortar in a wall are related to each other. We can use the metaphor to help the student see that the information is connected as a whole, rather than being a conglomeration of disparate facts.

When we use Brick and Mortar Notes we organize our lecture into several questions and their answers. Then we have the students use notebook paper and draw a box around the space between two lines with a pencil. This is the mortar. The mortar box is drawn with a pencil. Then, the students draw a brick by drawing another box around the lines and spaces representing five or six lines of notebook paper. The brick is drawn with a red (or other color) pen. The students continue down the page drawing bricks and mortar until the page is full.

Next, the students use a pencil to write the questions and a red (or other color) pen to write the answers.

When a student is ready to study the notes, he or she covers the page of notes with a clean sheet of paper. The student then moves the paper down until he or she can see one question (the mortar). Then, the student tries to answer the question. Next, the student moves the paper down to expose the answer (the brick). The student continues down the page in this way until he or she has tried to answer all of the questions.

Brick and Mortar Notes are an effective inclusion strategy because:

- Attention is increased because the student is actively engaged in the notetaking process.
- Comprehension is increased because of the deep processing involved in creating questions from the notes.
- Memory is increased because of the deep processing and the judicious review.

Here is an example from an English class in which the students were learning to develop an Idea Portfolio.

| **Brick and Mortar Notes on Creating My Idea Portfolio** |
|---|
| *What is an Idea Portfolio (IP)?* |
| An Idea Portfolio is a collection of things I find that might give me an idea that I could turn into a story, poem, etc. My Idea Portfolio could include photographs, newspaper articles, stories by other people, or interesting things I overhear people say. I don't have to have an idea at the time I include the document in my portfolio. If the document intrigues me, that's enough to include it. |
| *How can an IP help me write a Found Poem?* |
| A newspaper article or short story I find could result in a Found Poem. A Found Poem consists of words, phrases, or sentences from a selection that are chosen and arranged to communicate the essence of the selection. For example, a newspaper article describing someone's home burning to the ground could give me a Found Poem with its words such as *devastation, homeless*, and *destroyed*. |
| *How can an IP help me write a Character Sketch?* |
| A photograph I find could help me create a Character Sketch. I would put the photograph in my IP. Then when I had time, I could study it and look for evidence of how the person thinks, feels, acts, and so forth. For example, how the person dresses, the type of shoes, the jewelry, and the hair style could tell me a lot about the person. What the person was doing in the picture would also tell me a lot. |

## ⊷ Key 28 is Three-Column Personalized Notes

Because most students, but especially students with learning problems, understand best when new ideas are directly related to their personal experiences, the Three-Column Personalized Notes strategy is designed to help students make that connection. The first column, a narrow column, is for the chapter subheading or sub subheading. The second column, the widest of the three, is for the extended notes from that subchapter. The third column includes examples from the student's own life when applicable. This connection not only helps comprehension and retention because it explicitly connects the new learning to our student's existing schema, but it also increases motivation because our students are naturally interested in things that relate to themselves.

For example, in an economics class, several of our students had entries in their personal column on the "tax loopholes" their parents were able to use, many students had entries on the topic of "minimum wage," and all had stories about "scarcity."

We periodically have our students share their third-column entries with a partner or in a small group in order to provide multiple representations, which we know also increases comprehension and retention. Sometimes we have the entire group share, particularly if very few people have a personal story to relate to a topic. For example, when we studied "public works," only one or two students in a class would have personal stories about great grandparents who worked on WPA or CCC projects during the Great Depression; so we invited those students to share their stories with the entire class.

Three-Column Personalized Notes help unlock the doors to Knowledge and Comprehension because:

- 🔑 Motivation is increased when students can relate academic content to their own lives and share it with their classmates.
- 🔑 Attention is increased when students relate content to their own lives or hear stories about their classmates.
- 🔑 Confusion is decreased when real-life stories exemplify abstract concepts.
- 🔑 Memory is enhanced when abstract concepts are anchored to students' life experiences.

Here we have an example from a history class in which students were studying Alexander the Great.

### Three Column Personalized Notes on Chapter 4:
#### Alexander–Empire Builder

| Subsection Title | Details | My Thoughts/Experiences |
|---|---|---|
| Phillip II Builds Macedonia's Power | M's were tough people who lived in mountains; Greeks looked down on them but admired their kings | M's are like the Goth kids at school. Preps look down on them. |
| Phillip's Army (359 B.C.) | Phillip (only 23!) became king & made M's into fine army that was unbeatable. | I'm 16, and I think I be a good king. Our football team is unbeatable so far this season. |
| Conquest of Greece (338 B.C.) | M's army took Greece's independence. | When Mom took away my car, I lost my independence and was really mad. |
|  | Phillip is killed & his son Alexander the Great becomes king at age 20. |  |
| Alexander Defeats Persia | Alexander was well educated. He proved himself when he defeated Thebes, destroying the city & killing 6000. The other cities caved in. | New guys in school have to prove themselves sometimes by fighting the toughest guys there. |
| Invasion of Persia (334 B.C.) | Led 35K M soldiers to war. Persia responded with an army of 40K. M's won. | Sometimes brains beat braun. |
|  | Persia's King Darius III raised an army of 75K but Alex outsmarted him and won. | Ditto. |
| Alexander's Ambitions Grow | Darius offers Alex 1/3 of Persian Empire but Alex refuses & marched to Egypt, who considered him their liberator. He was crowned Pharaoh & founded Alexandria. | Sometimes I can get a better deal when I don't accept someone's offer at the flea market. |
| Conquering the Persian Empire | Darius raised an army of 250K but lost to Alex at Gaugamela. | Sometimes brains beat braun. |

## ⚬┭ Key 29 is Newspaper Notes

The use of Newspaper Notes is especially well-suited for literature or history classes. This strategy uses columns in the form of a table. The strategy is an adaptation of the 5 Ws and H of writing a news article: who, what, when, where, why, and how. The first column is When in order to help students with sequencing and usually cause and effect. When the events are cause and effect related, we use an arrow from one row to the next to indicate the relationship. Next column is Where so that the context of time and place are established before we examine the actual event. The Who column comes next, followed by the What and How columns. A To Whom column follows, and the Why column is last. This strategy is an excellent notetaking strategy that has the added benefit of being a graphic organizer. It also gives our students a good analytical tool, as well as a great tool to use to structure their writing.

One of our learning disabled students in a history class told us, "I never thought about history being about real people doing real things, sometimes to other real people. I knew that newspapers were about real people doing real things, but history just seemed like lists of facts, not connected to real people."

Another said, "This way of taking notes helps me make better sense out of our classes. I feel like my learning is more organized when I think about it as a newspaper article than when I used to take notes in history the old way."

A very bright student with learning disabilities and serious challenging behaviors told us, "I pretty much like the stories we read and talk about, but sometimes I just think of them as just bunch of things happening. With the Newspaper Notes, I get it, it's clearer, and I do better on the tests. Maybe I'll be a reporter when I graduate."

The Newspaper Notes help students unlock access to Knowledge and Comprehension because

- Motivation is enhanced because identifying the Ws and H is less daunting than trying to process the material more globally.
- Perception is enhanced by using all three modalities to process the material.
- Discrimination is ensured by the highly explicit nature of the graphic organizer.
- Sequencing the events correctly is ensured by the explicit method of recording the data.
- Organization is enhanced by the very nature of the strategy and its graphic form.
- Memory is enhanced by the explicit treatment of the material.

Here is an example of the strategy that one of our students used in a history class.

## Newspaper Notes: War of 1812

| When | Where | Who | Did What | How | To Whom | Why | Effect |
|------|-------|-----|----------|-----|---------|-----|--------|
| 1812 | Detroit | Gen. W. Hull | Surren-dered the fort | | Canadian General Isaac Brock | He was confused from a defeat by Tecumseh | Brock annexed Michigan to the British Empire! |
| 1813 | Lake Erie | Gen. Oliver Hazard Perry | Cleared Lake Erie of British ships | A naval war includ-ing many African American troops | British Navy | So Wm. Henry Harrison could invade Canada | Harrison could capture Detroit back |
| 1813 | Detroit and Thames River in Canada | Wm. Henry Harri-son | Captured Detroit and advanced to defeat Canadian troops and Tecumseh's warriors | By land warfare | British/ Canadian troops & Tecumseh's warriors | To win back the Great Lakes region for the U.S. | Tecumseh dies in battle; U.S. regains Great Lakes Region |

# ⚷ Key 30 is Power Notes

In 1987, the high school teachers in the Kalispell, Montana public schools were unsatisfied with their students' progress. They decided to work together to develop strategies that would increase the achievement of their student body. The result was the CRISS strategies (Kalispell, Montana Schools, 1987; Santa et al., 1988). CRISS was the acronym for Content Reading in Secondary Schools. The strategies were later repackaged and changed in name to Creating Independence with Student-owned Strategies and expanded to include middle school students. The training is available in a video training program. The CRISS strategies are effective, both for those who are going on to college and more importantly for those students not going on to college. Power Notes are one of the CRISS strategies.

Although they were originally developed for and evaluated on secondary school students, Buehl (2001) recommended Power Notes to middle school content area teachers as well; he also stressed that Power Notes are not the sole purview of reading teachers. They were specifically developed for content area teachers to increase their students' independent learning. The strategy is presented as one that promotes effective reading, related literacy skills, and study strategies that help students tackle increasingly complex materials.

When using Power Notes, students identify the title of the chapter as a Power 1 idea. Power 2s are usually bold subheadings within chapters, the concepts that support the Power 1. Power 3s are drawn from the text within each subheading; they are the supporting details for the Power 2s. This format helps students take comprehensive notes.

When we have used Power Notes with students, we have often allowed them to work with partners. We place them in heterogeneous pairs, each student with disabilities paired with a strong student. The students with learning problems have increased their understanding of their reading assignments, as well as increasing their understanding of text structure through the structured interaction with the stronger students.

Some students have told us that taking Power Notes is like a puzzle; they enjoy finding where the pieces of information fit. A junior student said, "Power Notes helps me see how it all fits together. When I write, I feel more like I know what I'm doing." Occasionally, we have to admonish students not to focus on the details, but how they support the higher Power Note.

Power Notes are explicit and structured and are an effective inclusionary practice because they provide a structure, therefore,

- Organization is provided by the nature of the strategy.
- Frustration is avoided when organization is provided.
- Motivation is increased when students view the task as a puzzle in which they are searching for missing pieces.

Here is an example from social studies.

| | *Power Notes for Tectonic Plate Boundary Motions* |
|---|---|
| *Power 1* | *Understanding Tectonic Plate Motions: Plate Movement Causes Changes in the Earth.* |
| *Power 2* | *Four types of plate boundaries are: Divergent, Convergent, Transform, & Plate Boundary Zones.* |
| *Power 3* | *Divergent boundaries: new crust is formed as plates move away from each other. Magma pushes up. Mid-Atlantic Ridge best known, spreading at 2.5 cm/yr. Most studied is Iceland, because ridge runs through it. Rifting & volcanic activity.* |
| *Power 3* | *Convergent boundaries: Two plates come together. One subducts under the other. Very slow collision. 4 types: Oceanic-Continental Convergence, which created Andes & Cascade Mountain range. Earthquakes & volcanoes result. Ring of Fire . . .* |

# 6

# Helping Students With Special Needs Maximize Learning From Reading the Textbook

## In This Chapter

*Textbooks are ubiquitous in middle and high schools, but they vary greatly in how friendly they are to readers. Some expository texts are better, and some are worse. But the strategies discussed in this chapter will help make all of them more effective in assisting students with special needs learn our disciplines. The strategies are inexpensive in terms of teacher time expended for the return received in student learning. Some of them, such as Highlighted Textbooks, do not have to be repeated after they have been done once; Universal Design Learning environments do not even require that. What great keys to help our students enjoy the treasures of our disciplines.*

The world of secondary students is an immersion into expository texts. In fact, secondary students spend as much as 75% of classroom time and 90% of homework time interacting with textbooks, and at each grade level, dependence upon textbooks increases, especially expository, as opposed to arrative, texts (Barton, 1997; Saenz & Fuchs, 2002; Woodward & Elliott, 1990).

But in the *Harvard Education Letter,* Webb (1995, p. 1) called the textbook industry "education's big dirty secret" because expository textbooks are "inconsiderate" texts and make comprehension unnecessarily difficult. In such inconsiderate texts, many students with special needs meet their nemesis.

Saenz and Fuchs (2002) have noted that many factors contribute to the difficulty that students who have learning problems experience with expository reading but that the four factors most commonly cited are prior knowledge, vocabulary knowledge, text structure, and conceptual density and familiarity. One type of inconsiderateness is making key concepts and relationships implicit rather than explicit.

Writing in the *Journal of Learning Disabilities*, DiCecco and Gleason (2002) argued that textbooks include too much factual knowledge, and they noted that

> not all levels of knowledge are equally important. Alexander, Schallert, and Hare (1991) proposed a framework that differentiated content, domain, and discipline knowledge. Content knowledge is the factual information that people gather formally or informally about the world around them. Domain knowledge makes concepts or principles a more formal part of a system of learning. Concepts or principles become discipline knowledge when understanding becomes more specialized. (p. 306)

Jitendra et al. (2001) examined four middle school geography textbooks. Among their findings was that the readability of the texts was about tenth grade and that the books were not supportive of students who had learning difficulties. Among their recommendations were that when working with students who have disabilities that teachers should develop textbook enhancements such as reading guides, graphic organizers (GOs) and carefully structured discussion questions. They noted that this is especially important for students who may lack prior knowledge.

The difficulties that students with learning problems have with making inferences from implicit text is compounded by their other difficulties: understanding relationships and connections in general, distinguishing between main ideas and insignificant details, and understanding the main idea of a passage. They have less awareness of the structure of a text and have poor recall of text ideas. In addition, the passive learning style of students with learning problems and their usual lack of processing skills and skills related to organizing written information makes their understanding of text difficult. Therefore, textbooks must make relationships among concepts explicit (Alexander et al., 1991; Bos & Vaughn, 1994; Kameenui & Simmons, 1990; Lenz, Alley, & Schumaker, 1987; Oakhill & Patel, 1991; Torgesen, 1982).

Textbooks can be daunting to our students with disabilities; however, we can assist them in tackling the material by using these strategies.

- Key 31: Using Graphic Organizers to Make Relationships Within Domain Knowledge and Discipline Knowledge Explicit
- Key 32: Preteaching Vocabulary
- Key 33: Explicitly Teaching Text Structure
- Key 34: Highlighted Textbooks
- Key 35: Recorded Textbooks
- Key 36: Universal Design Learning
- Key 37: Peer Reader
- Key 38: Study Guides

## ⚷ Key 31 is Using Graphic Organizers to Make Relationships Within Domain Knowledge and Discipline Knowledge Explicit

DiCecco and Gleason (2002) created a well-controlled experiment in which they tested the impact of GOs on domain knowledge gleaned from text by 24 learning disabled middle school students in a social studies class. Although the GOs did not increase factual recall (and were not expected to), they significantly increased students' relational knowledge as demonstrated by frequency of relational statements in essays.

On the pretest of domain knowledge that was directly taught, the group who received instruction using GOs averaged 12 statements on the pretest essay as compared to the No GO group, who averaged 18 statements. The treatment consisted of type of explicit instruction following each section read in the history textbook used by both classes. The GO group received explicit instruction using GOs, and the No GO group received the same number of minutes of instruction using strategies traditionally used in social studies classes, such as examining photographs of Henry Ford's first assembly line, class discussion, guided notes, and acting out an assembly line. On the first essay, after seven days of instruction, the GO group made 47 relational statements as compared to 34 relational statements made by the No GO group. On the second essay, at the end of 20 days of instruction, the GO group made 57 relational statements as compared to only 27 relational statement made by the No GO group. The authors argued that this provides support not only for explicit instruction using GOs to help students understand relational knowledge in textbooks, but also that a protracted period of instruction using GOs is a stronger intervention than a shorter period of intervention.

The researchers also noted their amazement that although the No GO group discussed assembly lines and also acted out being in an assembly line that assembly lines were only mentioned in the essays of the No GO group 7 times as compared to being mentioned 21 times in the essays of the GO group.

Using Graphic Organizers to Make Relationships Within Domain Knowledge and Discipline Knowledge Explicit before students tackle the text is an effective inclusion strategy to help students comprehend text because

- Confusion is conquered when students have visualized the relationships before they begin to read.
- Frustration is eliminated when confusion is conquered.
- Completion of the reading assignment is more likely when students comprehend the text.
- Reasoning is supported as students encounter the text because they have been introduced to the relationships before they have read about them.

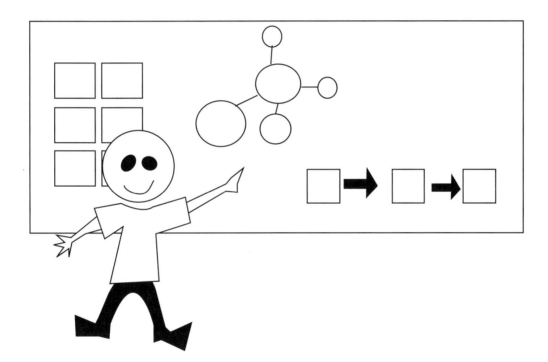

## ⚏ Key 32 is Preteaching Vocabulary

Saenz and Fuchs (2002) have found that lack of vocabulary knowledge is a major cause of the content area reading problems of students who do not have general reading deficits. In fact, vocabulary knowledge is the number one predictor of reading comprehension of content area textbooks in secondary students both with and without learning disabilities.

Many students will learn the meaning of new vocabulary words by inference, but students with special needs probably will not learn the vocabulary inferentially. So we have to teach it explicitly.

One of us was teaching our students with special needs using the book *White Fang* by Jack London. We wanted to strengthen their understanding of the relationship between a dog and a wolf and the meaning of the word *wolf* in context. So in addition to such words in the story as *conjecture*, we had our students look up the word *wolf* in the dictionary. Every single student wrote down the definition as "a man who relentlessly pursues a woman." They simply did not see a discrepancy between that definition and the use of the word *wolf* the book. We were surprised, but we should not have been because the inability to discriminate between the meanings of a word in context is a hallmark of mild learning problems.

Using the dictionary is a skill that all students should master, but when our intent is to get students to start reading a chapter, we are best served by explicitly preteaching the vocabulary ourselves.

Preteaching Vocabulary is a good strategy for helping special needs learners succeed because

- Confusion is diminished when students begin reading with the big picture in mind.
- Frustration is prevented when confusion is not a problem.
- Completion of the reading assignment is more likely when students are not frustrated.

| Word | Definition | Root | Definition |
|------|-----------|------|-----------|
| Tectonic | Relating to structure | | |
| Converge | Move together | Verge | Move |
| Diverge | Move apart | Verge | Move |

Write in your dictionary.  Then read pp. 142-147.

## ⚡ Key 33 is Explicitly Teaching Text Structure

Reading expository text is much more difficult for students with learning problems than is reading narrative text (Saenz & Fuchs, 2002). That difficulty may be aggravated by poor text structure. Some textbooks are worse than others at providing a good text structure that will assist students with learning problems.

But however good our textbook's structure, we explicitly teach our students what that structure is. One common structure is for the title of the chapter to be the organizing idea, with the titles of subsections in bold letters. Our text may have a specific structure for presenting items in seriation, for presenting parts of a whole, for comparing and contrasting, or for presenting cause and effect. We ferret out what those structures are and explicitly teach them to our students.

Downing, Bakken, and Whedon (2002) explain five types of expository text structure: main idea, list, order, compare/contrast, and classification. They provide the following keys to identifying the type of text structure.

Main idea structure is characterized by a passage focusing on a single idea. The other sentences in the passage provide details, extend support, clarify, or illustrate the main idea. Words that signal that the passage is a main idea text include *principles, laws,* and *definitions*. The authors suggest that the appropriate study strategy is to state the main idea and provide at least three supporting details.

Semicolons, numbers, or letters in parentheses signal that the text structure is a list format. This type of passage focuses on a general topic followed by a list of characteristics that describe the topic. The suggested study strategy is to state the topic and list at least four characteristics.

Order structure is the third text structure, and the signals for this type of structure are the words *first, second, stages, next,* and *then*. The order structure text focuses on a single topic and then consists of a series of ordered steps or events.

In compare and contrast structure, the text focuses on the relationship between or among two or more things. Signals are phrases such as *in contrast to* or *in comparison*. Downing et al., (2002) suggest having students list the two or more items being compared and then list similarities in one column and differences in another column.

The authors explain that the classification structure is the fifth structure and that the signals for this type of structure are phrases such as *two types of* and *can be classified as*. The classification structure explicates a scheme to be used later in classifying items. The suggested study strategy is to write down the topic and the related items in column form.

Smith (1986) investigated the effects of teaching text structure on the reading comprehension of 73 adolescents who had learning disabilities. The students were randomly assigned to one of two groups. The experimental group was instructed on how to recognize and use an author's organizational structure while reading and taking notes on an expository passage. The control group was instructed on how to use a generic problem-solving model. The results demonstrated that the experimental group recalled more of the information in the selection immediately and one week later and were able to recognize the specific text structure when they again encountered it. Smith and Friend (1986) reported the same findings with 27 more adolescents who had learning disabilities.

We made a wall chart designed to help students remember how to identify the various structures, and we permanently posted it on the wall in our classroom so students would be able to consult it when they could not remember the structures.

Explicitly Teaching Text Structure is a good inclusion strategy because

- Confusion is decreased when students comprehend what the text is trying to communicate.
- Frustration is eliminated when confusion is decreased.

| Compare & Contrast Text Structure | Cause & Effect Text Structure |
|---|---|
| In contrast. . . | Because. . . |
| As compared to. . . | Therefore. . . |
| As opposed to. . . | As a result. . . |
| On the other hand. . . | For this reason. . . |
| Different from. . . | In order to. . . |
| But. . . | Thus. . . |
| However. . . | So that. . . |
| Unlike. . . | Causes/is caused by. . . |
| Similarly. . . | Consequently. . . |
| In the same way. . . | Due to. . . |
| Like. . . | So that. . . |
| Both. . . | Contributes to. . . |
| Likewise. . . | |
| In sharp relief to. . . | |
| Any sequence words | Any sequence words |

## ⌐ Key 34 is Highlighted Textbooks

Highlighted Textbooks are a type of glossing. *Glossing* refers to notes in margins and other intratext devices, such as highlighting, that assist with text comprehension.

Highlighting textbooks takes work the first time we use them, but after that, all we have to do is be certain that the students with special needs are the students who get the Highlighted Textbooks.

First, we take a textbook and a highlighter and go through the book highlighting the most critical information. We think of the information as Critical, Important, or Just Interesting. After we have completed the process in one book, we have a student assistant highlight three or four additional books to be reserved for students with special needs.

Alternatively, we highlight one chapter at a time as the year progresses, and we teach the chapter. We stay at least one chapter ahead of our students, our student assistant highlights the additional books using ours as a model, and we have students with special needs drop by before or after school to pick up their books.

Our students with special needs may have many problems that make reading an entire chapter almost impossible, ranging from problems decoding the text, comprehending it, and discriminating between critical and just interesting information. By highlighting the critical information, we will ensure that our students are spending their study time effectively.

Lomika (1998) investigated glossing with college students studying French. The interventions were no glossing, limited glossing, or full glossing on a computer screen reading assignment. Lomika found that the full glossing strategy produced increased comprehension.

Using Highlighted Textbooks is a good inclusion strategy because

🎶 Discrimination between critical and not-so-critical information is assured.
🎶 Attention is focused on the most important information.
🎶 Frustration is eliminated when discrimination is assisted.
🎶 Motivation is increased when frustration is eliminated.

## ⊶ Key 35 is Recorded Textbooks

Many of our districts have recorded textbooks available. If our district does not have the recorded textbook available, the student's IEP committee can require it, and one will have to be provided. In addition, the recorder and earphones, batteries, and so forth that the student would need to have at home would be considered assistive technology and must be provided by the district if the IEP committee deems that it is necessary.

Using tape recorders across contexts in teaching students with learning problems has a long history. In an early study, Gates (1970) tested the effects of tape-recorded texts with 100 secondary science students who were classified as poor readers. The students were divided into four classes of which two were taught with tape-recorded textbooks and two were taught without the tape recordings to assist them in reading the text. The same teacher taught all four classes that in all other ways were treated in an identical manner. The experiment was conducted over a full academic year.

At the end of the study, the experimental group significantly outperformed the control group in academic performance on the course-specific science concepts, as well as on science understanding, reading science vocabulary, reading vocabulary, reading comprehension, reading grade level, and subject preference.

Using tape recorders to assist learning disabled secondary students in the content areas is particularly appropriate and is even recommended in *ERIC Digests* for adult students with learning difficulties (Lowry, 1990) and low-level adult ESL learners (Holt, 1995).

In Texas, all state-adopted textbooks are available on audiotape through the state, but it was not always so. In previous years, a strategy that we used with success was contacting a prison and having inmates record the book. We used two different prisons for this function over the years. First, we contacted the educational officer of the institution and explained what we needed. The officer agreed that selected inmates could record the books in exchange for "good time," which helps them earn early release. We had to provide the books, blank cassettes, and a signed statement that our district would hold the prison harmless if a prisoner spiced up his reading with colorful words. (That never happened.)

In those earlier days, we had a listening station with multiple headphones set up in our classroom, and we made sure that every student had access to a cassette player at home. Now, we have a wireless transmitter connected to a tape player at the front of the room. We also have six sets of wireless headphones available so that any student who desires to can listen to the chapter at their desk as they follow along in the text. This assistive technology can be required by a student's IEP committee, especially if they deem that being singled out by using headphones would be harmful to the student.

Providing Recorded Textbooks is an excellent inclusion strategy because

🎵 Perception is strengthened by providing the auditory input to a visual medium.
🎵 Comprehension is assured when the material is made accessible.
🎵 Confusion is eliminated when material is understood.
🎵 Frustration is avoided when confusion is eliminated.
🎵 Motivation is increased when material is understood.
🎵 Attention is stronger when motivation is increased.

## ⚬┱ Key 36 is Universal Design Learning

The bad news is that Universal Design Learning (UDL) environments do not exist yet. UDL is a process that will lead to curricula that are fully accessible, flexible, and supportive of diverse learners (C. Hitchcock, personal communication, January 23, 2003).

The good news is that UDL materials will exist sooner or later, and when they do, they can be required by the IEP or 504 plans of students with disabilities. After that, it should not be long before all of our students have Universal Learning Environments (ULEs).

ULEs are electronic books, including textbooks, which change language, reading level, and a host of other options that make them suitable to every learner. The student whose dyslexia gets in the way of learning science can have the computer read the material to him or her. The student who reads only one or two years below grade level can have the text modified to his or her reading level. The student who is fluent in Spanish but not English can read it in his or her preferred language. The student who needs more examples about a particular concept can click on a hot button and see as many representations as he or she needs. The ULE research that is under way at the National Center on Accessing the General Curriculum (CAST) will provide the foundation for new research-based approaches to meeting the needs of diverse learners.

Chuck Hitchcock, Director of the National Center on Accessing the General Curriculum (www.cast.org ), sharing his dream of schools in 2006, wrote in the Fall 2001 issue of the *Journal of Special Education Technology* (JSET is available on-line at http://jset.unlv.edu/),

> The basic premise behind UDL is that curricular content should be provided in a transformable format or as multiple representations such that multiple means for recognition, strategy, and engagement are built into each learning activity. Individual differences in the ability to recognize information are accommodated by providing multiple examples of content in multiple media and formats, with critical features highlighted and background context supported. To accommodate individual differences in the ability to be strategic and express oneself, the curriculum is designed to provide flexible supports, ongoing relevant feedback, and opportunities to demonstrate skill in a variety of ways. Individual differences in the ability to engage with learning are accommodated through choices of content and tools, learning context, and rewards as well as adjustable levels of challenge. Moreover, in a universally-designed classroom not only are students given the tools necessary to adapt methods and materials to their individual needs, but also the goals for learning are flexible and assessment is continuous.

We should inquire often of our textbook publisher about the availability of our adopted texts in UDL format. The more of us who inquire and the more often inquiries are made, the sooner our materials will be available.

Universal Design Learning will revolutionize text-based delivery because

- Perception problems will be circumnavigated as material is delivered both auditorily and visually.
- Discrimination problems will be bypassed as material is delivered both auditorily and visually.
- Sequencing will be supported by flowchart features.
- Memory will be supported as materials will provide for deep elaboration, the provision of mnemonic devices, and repetition as necessary.
- Organization will be provided through structured overviews and graphic organizers.
- Motivation will be ensured as students work at their own levels, with materials designed to meet their individual needs, and reward systems and stimuli tailored to their specific interests.
- Attention will be focused because motivation is heightened.

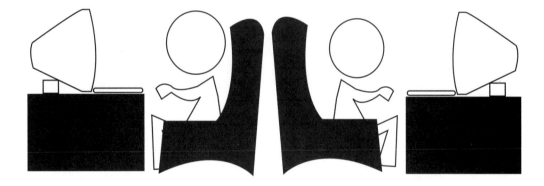

## ⌐ Key 37 is providing a Peer Reader

A high school social studies teacher we know used Peer Readers to help his students with reading problems learn the textbook content. In his classes, all of the nonreaders were boys. He asked the principal's office to assign him a student aide for each period in which he had one or more students who could not read the textbook. The office complied, and all of the Peer Readers happened to be girls. Each period, the Peer Reader would go with the boys who needed reading help to a place where reading aloud would not disturb the rest of the class. Some periods they could use an empty room next door. Other periods they worked in the hall outside of the classroom.

The teacher reported that the poor readers dramatically improved their academic achievement in social studies. (He quizzed them orally so their reading and writing disabilities would not confound their test results.) He also reported that the boys enjoyed the privilege of working with a girl in a one-on-one or small group setting. We worried that the boys might feel embarrassed to have a Peer Reader, but he assured us that his particular students were not. He indicated that in the small community in which he taught, the students had known each other all their lives. They knew who could read and who could not, who was mathematically capable and who was not, and who was a good football player and who could not make the team. He said he stressed that the boys could learn the content but had word blindness. This approach satisfied them and circumvented their embarrassment.

Although we think this is a good strategy, we would use it as a stopgap while we were either acquiring Universal Design Learning materials or having our textbooks tape-recorded. Those are better alternatives because they allow the student to study independently. However, in this context, Peer Readers are a good strategy because

- Perception problems are circumnavigated because the students do not have to be able to read in order to learn the material.
- Frustration is avoided because students can access the material without being able to read the textbook.

## ⊶ Key 38 is providing Study Guides

Providing Study Guides deserves a chapter of its own; so in the next chapter, we discuss Study Guides at length.

# 7

# Increasing Learning by Using Guides

## In This Chapter

*Study guides are keys to helping students with disabilities access the Knowledge and Comprehension domains and the Analytical domain. In general, study guides help students by providing (1) an encoding function that causes them to process information deeply and (2) an external storage function that provides access to information that is not yet stored in long-term memory.*

*Study guides are cognitive frameworks that help motivate students and assist them in focusing their attention. They can increase perception by providing for multicoding of information. They also assure that students will discriminate between what we think is critical in a reading selection (or videotape) and what is less important. Study guides such as flowcharts can help students with sequencing and organization. They can assist students in analytical thought by directing their attention to seeking evidence, comparing and contrasting, or seeking causes and effects. Finally, study guides assist in helping students retain information in long-term memory because they provide for increased depth of processing.*

*For information that we cannot directly control in the way that we can control our classroom activities, study guides provide a way for us to help students interact with the information we consider crucial.*

The use of textbooks is ubiquitous in secondary education. Students with special needs often experience difficulty learning from textbooks, and guides are excellent tools for use in this context. In addition, many teachers use videotapes in their instruction, and viewing guides can be important tools in increasing the learning of special needs students with this medium.

Boyle and Yeager (1997) argued that teachers can help students counteract their difficulty in learning from reading assignments by creating cognitive frameworks. Study guides provide such cognitive frameworks. Cognitive frameworks help students transfer and retain information; they help support students' learning by helping them organize information and link the various parts of that information together. Frameworks highlight important points and serve as guides for studying.

Study guides come in a variety of formats; the format we select depends on our purpose. Possible purposes may include having students identify the most important information during a lesson, having them create notes for later study, or providing them with an overview before learning new information. Wood, Lapp, and Flood (1992) explained that the use of a study guide differs from having students answer the questions at the end of the chapter in two critical ways. First, the teacher has control of the questions and second, the students know what the teacher wants them to learn before they begin to read, rather than having to wait until they have finished reading.

Fisher et al. (1995) noted that like graphic organizers, study guides are characterized by flexibility of purpose and type: they may be a teacher-prepared list of questions or an outline given prior to students' reading a chapter or listening to a teacher presentation. They may be used to teach vocabulary terms or important main ideas in a unit of study. They may be used to promote higher-order thinking.

Wood (1988) argued that teachers should provide companion study guides when assigning textbook reading because textbooks are often poorly organized and hard to understand. In their review of the literature on study guides, Wood et al. (1992) noted that study guide questions interspersed throughout the text can make significant contributions to students' understanding.

Horton and Lovitt (1989) compared the effects of using a teacher-directed study guide to self-study for 121 high school students in science and social studies classes, of whom 8 had learning problems. The study guide consisted of 15 short answer questions on main ideas taken from throughout the textbook assignment. The teacher instructed the students on how to use the study guide. The students were divided into two groups; in the first part of the experiment, Group A used the study guide while Group B used self-study. In the second part of the experiment, the groups switched interventions. The results were statistically significant. The average test score of the students with learning problems during the self-study condition was 49%; their average test score on the study guide condition was 68%. Of the students without learning problems, the self-study mean score was 80%, and the study guide mean score was 93%.

Horton and Lovitt (1989) repeated their experiment with a student-directed (as opposed to teacher-directed) study guide condition as compared to the self-study condition on recall of main ideas from a reading assignment. In this experiment, the students with learning problems had a mean score of 43% on the self-study condition and a mean score of 77% on the student-directed study guide condition. The students without learning problems scored 55% on the self-study condition and 87% on the self-directed study guide condition.

The results of the treatment on the students with learning problems is especially encouraging because any treatment that moves a student with a failing score into the range in which the score is passing is known as socially significant.

Horton, Lovitt, Givens, and Nelson (1989) then investigated the use of study guides on computer. The study involved 31 freshman students, of whom 13 had learning disabilities; the students were all enrolled in a low-track world geography class. Using the computer in all phases, the students read a selected text, completed a 15-question short answer, main idea study guide, and took a test. The intervention took 40 minutes.

The students with learning disabilities scored 42% correct on self-study and 76% correct during the computerized study guide treatment. The students without learning disabilities scored 58% on the self-study and 77% on the computerized study guide. When a follow-up study was conducted, 86% of the students reported that they were more highly motivated when using the computer than the textbook.

When we first heard about how little students learn from videotapes without study guides, we were skeptical; so we tried an experiment with a videotape study guide. First, we showed a videotape from a series on human development to a group of 36 college juniors who were education majors and told them that they would be given a quiz at the end of the videotape. Then, we gave the students a 15-question short answer quiz. The mean score of the group was 48%. We then asked ten randomly selected students to show us their notes. Seven of the students had not taken notes at all, and of the three who had, their sketchy notes had touched on both the important and unimportant information, demonstrating that they could not discriminate between the two.

The following week, we showed a videotape from the same series on a different topic; the material was of equivalent difficulty to the first videotape. This time, however, we gave the students a videotape study guide and instructed them to study the guide for five minutes before viewing the videotape. They were to then complete the study guide as they viewed the second videotape; after completing the videotape and study guide, we gave a posttest with difficulty equivalent to that given in the control condition. The mean posttest score for the videotape condition was 92%. We were sold!

In this chapter, we will address the following keys to help students with learning problems open the doors of Acquisition and Proficiency and Fluency to enter the rooms of Knowledge and Comprehension in our disciplines:

- Key 39: Content Guide
- Key 40: Process of Reading Study Guide
- Key 41: Analogy Study Guide
- Key 42: Extended Anticipation Guide
- Key 43: Point-of-View Guide
- Key 44: K-W-L Study Guide
- Key 45: Flip Flop Study Guide
- Key 46: Cause and Effect Study Guide
- Key 47: Hypertext Study Guide
- Key 48: Videotape/DVD Viewing Study Guide

## ☛ Key 39 is the Content Guide

The Content Guide (Karlin, 1964) identifies much focused purposes for reading. Students with learning problems often fail to differentiate well among reading strategies, reading the same way whether skimming is called for or studying with notetaking is the appropriate strategy. The Content Guide helps them learn to use context-appropriate strategies. The Content Guide also helps them master content because it helps them locate answers within the text.

The questions on the Content Guide are written in the order that their answers appear in the text, and the pages on which their answers occur are specified. This allows struggling readers to learn the content that we most want them to learn. We provide the Content Guide and the instruction to skim the material that is not called for on the Content Guide.

Wood et al. (1992) have noted that optional questions may be included to differentiate instruction for more able students. These questions may require divergent thinking and do not have a "correct" answer, such as those we included for our biology class in the example (see page 117).

This Content Guide helps students Acquire, become Proficient and Fluent, and Maintain Knowledge and Comprehension because

- Motivation is increased by making the chapter-reading task more manageable.
- Attention is enhanced because the task of completing the content guide, instead of strictly reading the chapter, causes them to be actively, rather than passively involved.
- Frustration is decreased because the student knows exactly what he is supposed to do.
- Discrimination is supported because the guide shows the student what is important and what is not so important.
- Memory is enhanced because the student processes the important material more deeply by reading it thoroughly and transferring it to the guide.

## Content Study Guide for Biology–*The Autoimmune System*

Answer the following questions as you read pp. 876-885 in your text.

| Question | Your Answer |
|---|---|
| What happens in an autoimmune disease? (p. 877-878) | |
| What are some autoimmune diseases? (p. 879) | |
| How does HIV attack the immune system? (p. 881-882) | |
| How is HIV transmitted? (p. 883) | |
| How is HIV **_not_** transmitted? (p. 883) | |
| Optional question: What is a good analogy for studying autoimmune disease? Explicate. | |
| Optional question: What should schools do to slow the rate of transmission of HIV among teenagers? | |

## ⬤━ Key 40 is the Process of Reading Study Guide

Singer and Donlan (1980) described the Process of Reading Study Guide. These study guides are used to teach specific thinking skills to students in a step-by-step manner. For example, Singer and Donlan would use a Process of Reading Study Guide to teach students how to compare and contrast. Likewise, Olson's (1980) Pattern Guide teaches students to look for text structures as they read and to use the structure to cue them as to what is important in the selection. In most textbooks, the structures are one of the following: hierarchical, time order, cause/effect, description, or comparison/contrast.

Because the Process of Reading Study Guide is specific to specific processes, we will discuss a guide for the compare and contrast process.

Wyatt and Hayes (1991) compared two types of compare and contrast study guide approaches in teaching an obscure religion to 87 undergraduate college students. In the first condition, the students read a selection about a religion that was similar to the target religion. They compared and contrasted the two similar religions.

In the second condition, the students read a passage about a religion that was quite different from the target religion and then read the passage about the target religion. They then compared and contrasted the two dissimilar religions.

When the students were asked to list the facts they remembered about the target text, they made many more correct responses about the target text when they had studied dissimilar texts. When they had studied similar texts, they made many more wrong responses about the target text, instead making statements that referred to the similar religion instead of the target religion. Therefore, one criterion for deciding to use a Compare and Contrast Study Guide is that our concepts should be very different from each other.

Here is how we prepare a Compare and Contrast Study Guide. First, we prepare a three-column graphic organizer. The first column identifies the dimensions along which the students are to compare and contrast the concepts. The other two columns hold the information on each concept.

Process of Reading Study Guides such as the Compare and Contrast Study Guide are good inclusion strategies because

- ♪ Attention is captured because the student is actively engaged.
- ♪ Discrimination is enhanced because the student explicitly discriminates between the target concept and another concept; discrimination between critical and less important information is assured because the student is directed to seek the analogous information only.
- ♪ Memory is strengthened because of the level of processing.
- ♪ Reasoning is supported because the student must identify the target concept's analogous information from the text.

Here is our example from a class that was comparing the Age of Reason to the Age of Romanticism, two very different concepts.

## Compare and Contrast Study Guide for World History:
## The Age of Romanticism

As you read pp. 437-445, complete this chart to compare the Age of Romanticism to the Age of Reason/Enlightment which we have already studied.

|  | **Age of Reason/Enlightenment** | **Age of Romanticism** |
|---|---|---|
| When? | 1750s | |
| Birthplace? | France | |
| What did it emphasize? | Reason and logic | |
| How can the world be improved? | People can improve themselves and the world by careful study and rigorous thinking. | |
| Who were the initiators? | Scientists | |
| What contributed to the movement? | Galileo's telescope: showed the universe as an orderly place. | |
| Why? | Newton's Law of Gravity: showed the world followed rules which could be learned through study. | |

## ⌗ Key 41 is the Analogy Study Guide

Bean, Singer, and Cowan (1985) explained that an Analogy Study Guide is especially helpful in assisting students understand complex or unfamiliar material. The strategy allows them to connect the foreign material to concepts that are well-known and comfortable to them. The strategy also helps the students engage in higher-order thinking because they must analyze both the lecture material and the referent to which they are comparing it.

Bean et al. (1985) wrote that when we construct an Analogy Study Guide, we should think only about the critical concepts and eliminate the rest of the material in the chapter; that means that we only have our students read the critical material. This will help reinforce to our students that the textbook is a learning resource, and reading a textbook is not an end onto itself.

Next, we construct the analogy. Not only do we need an analogy to fit our concept, but we need it to have subordinate concepts that we can use to construct analogies for all the critical subordinate concepts of our topic. Many concepts that we need to teach do not lend themselves to analogies, but for those concepts that do, we find the Analogy Study Guide to be a powerful tool.

We place our concept at the top of the page, our subordinate concepts down the left side of the page, our analogous elements down the right side of the page, and the functions of each down the middle of the page.

Finally, when we are first using the Analogy Study Guide, we explicitly teach the students how the guide works. In future lessons, we may want to have the students construct their own guides.

Bean and colleagues (1985) conducted their research in science and used the example of teaching the functions of the cell in biology by using the analogy of a factory. They suggested, for example, that the cell membrane is like a security guard at the factory. As they read, the students must explain the function that would complete the analogy: Why is the cell membrane analogous to a security guard?

Hayes (1986) tried out an Analogy Study Guide experiment with 52 eleventh grade students. The students were divided into four groups and were assigned to read a selection about the game of cricket. All four groups were given study guides. Two of the study guides included diagrams, and two of the study guides included analogies to baseball. Both interventions were highly effective on a 20-question posttest, but the analogy groups scored higher than the diagram groups on a follow-up test at a later date on both understanding and retention. Hayes recommended the use of visual tools in assisting students to originally learn new material, but analogies to help students retain the information longer.

We tried out this strategy with students in an economics class. Our topic was "What are the five basic economic questions?" We likened this to "What's for dinner?" We discovered that the hardest part of this strategy is selecting an appropriate topic and an appropriate analogy. Not every topic works. But once we selected an appropriate topic and analogy, the strategy worked effectively; the students comprehended the material well and retained it when retested two weeks later.

The Analogy Study Guide helps students unlock the barriers to Acquisition and Proficiency and Fluency in Acquisition and Comprehension because

- Frustration is decreased because the new material is compared to something the student knows well.
- Perception is enhanced because of the use of three modalities.
- Sequencing is ensured if the material involves seriation because of the comparison to a well-understood sequence of steps.
- Confusion is decreased because the new information is compared to well-known information.
- Memory is assured because of the connection of the new material to the known material.

Here is our completed study guide for a biology lesson.

## Analogy Study Guide for The Immune System

| Element of the Immune System | Function | Element of Medieval City |
|---|---|---|
| Skin & Mucous Membranes (Guard Nasal Passages, Lungs, Reproductive Tract, Digestive System, etc.) | First Line of Defense: Blocks Entry | City's Outer Walls |
| *Secretions of Sweat & Oil Glands & Mucous* | *Weapons That Protect External Surfaces* | *Boiling Oil Poured Down Water in Moat Surrounding* |
| Microbes | Enemy | Nomadic Invaders From Outside City |
| Cells That Kill Invading Microbes | Second Line of Defense: Counter Attacks | Armed Guards Inside City |
| *1) Macrophages (Type of White Blood Cell)* | *Kill Invaders One at a Time by Eating Them* | *Cannibal Guards* |
| *2) Neutrophils (Type of White Blood Cell)* | *Kill Invaders by Poisoning Them and Simultaneously Sacrifice Themselves* | *Suicide Guards* |
| *3) Natural Killer Cells* | *1) Kill Cells Infected by Microbes; 2) Immune Surveillance* | *1) Executioner; 2) Police Guards* |

## ⌖ Key 42 is the Extended Anticipation Guide

Duffelmeyer et al.'s (1987) Extended Anticipation Guide is appropriate across the curriculum and builds on natural curiosity. Here is how it works. The teacher introduces the reading assignment by asking the students the questions in the first part of the guide and stimulating discussion about what the students think they know about the topic. Then, the students place a check in a column that notes whether they agree or disagree with a statement. Having thus invested themselves in the assignment, the students read the selection in order to determine whether their opinions are or are not supported and if they are not supported, why.

In the second part of the guide, the students record whether or not their preconceptions about the subject expressed in the first part of the guide were supported; for each preconception that does not receive support, the students summarize the material in the text that disproves their hypotheses.

We amend Duffelmeyer et al.'s (1987) guide in several small ways. First, we title the first section of the guide as "Pre-Reading Ideas." We think this helps the students learn to view many things that they think they know as unsubstantiated preconceptions. We use the term "Post-Reading Ideas" to highlight the fact that our ideation can change when we encounter evidence that refutes our ideation.

The Extended Anticipation Guide helps students with special needs access and develop Knowledge and Comprehension and Analysis skills because

- Motivation is increased when natural curiosity is aroused and because students often want to "prove" a preconception. (Although we would rather they seek evidence in a more detached manner, at least they are motivated.)
- Attention is heightened because motivation is increased.
- Discrimination between crucial and less important material in the text is supported because the students are searching for specific material.
- Memory is enhanced because students must process the new information by summarizing what is contrary to their preconceptions.

We used this guide in an economics class with good results.

**Pre-Reading Ideas**

| I Think That the Statement is Accurate. | I Think That the Statement is Inaccurate. | Statement |
|---|---|---|
|  | X | 1. Free room and board for a summer camp counselor count as income. |
|  | X | 2. When employed as a piece worker, an employee gets sick leave if he or she can't work due to a legitimate illness. |
| X |  | 3. Many sales people are paid by commission, a fee based on the number and value of sales made. |
|  | X | 4. Employees in businesses must be paid bonuses if they have performed at an exemplary level. |

Now read pp. 187-201 in your textbook. If the information supports your answer in Pre-Reading Ideas, place a check in the Support column. If the information refutes your answer in Section I, make a check in the Refutes column and write the information that refuted your claim in the appropriate space.

**Post-Reading Ideas**

| The Information Supports My Hypothesis. | The Information Refutes My Hypothesis | Write What the Textbook Says in Your Own Words |
|---|---|---|
|  | X | Food and a place to sleep are worth something to you, so they are part of your income. |
|  | X | The pieceworker gets paid only for each item completed. |
| X |  |  |
| X |  |  |

## ⊶ Key 43 is the Point-of-View Guide

By using Wood's (1988) Point-of-View Guide, students are able to access varying perspectives on the events in a reading selection by allowing them to "get inside the head" (p. 913) of participants in that event. This is accomplished by posing the questions in an interview format.

We first encountered this strategy in an American history class that was studying Westward Expansion. By having the students examine the coming of European Americans from the viewpoint of Native Americans, the teacher opened their eyes and caused them to reexamine their assumptions about Manifest Destiny.

The purpose of Wood's (1988) Point-of-View Guide is to help students to process material deeply and to encourage mental recitation. They process the material by adding their own information as they are reading and by translating the material into their own words.

Seeing the usefulness of the Point-of-View Guide in history and literature is easy, but creative science teachers grab the idea and run with it, too. A caveat is that we must be certain that students understand the difference between making the mistake of anthropomorphizing when it is not appropriate and using anthropomorphizing as a learning tool. With that assurance in place, we find the Point-of-View Guide an excellent tool.

The Point-of-View Guide is effective in helping students access Knowledge, Comprehension, Analysis, and Synthesis because

- ♪ Motivation is enhanced because the strategy personalizes impersonal material.
- ♪ Attention is focused because motivation is enhanced.
- ♪ Sequencing becomes easier when we imagine ourselves in a series of events.
- ♪ Memory is strengthened because we have imagined ourselves experiencing something.
- ♪ Reasoning is promoted as we analyze an event from different perspectives.
- ♪ Synthesis is promoted as we create an imaginary persona.

Here is a partially completed example (from a gifted student with learning disabilities) we used in a unit on the muscular system.

## Point-of-View Guide for Biology–*The Muscular System*

You are Senator Biceps, a (flexor) muscle. Ms. Reporter, who is an anchor for the evening news, is interviewing you. Please respond to her questions.

| Question | Your Response |
|---|---|
| Senator Biceps, how do you manage to move parts of the body? | Well, you see, I am deeply attached to bones by tendons. One end of me, the <u>origin</u>, is attached to a bone that remains stationary when I contract. It gives me something to pull against, my foundation, if you will. My other end, the <u>insertion</u>, is attached to a bone that moves when I contract. My insertion always moves toward my origin. Insertion to origin, insertion to origin. It never works the other way. I am adamant about that.<br>Now, I have a colleague on the other side of the aisle, Senator Triceps, who is an extensor, and I am in strong opposition to him. He's so reactionary! I get limbs to bend at a joint, and he just wants them to straighten out! I pull the bone in one direction, and he pulls it in the other! We seem locked in an endless debate! |
| Senator, please describe your response to Myosin and Actin. | |
| You seem to grow larger and more efficient with exercise. How is that? | |
| I understand that you are sometimes subject to overexercise. Please explain why you are so averse to it. | |

## ☛ Key 44 is the K-W-L Study Guide

Ogle (1986) recommended using the K-W-L strategy as a study guide for reading a chapter. The K-W-L strategy has long been used as a pre-reading and post-reading activity to develop comprehension. K stands for "What we KNOW about the topic." The W stands for "What we WANT to learn about the topic from the reading." The L stands for "What we LEARNED about the topic from the reading." The method commonly used is that the teacher writes K-W-L in table form on the board. Before the students begin reading, the teacher asks them what they already know about the topic. The teacher lists the things the students know (or think they know) under the K. Then with the teacher's help, the students generate questions about what they want to learn about the topic from their reading, and the teacher writes the questions on the board under the W. After the students finish reading the material, they return to the chart. The students tell the teacher what they learned from the reading, and the teacher writes what they learned under the L.

Using Ogle's (1986) strategy, students (or the teacher) complete the K and W parts of the chart on a handout. Then, when they complete the reading, the students complete the L part of the chart.

A number of authors have recommended the use of K-W-L charts with secondary and postsecondary students (Wilson, 1997; Yopp & Yopp, 1996). The strategy is recommended widely; it is lauded both for students in adult basic education classes and for those in university courses. Meyer and Keefe (1998) include a fourth column in their K-W-L guides: "Confused."

One advantage of the K-W-L guide is that the "What do I know?" question stimulates the students' schema; another advantage is that the "What do I want to know?" question motivates students to answer their own questions, which is more appealing than answering the teacher's or a textbook's questions (Ogle, 1986).

The problem is that what students want to know about a topic is not always what their teachers want them to learn; therefore, the teacher often must help guide them to identify critical questions that the material will address.

Ciardiello (1998) argued in the *Journal of Adolescent and Adult Literacy* that students must be taught to ask good questions; students need direct instruction, in self-questioning in order to generate higher-order questions. In response, Ciardiello developed an explicit instructional model to teach inner city high school students to ask four types of questions: memory-based, convergent, divergent, and evaluative. She then uses a direct instruction model that she calls TeachQuest to help students learn to ask the four kinds of questions. The TeachQuest model uses three sequential stages: identification, categorization, and construction of questions. By direct instruction methods including modeling, guided practice and feedback, and independent practice, the students learn to ask higher-order questions of themselves. This method will ensure that students using the K-W-L method will ask worthwhile questions.

The K-W-L Study Guide is a key to help unlock the locks that block the way to Acquisition and Proficiency and Fluency in Knowledge and Comprehension because

- Motivation is enhanced because students are answering their own questions.
- Attention is enhanced because students are motivated.
- Perception is enhanced because the student receives the material through auditory, visual, and kinesthetic channels.
- Discrimination between important and unimportant information is enhanced because the students have identified important questions to answer.
- Confusion is decreased because students know the specific questions which they will answer in their notes.
- Memory is enhanced because of the depth of processing as well as because of the increased motivation and attention.

Here is an example from one of our students in a soil sciences class.

## K-W-L Study Guide: *Life in the Soil*

| What I Know | What I Want to Know | What I Learned |
|---|---|---|
| Lots of microorganisms live in the soil. | What kinds of microorganisms live in the soil? And how many in a square foot? What do they do? | Every acre of soil contains two or more tons of living things. 1 teaspoon is home to: 200 nematodes 250,000 algae 288,000 amoebae 444,000 fungi 11,680,000 actinomycetes 101,120,000 bacteria<br><br>*4 Roles* *Autotrophs* are producers. All others are *heterotrophs*. *Parasites* feed on roots and often cause disease. *Predators* prey on other soil life. They help keep parasites in check. *Saprophytes* are decomposers.<br><br>*4 Important Categories* *Bacteria* are main decomposers of organic matter; a few are parasites; a few others are autotrophs. *Fungi* are other main decomposers. Can work on resistant matters. Many are parasites; a few are predators! *Actinomycetes*, aka mold bacteria, can work on resistant matter. Are antagonists: antibiotics. Protect some plant roots. A few cause diseases. *Algae* are autotrophs that add a little matter to the soil. |

## ⚷ Key 45 is the Flip Flop Study Guide

Chalmers (1995) developed the Flip Flop Study Guide to help students master key vocabulary and concepts in content areas. As compared to study guides that list terms and have students provide the definitions, the Flip Flop Study Guide lists definitions and has students find the terms in the text and match them to the definitions. If the guide is used for textbook study instead of lecture notetaking, the teacher may include the page number where each key term can be found.

Chalmers noted that this strategy helps students with writing difficulties because writing one word is much quicker than writing an entire definition. She claimed that the strategy also eliminates students' writing down the definition incorrectly.

Chalmers (1995) stated that such guides help the teacher focus on specific concepts and provide repetition of information for students with disabilities who are included in general education classes. She noted that an advantage of the study guide is that the special education students can be completing the Flip Flop Study Guide while the general education students are completing a guide that involves more writing.

Chalmers also noted that the special education students could complete the Flip Flop Study Guide and use it to complete the guide that the general education students are using, thus having additional exposure to the content.

Although little empirical evidence supporting the Flip Flop Study Guide strategy exists, its characteristics suggest that it would be effective because

- ⚷ Motivation is increased because the amount of work does not seem overwhelming.
- ⚷ Frustration is decreased because of the ease of writing a term instead of writing the more wordy definition and because the page numbers (if in a textbook reading) make the task more manageable.
- ⚷ Memory is increased because of the repetition of completing the Flip Flop Study Guide and then transferring that information to the standard study guide.

Here is an example of a Flip Flop Study Guide in an American history context.

## Flip Flop Study Guide for Chapter 18: The Development of Modern America

Find the word or concept that matches the following definitions. Write the word in the appropriate box.

| Word/Concept | Definition |
|---|---|
| | Legal agreements designed to regulate industry production and eliminate business competition |
| | Breaking down manufacturing into many small steps in which each worker plays only a small part in the making of a product |
| | The right of a labor union to bargain for better wages, benefits, or conditions for workers employed in a business |
| | Refusal of employees to work until their demands for better wages, benefits, or working conditions are met |
| | A big city organization run by bosses who won elections by controlling poor and immigrant voters |
| | The leader of a political machine |
| | Effort to improve government service by creating an employment system based on skill and merit rather than on politics |
| | A farmers' organization that became politically active during the 1870s |
| | A third party formed in 1862 that represented the interests of farmers and labor unions; also called People's Party |

## ⚷ Key 46 is the Cause and Effect Guide

Like the Compare and Contrast Study Guide, the Cause and Effect Study Guide finds its roots in Singer and Donlan's (1980) Process of Reading Study Guide and Olson's (1980) Pattern Guide. It not only teaches students the text structure of cause and effect, but it helps them learn content at the same time.

Ciardiello (2002) noted that not only do adolescents have a difficult time understanding an author's logical arrangement of ideas (text structure) in expository text, but they also have a particularly difficult time identifying the organizational text structure of cause and effect. That makes our use of Cause and Effect Study Guides essential when we want students to read an expository selection using that text structure.

We like to place the Cause and Effect Study Guide in a graphic organizer form. Even though a timeline is an appropriate graphic organizer, we like to use a flow chart whenever possible because we have found that students with special needs often see the timeline simply as a series of unrelated events, rather than related events. For junior high school students or special needs high school students who require more help, we use a simplified form that only asks them to identify one cause and one effect of each event, and we supply the events that we want them to examine. For more capable high school students, we use a more complex flowchart that shows each event as both the cause and effect of other events. We do not specify events; the students identify the events.

After using the more complex flowchart Cause and Effect Study Guide, a student told us, "I never thought about history as things causing other things. I thought that stuff just happened. Now I see that stuff is connected to other stuff! Stuff causes other stuff!"

The Cause and Effect Study Guide helps students as they read because

- ⚷ Sequencing is clarified because the very nature of a flowchart is to sequence.
- ⚷ Memory is enhanced because of the level of processing.
- ⚷ Organization is developed by practice with sequencing.
- ⚷ Reasoning is developed by looking for causes and effects.

Here are two Cause and Effect Study Guides on the same material. We used the more complex guide for our general education students and our more skillful students with special needs; we used the simplified form for our students who had more challenging learning problems.

## Complex Cause and Effect Study Guide – American History

As you read the assigned pages, complete this Cause, Event, Effect study guide.

> *The end of the American Revolutionary War.*

> *Normal life resumed. American ships could sail the seas in safety. Merchants could buy and sell in China and other previously-closed markets. HOWEVER, the states went their separate ways.*

> *State rivalries worsened. A depression followed (1784-1786). States wouldn't pay their fair share of funding the federal government, for example, for national defense, unless they were direct recipients.*

> [blank box]

## Simple Cause and Effect Study Guide – American History

As you read the assigned pages, complete this Cause, Event, Effect study guide.

Cause:

Event: *Normal life resumed. Ships could sail the sea safely. Merchants could buy goods from other countries.*

Effect:

## ⌐ Key 47 is the Hypertext Study Guide

Higgins and Boone (1990) are leaders in the use of Hypertext Study Guides with junior high and high school students who have learning disabilities or other learning problems that prompt their placement in remedial classes. Writing in the *Journal of Learning Disabilities* in 1990, they investigated the effects of (1) a hypertext text-only (as opposed to text and graphic) study guide with pop-up window notes to (2) teacher lecture and the hypertext text-only study guide with pop-up window notes to (3) teacher lecture and textbook reading. Their participants were 13 learning disabled students and 12 remedial students in a ninth grade state history class. The first group (after all students had been trained to use hypertext) used the hypertext text-only study guide with pop-up window notes for 30 minutes per day for the ten days of the study. The second group listened to a 15-minute lecture and followed that with 15 minutes of the hypertext text-only study guide with pop-up window notes. The third group listened to the 15-minute lecture and followed that with 15 minutes of textbook reading on the topic.

Although the groups were too small for inferential statistics, the effects of the hypermedia study guide were encouraging. On a retention test, the combined group of lecture/textbook students averaged 54%, the hypertext-only group averaged 65%, and the lecture/hypertext group averaged 73%. On the ten daily quizzes, the mean scores were lecture/textbook, 62%; hypertext, 75%; and lecture hypertext, 73%.

In another study cited in the same article, Boone and Higgins explored the use of Hypertext Study Guides in a ninth grade class with 15 nondisabled, 15 remedial, and 12 learning disabled students. The students were tested on information they had been presented in a lecture, a lecture/computer study guide condition, or a computer study guide-only condition. Boone and Higgins then repeated the study with the lowest-achieving students from the first study. They found the Hypertext Study Guide to be more effective than either the lecture-only condition or the lecture/computer study guide condition on both posttest and follow-up retention scores.

Even though creating Hypertext Study Guides may be time-consuming, the benefits should be worth the time and effort. Hypertext Study Guides should help students open the doors of Acquisition and Proficiency and Fluency to the rooms of Knowledge and Comprehension because

- Motivation is improved because many students enjoy working with computers and because the student can explore links as desired.
- Attention is improved because motivation is improved.
- Perception is improved by having the hypertext material in visual and auditory form. ,
- Frustration is reduced because the student can work at his or her own speed and examine the hyperlinks that he or she needs to examine.
- Memory is enhanced because the student can revisit each link as often as necessary.

---

*Accept* is a verb that means "receive."

*Except* is usually a preposition. As a preposition, except means "other than" or "excluding."

---

Press the hot button after the sentence that is correct.

**Everyone is going to the assembly accept Chad.**  ☐

**Everyone is going to the assembly except Chad.**  ☐

## ⟊ Key 48 is the Videotape/DVD Viewing Study Guide

We include the Videotape/DVD Viewing Study Guide here rather than with the chapter on lectures because study guides are more appropriate for students viewing instructional videotapes than are notetaking strategies. First, in a lecture or other classroom presentation, we can tightly control what points are addressed, whether they are cued as important, when to pause to allow students to catch up on their notetaking, and so forth.

In contrast, when we show a videotape, we can control only whether or not to show a videotape and which videotape to show. How the material is organized and treated is beyond our control unless we want to jump around on the videotape, rewinding and repeating this section, fast-forwarding and skipping over that section, and so forth.

When we show a DVD, we have much more control than with a videotape; we can skip around easily repeating sections or skipping over other sections. Therefore, notetaking can be appropriate because we can cue as we direct the viewing. However, most of us have a much more extensive library of instructional videotapes than we do of instructional DVDs at this point.

Creating a Videotape/DVD Viewing Study Guide is more time-consuming than creating a study guide to accompany a textbook. First, we have to view the videotape and take notes, unless we know the videotape well. We may have to stop several times to catch up on our notes. Then, we have to organize those notes into a format that will work in a study guide. Finally, we have to construct the study guide itself. However, the work is worth the payoff. As we noted in the beginning of the chapter, we increased the average of a class of 36 college students in teacher education from 48% on a videotape for which we did not construct a study guide to 92% on a videotape of similar difficulty when we had them use a study guide we constructed.

Videotape/DVD Viewing Study Guides help students maximize their learning from videotapes because

- Motivation increases when students are actively involved in seeking information rather than passively watching and listening.
- Attention is increased when students are active rather than passive.
- Discrimination is assured because the students know exactly what is critical and what is not.
- Memory is supported by the level of processing target information.
- Reasoning is developed as students search for evidence for which we have primed them.

Here is a Videotape/DVD Viewing Study Guide we used in a literature class when we were teaching character development using the popular movie adaptation of J. R. R. Tolkien's *Lord of the Rings*.

## Video Viewing Guide for the Characterization of Gandalf in *Lord of the Rings*

As we view the video, look for evidence that develops the following character traits of Gandalf. Jot quick notes in the left-hand column, and when we pause, complete your notes in the right-hand column.

| Characterization/ Jotted Notes | Evidence |
|---|---|
| Gandalf has a sense of humor. | |
| Gandalf is fond of hobbits. | |
| Gandalf is especially fond of Bilbo and Frodo. | |
| Gandalf has a temper. | |
| Gandalf is courageous. | |
| Gandalf has a deep sense of right and wrong. | |

# 8

# Increasing Understanding of Higher-Order Thinking Skills

## In This Chapter

*We often think that we are teaching students to use higher-order thinking skills when what we are actually doing is giving them problems upon which to use such skills, without teaching them the skills required to tackle the problems. General education students may develop their own workable strategies without our help, but special education students almost certainly will not. However, teaching students strategies and heuristics for analyzing, synthesizing, and evaluating is possible. In fact, it is not difficult at all. By explicitly teaching these strategies, not only will our special needs students increase their academic achievement in our classes, but they will also transfer the skills to new settings if we encourage them to do so.*

*In this chapter, we will address strategies to help students analyze and evaluate. In the following chapter, we will discuss ways to help students with the synthesis skills involved in expository writing.*

Teaching that involves Higher-Order Thinking Skills (HOTS) is what most of us teachers love to do best, but we sometimes wish we knew more effective strategies for doing it. These strategies help all of our students use HOTS more effectively, but they are especially important if we are to help our students with learning difficulties develop those crucial HOTS.

Ivie (1998) argued that three criteria exist for defining HOTS. First is the use of abstract structures for thinking, and we have already explained that structure is one of the keys to special education. He wrote, "If we wish to think in abstract terms, we must necessarily come to grips with the structure of knowledge" (p. 35). This implies that we must master the basic facts of a discipline, which we may then construct into hierarchies and manipulate with HOTS.

Ivie's (1998) second principle is the organization of knowledge into an integrated system. Poor learners and effective learners differ in their conceptualization of knowledge. Problem learners see only an unrelated conglomeration of facts; effective learners see classes, systems, relationships, and analogies. This implies that we must make instruction explicit and structured.

Ivie's (1998) third principle is the application of sound rules of logic. Logic is a structure for thinking. We must explicitly teach structures of logic in order for students with special needs to be able to learn them. He also argued that logic is metacognition: thinking about thinking.

The ERIC Digest No. 127, *Order Thinking Skills in Vocational Education* (accessible at www.eric.ed.gov), written by Sandra Kerka (1992), stated,

> Thomas (1992) identifies three types of cognitive theories upon which teaching strategies can be based. Information processing theory explains how the mind takes in information. Knowledge structure theories depict how knowledge is represented and organized in the mind. Social history theory explains the vital role of cultural context in the development of individual thinking. Together, these three perspectives offer a comprehensive view of cognition. In this view, learning is characterized as an active process in which the learner constructs knowledge as a result of interaction with the physical and social environment. Learning is moving from basic skills and pure facts to linking new information with prior knowledge; from relying on a single authority to recognizing multiple sources of knowledge; from novice-like to expert-like problem solving.

The ERIC Digest further identified five general principles for teaching HOTS outlined by Johnson and Thomas (1992). The first principle is to help students organize what they know, and the authors noted that use of graphic organizers (GOs) helps students structure their knowledge. They explained that GOs help ease the cognitive load and free up working memory for higher-order tasks. Their second principle is to build on what students already know. Again, they supported the use of GOs for this principle.

The third principle is to facilitate information processing through explicit modeling of problem solving, including selection of strategies. (This explicit modeling is explained in the fifth principle.) The fourth principle is to facilitate thinking through elaboration. Their fifth principle is for teachers to make their thinking processes explicit, a strategy that Vygotsky (1962) called Cognitive Apprenticeship. Teachers can also use GOs to implement these three principles in teaching students HOTS.

Most secondary students with special needs are concrete thinkers; in fact, Collea (1981) stated that the typical college freshman functions at the concrete level of intelligence. ERIC Digest *Teaching Problem Solving — Secondary School Science* (Blosser, 1988) cited research by Powers (1984) stating that 50% of all college chemistry students are concrete thinkers and have not reached the level of abstract operations.

HOTS can be taught to students with learning problems, as evidenced by increased performance among secondary students studying Spanish as a second language, Chapter I students, seventh and eighth grade poor readers, and sixth grade mathematics and reading students. In addition to increased thinking ability, mastery of HOTS results in higher self-esteem and increased confidence in the ability to solve problems (DeWispelaere & Kossack, 1996; Eisenman & Payne, 1997; Jackson, 2000).

GOs are effective at helping us teach HOTS. DeWispelaere and Kossack (1996) used GOs to teach the HOTS skills of sequencing, classifying, and comparing and contrasting. Their participants were secondary students who were studying Spanish as a second language. Appropriate GOs were used for instruction in course content and testing, and the students were provided with feedback. Students also made their own GOs. Increased performance was demonstrated in written tests, organization of projects, and improved behavior.

GOs are excellent tools for teaching HOTS to students with learning problems. They work because they help make highly abstract and usually verbal information into a representational form.

In this chapter, we will address the following HOTS strategies:

- Key 49: Storyboards
- Key 50: Flowcharts
- Key 51: Timelines
- Key 52: The Forest and the Trees
- Key 53: Venn-Euler Diagram
- Key 54: Use of the Venn-Euler Diagram to Help Students Develop Analytical Ability
- Key 55: Apple Orange Tree
- Key 56: Compare and Contrast Matrix
- Key 57: Campfire
- Key 58: Evaluation by Elimination Matrix
- Key 59: Evaluation by Addition Matrix

## ⚷ Key 49 is Storyboards

From the earliest research on learning disabilities, sequencing has been identified as a major problem area (Cruickshank, 1977; Johnson & Myklebust, 1967). In fact, McLeod (1966) noted that difficulty sequencing was the primary factor in predicting whether or not a child was learning disabled, and sequencing skills are requisite for understanding cause and effect.

Creating Storyboards, sequencing strips, or cartoon strips can help students improve their sequencing skills. The strategy helps students visualize what they read (Schur, 1980), thereby helping them understand sequences, which in turn increases comprehension and analysis skills. Students with learning problems are often nonlinear thinkers and need help in conceptualizing in a linear fashion. This very graphic tool helps with that and can be extended to as many cartoon frames as required. Rubman and Waters (2000) found that Storyboards also enhanced the integration of text propositions and helped students discover inconsistencies in text.

As part of a larger study on using GOs to teach HOTS, DeWispelaere and Kossack (1996) used cartoon frames to help students who were learning Spanish as a foreign language develop HOTS. The strategy increased the students' sequencing skills, and the overall treatment improved not only performance on examinations, but also on the organization of their projects and eventually their behavior.

We even used cartoon frames to help adults increase their ability to follow a convoluted legal case; as the students read aloud, we stopped periodically and drew cartoon frames that depicted each event. Not only did the process help students better comprehend the material, but they also reported that the strategy helped them understand the cause and effect relationships of the events as each event led to the next. That is our great attraction to sequencing strategies: they help our students learn cause and effect.

Storyboards are effective strategies for helping students with disabilities learn cause and effect relationships and thereby Acquire Analytical skills because

- 🎵 Confusion is eliminated because the causes and effects of events are made explicit.
- 🎵 Reasoning is developed as the cause and effect nature of events is demonstrated.

Here are three frames we used involving the Honey War, a little known war between Missouri and Iowa.

Missouri and Iowa dispute ownership of three bee trees.

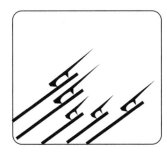

The governors of both states send troops to fight.

The troops do not want to kill their neighbors, so they kill a deer and have a party instead.

## ☛ Key 50 involves using Flowcharts

We like to use storyboards as an introduction to Flowcharts because Flowcharts are more abstract than storyboards. Helping students make the move from less to more abstract is good inclusion teaching.

We all know what Flowcharts are, but we tend to underutilize them in the classroom. When we are teaching a process that involves several steps, we use a Flowchart. A Flowchart can represent a simple, straightforward, one-way process, such as a simple science experiment or mathematical process, or it can represent a more complex scientific, mathematical, or other process with loops and decision-making points.

However, Flowcharts can also be used to help teach the analytical skills involved in identifying cause and effect in science, history, current events, the behavioral sciences, or literature. Flowcharts are excellent tools for analytical thinking because they help students see how Event B is both an effect of Event A and a cause of Event C (Moon, 1992; Ollmann, 1989).

A disadvantage of Flowcharts is that unlike timelines, they generally do not provide a visual representation of the relative amount of time between cause and effect events. So when using Flowcharts, it is often helpful to place the date of an event in the box in which the event occurred. For example, on one Flowchart, we place the following: Hitler created Dauchau concentration camp in 1933; announced the anti-Semitic Nuremburg laws in 1935; and ordered Krystallnacht in 1938. On a second Flowchart, we place: Japan attacked Pearl Harbor December 7, 1941, and the U.S. entered the war December 8, 1941. A Flowchart does not differentiate between the difference in years of three events on the first Flowchart and the difference of only hours of the 1941 events on the second Flowchart.

However, Flowcharts are good tools for helping students Acquire the Analytical skill of cause and effect when used with those caveats in mind because

- ☙ Confusion is eliminated when causes and effects are made explicit in a visual form.
- ☙ Reasoning is developed when the relationships between events and their causes and effects are elucidated.

We used this Flowchart to demonstrate how a new word can enter the lexicon.

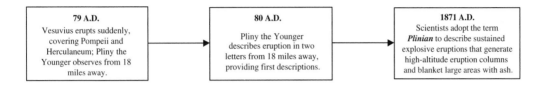

**79 A.D.**
Vesuvius erupts suddenly, covering Pompeii and Herculaneum; Pliny the Younger observes from 18 miles away.

**80 A.D.**
Pliny the Younger describes eruption in two letters from 18 miles away, providing first descriptions.

**1871 A.D.**
Scientists adopt the term *Plinian* to describe sustained explosive eruptions that generate high-altitude eruption columns and blanket large areas with ash.

## ☛ Key 51 involves the use of Timelines to teach cause and effect

Timelines are excellent inclusion tools. Writing in the *Journal of Learning Disabilities*, Kinder and Bursuck (1991) especially recommended timeline note-taking for teaching students with learning disabilities.

Hoone (1989) noted that Timelines reveal history's unfolding more effectively than fact-recall strategies do. She recommended using autobiographical, biographical, large display, and manipulative Timelines. In addition, Timelines are important tools in helping students infer relationships and understand causes and effects.

Harris, Kohlmeier, and Kiel (1999) encouraged teachers to use Timelines to help integrate interdisciplinary curricula. They used Timelines with high school and middle school students in an interdisciplinary activity called Crime Scene Investigation. Cast as investigators, reporters, and lawyers at the scene of a crime, the students used Timelines (as well as other strategies that support thinking skills) to analyze evidence to solve the crime.

While Timelines are a tool of every history teacher's trade, teachers in other disciplines can use them to help students understand cause and effect. A Timeline has the advantage of showing the relative temporal difference in when causes and effects occur: a long time may separate a cause and an event or only a short time may separate them. They are also better at indicating multiple distal and proximal causes than Flowcharts are; the nature of a Flowchart suggests that A causes B, B causes C, C causes D, and so forth. The Timeline makes it easier to see A as a distal cause of D, B as a distal cause of D, and C as the proximal cause of D without A being a cause of B. The Flowchart does not make such distinctions as clearly.

Timelines are useful in science classes, literature classes, and other classes in which they are underutilized. Timelines are a good inclusion strategy because

- Confusion is eliminated when causes and effects are made explicit in a visual form.
- Reasoning is developed when the relationships between events and their causes and effects are elucidated.

We use the following Timeline to highlight the lapse in time between the beginning of Hitler's atrocities and the entry of the U.S. into World War II. Our students are always astonished to see how long the U.S. maintained an isolationist policy when they see this graphic display; they come to class thinking that the U.S. entered into combat as soon as Hitler took office.

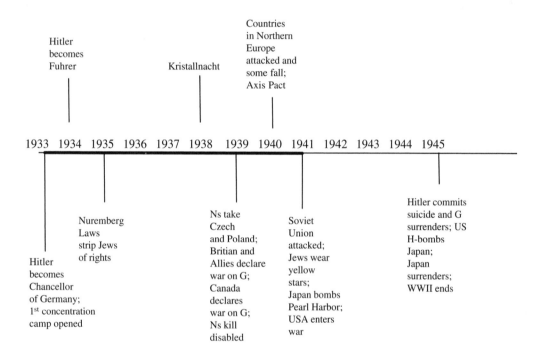

## ☛ Key 52 is the Forest and the Trees, one of the Graphic Analysis Notes strategies

Flynn, Dagostino, & Carifio (1995) argued that metaphor influences a reader's ability to assimilate new concepts into existing conceptual schema and accommodate new concepts by creating new conceptual schema for formal thinkers. Metaphors can be used to clarify and elaborate on ideas and help students move from the concrete and the familiar to the abstract and strange.

In a collaborative interdisciplinary project, Barrell and Oxman (1984) and their colleagues had secondary students explore the meaning of metaphors in everyday language, analyze more formal metaphors from various subject areas, create their own metaphors moving from familiar concepts to more abstract concepts, create metaphors for subject-related concepts, and evaluate the final metaphors in general classroom discussions. From their successful experiment, Barrell and Oxman and their fellow teachers concluded that metaphoric thinking is especially useful in developing critical thinking skills.

Because our students with disabilities have trouble seeing the forest for the individual trees and vice versa, we use the "can't see the forest for the trees" metaphor for teaching the parts of a whole. By making each tree a part of a whole that we are studying and by then drawing a circle around the trees and placing a sign that says "Forest" in front of it, we are able to help our students better understand the part to whole to part concept. By using different shapes of trees, we are able to demonstrate that each part of the whole has unique characteristics.

The first time we use this strategy to teach analytical skills, we have to be sure to tell students to draw their trees large enough to write notes inside of each, and we demonstrate this on the board. It is helpful to have students block out an area with a light pencil sketch, write the notes in the area, and then draw the tree around it.

Using the Forest and the Trees Graphic Analysis Notes is a good strategy to help inclusion students Acquire Analyzing the parts of a whole because

- ♪ Comprehension is increased when the abstract is made concrete and the strange is made familiar.
- ♪ Analytic reasoning skills are developed as students begin to see that wholes can be analyzed by examining their parts.
- ♪ Synthetic thinking skills are developed as students are encouraged to begin thinking about ways they can use metaphors.
- ♪ Attention is garnered when information is presented or manipulated in creative ways.

Here is an example we tried in a mathematics class using the Basic Theorems of Modular Arithmetic. We introduced the forest metaphor on the first day, and on the last day, we had our students role-play explaining the basic theorems to another student. All of our students used the metaphor by choice. We looked over the shoulder of one of our learning disabled students, saw him drawing the trees, and heard him saying, "Together, these different theorems, like the trees, make up something more than just individual trees; they make up Modular Arithmetic, just like individual trees can make up a forest."

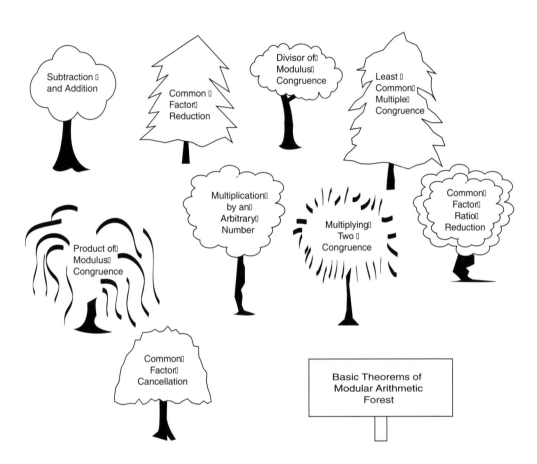

## ☞ Key 53 is a Venn-Euler Diagram for comparing and contrasting

The Venn-Euler Diagram was first described by the eighteenth century mathematician-logician Euler and made famous by the nineteenth century cleric Venn. When using the Venn-Euler Diagram, we draw circles that may or may not overlap to show relationships among classes. But to compare and contrast, a different purpose from that for which the strategy was originally developed, we overlap the circles.

Each circle represents one concept, and the overlapping area represents the commonalities of the concepts. The commonalities are written in the overlapping area. The differences that discriminate one concept from the other are written in the nonoverlapping areas.

In the social studies, teacher-researchers have recommended using Venn-Euler Diagrams in history classes to teach students to compare and contrast Roosevelt and Churchill; in world culture classes to teach students to compare and contrast the Qur'an and the Old Testament; and in American Government classes to teach federalism as a source of conflict and cooperation. In the language arts, Yopp and Yopp (1996) recommended their use in teaching literature; others have recommended their use in teaching developmental college students to compare and contrast in writing and in teaching English to secondary ESL students (Gray, 2000; Hartman & Stewart, 2001; Michalak, 2000).

Boyle (2000) used Venn diagrams to improve the reading comprehension of 26 high school students who had mild disabilities and were poor readers. The students who were taught the strategy demonstrated gains in both literal and relational comprehension.

Venn-Euler Diagrams are effective at helping students with special needs Acquire the Analysis skill of comparing and contrasting because

🔊 Reasoning is supported when the invisible is made visible, and the abstract is made representational.

Here is an example we used to teach students how metaphors and analogies are similar and different.

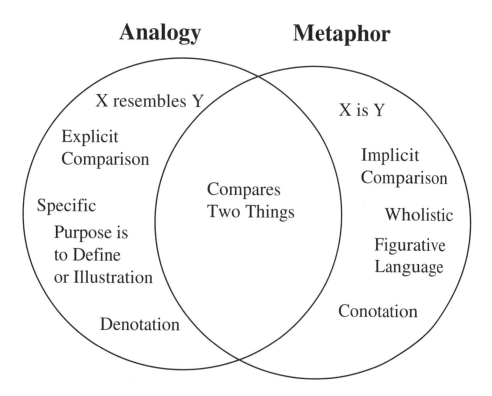

## Analogy    Metaphor

X resembles Y

Explicit
Comparison

Specific
Purpose is
to Define
or Illustration

Denotation

Compares
Two Things

X is Y

Implicit
Comparison

Wholistic

Figurative
Language

Conotation

## ⟶ Key 54 is the Use of the Venn-Euler Diagram to Help Students Develop Analytical Ability

While the Venn-Euler Diagram is an excellent tool for comparing and contrasting, its original function was to assist in developing logic through examining class membership; so instead of only having overlapping circles, this application has circles within circles, circles outside of circles, overlapping circles, and combinations thereof.

VanDyke (1995) recommended teaching secondary mathematics students to use logic with the aid of Venn diagrams. They have also been recommended in teaching deductive reasoning to secondary students and developing cognitive processes in adult students. Still other teacher-researchers have recommended teaching them as life-long learning strategies beginning in middle school and continuing on through high school.

Using Venn-Euler Diagrams, the student can make 16 statements such as Every A is a B, No A is a B, Some As are Bs, Some As are not Bs, and so forth. By using this strategy, teachers not only help their students have a deeper understanding of their content area, but they also help students develop logic, an area which is problematic for many students with learning problems. The following diagram shows a Venn-Euler Diagram used in an English composition class.

Using Venn-Euler Diagrams to Help Students Develop Analytical Ability in inclusion classes is a good strategy because

🔒 Reasoning is supported when the invisible is made visible.

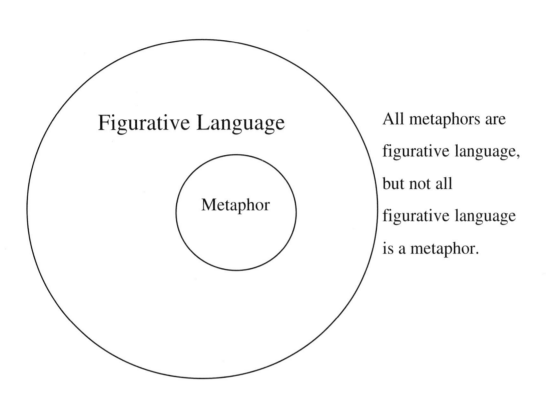

## ⌗ Key 55 is the Apple Orange Tree, a Graphic Analysis Note Strategy for Comparing and Contrasting

People often say, "You can't compare apples to oranges." We can compare apples to oranges; we can compare anything to anything else. Comparing apples to oranges is easier, though, if we keep in mind that apples and oranges share a critical attribute — they are both fruit.

When we introduce the Apple Orange Tree for comparing and contrasting, we start by talking about grafting two trees into one, how they share a common trunk, but each half produces a different fruit. Then, we draw a tree on the board, half apple and half orange. We compare and contrast the apples and oranges by writing their common attributes on the trunk of the tree and their differences on the divided branches of the tree. We draw a line between the opposing branches to further emphasize the dissimilarities of the characteristics on the branches. Next, we use the tree to compare and contrast two concepts from our discipline.

Writing in *History and Philosophy of Logic*, Gasser (2000) wrote that "the pervasiveness of figurative language is to be counted among the features that characterize logic and distinguish it from other sciences. This characteristic feature reflects the creativity that is inherent in logic and indeed has been demonstrated to be a necessary part of logic" (p. 227). Worsley (1988) explained that metaphors such as the Apple Orange Tree are effective because they help students visualize information. For the last two decades, many researchers have agreed that one subject in which metaphors are particularly useful is mathematics, and Burton (1986) especially recommended the use of metaphors in teaching mathematics to students in remedial programs.

Chiu (1994) explored the use of metaphor in mathematics with 12 middle school novice mathematics students and explained that metaphors helped the students understand mathematics for several reasons. First, metaphors intuitively justify mathematical operations. Second, they help students integrate mathematical knowledge into their knowledge structures. Third, metaphors enhance the students' computational environment; and fourth, metaphors assist students' recall.

An even greater number of researchers have recommended the use of metaphor in the science classroom. For example, in *Scientific Thinking is in the Mind's Eye*, Ganguly (1995) wrote,

It is important to incorporate visual thinking into science instruction. Imagination and perception play vital roles in scientific inquiry. Metaphors, like perceptions, are drawn from common experiences and are a means to anchor scientists' thought processes in generating a pattern that bridges the gap between the seen and the unseen.

The Apple Orange Tree Graphic Analysis Note Strategy is an effective strategy because, as Gasser (2000) wrote, figurative language is essential to logic and because

- Reasoning is supported when the invisible is made visible.
- Synthesis is developed when students begin thinking about new ways to apply metaphors.
- Attention is captured when information is presented or manipulated in a creative way.

Here is an Apple Orange Tree comparing and contrasting the Marshall Plan with the Truman Doctrine.

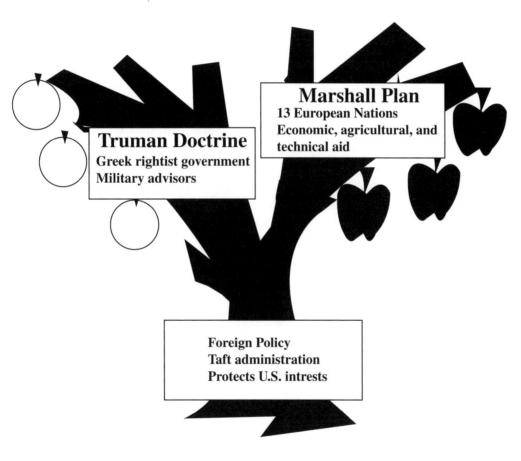

**Apple Orange Tree**

## ☞ Key 56 is a Compare and Contrast Matrix

Here is our matrix again; this time it is used to compare and contrast. We like to use an Apple Orange Tree when we are comparing and contrasting two things, but for comparing and contrasting three or more things, we use a matrix. When we use the term *contrast*, we are referring to how things differ from each other; when we use the word *compare*, we are referring to how things are similar. We explicitly teach these cue words to our students: compare for similarities and contrast for differences. First, we place the characteristics which we are comparing and contrasting across the top of the matrix. Then we place the concepts/people/places and so forth that we are comparing down the left-hand side of the matrix. The students then fill in the boxes with a word, a plus or minus, or any other scheme or even collection of schemes.

Instruction in teaching students to use graphic organizers to compare and contrast has been found to transfer to new settings. For example, Weisberg and Balajthy (1989) taught 16 below-average high school readers to summarize material and construct graphic organizers to compare and contrast in social studies selections. A control group of 16 students was provided with alternate instruction. One month after the instruction, the students were given a high-prior-knowledge selection on nuclear power plant disasters and a low-prior-knowledge selection on the death penalty. Transfer of the summarization and compare and contrast graphic organizer skills occurred on both the high-prior-knowledge and low-prior-knowledge selections. When the researchers had tested the strategy with college freshmen who were required to take a developmental reading course, they found that those students also transferred the knowledge to other contexts.

The Compare and Contrast Matrix is an effective tool for helping students with disabilities increase their analytical skills because:

❧ Reasoning is supported with the invisible is made visible.

Here is an example using three foreign policies, using the table function of a word processing program.

## Compare and Contrast Matrix of Foreign Policies

| Policy | Countries | Type of Aid | Purpose | Administration |
|---|---|---|---|---|
| **Dollar Diplomacy** | Latin America, China | Economic | Protect U.S. interests | Taft |
| **Marshall Plan** | 13 European nations | Economic, agricultural, technological | Protect U.S. interests | Truman |
| **Truman Dotrine** | Greek rightist government | Military advisors | Protect U.S, interests | Truman |

## ⊶ Key 57 is Campfire, one of the Graphic Analysis Notes strategies

The Campfire strategy is for helping students understand multiple causality and multiple effects of an event.

First, the students write the name of the event and a description of it in the middle of a page; then the students draw a fire around it. Next, as the students discover the proximal cause, they write it next to the campfire and draw a match around the cause. As they discover each of the other causes, they draw a log under the fire and write their notes about the cause inside of the log. They stack the logs (down) until all of the distal causes have been identified.

The effects of the event are symbolized by the smoke from the campfire, the more far-reaching the effect, the larger the cloud.

When our students used this strategy in a psychology class, one of them said, "The idea of proximal and distal causes has more meaning to me now. I can see how the distal causes set up (the event) and how the proximal cause set (the event) off!"

Meyrowitz (1980) noted that the use of metaphor for developing critical thinking skills is a particularly useful and a powerful strategy, in part because it helps students to begin to think metacognitively. Using a graphic metaphor renders the metaphor even more effective; when McKay (1999) compared the use of text with textual organizer to text with graphic organizer, she found that the 37 adults in the study increased their understanding of difficult content significantly in the graphic metaphor treatment.

The Campfire strategy is a good strategy to help students understand because

- Reasoning is supported when the unfamiliar is made familiar and when the invisible is made visible.
- Attention is garnered when information is presented or manipulated in a creative way.
- Synthesis skills are developed as students begin thinking metaphorically about other topics.

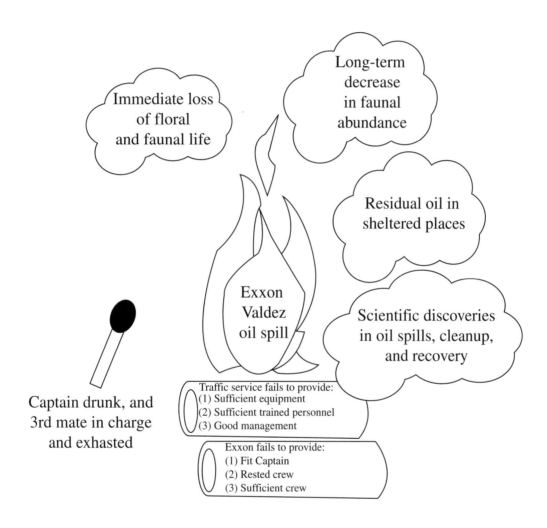

## ⚷ Key 58 is the Evaluation by Elimination Matrix

The Evaluation by Elimination Matrix teaches students a strategy for evaluation by external criteria. Bloom's taxonomy lists evaluation as the highest level of thinking and identifies only two types of evaluation: evaluation by external criteria and evaluation by examination of internal consistency. We will discuss two ways to conduct evaluations by external criteria.

Evaluation by Elimination, formally called Elimination by Aspects (Tversky, 1972), is a heuristic for helping us make decisions when the greatest number of criteria for making a decision must be met. We eliminate each alternate solution as it fails to meet a criterion and continue until only one solution is left. This is the simpler of the two strategies presented here.

In order to help students with disabilities learn this evaluation model, we first help them identify the criteria on which their decision is to be made. Because they have difficulty learning inductively, we will need to explicitly teach what criteria are appropriate for making a particular decision. Then, we help the students prioritize the criteria or teach them a strategy for prioritizing the criteria themselves. Next, we help students select options upon which to test their criteria. We have them enter the criteria and the options into a rubric matrix and determine whether each option meets each criterion. Each option is eliminated when it fails to meet a criterion. The last option standing is selected.

We have taught students to use this strategy with great success. In our classes, they have used the strategy to select the best site for establishing a frontier town, given factors such as the availability of water, game, and so forth. They have selected a menu for a picnic, given such factors as the temperature and accessibility, and have even explored the ethical issues involved in stem cell research and cloning. They have reported back to us how they have transferred the skill to their lives outside of school, such as deciding what videotape to rent, what recreational activity to enjoy over the weekend, and what theme to use for the senior prom.

The Evaluation by Elimination Matrix is effective because

- Motivation is increased when what seems like an undoable task is made doable.
- Attention is secured when students are asked to make judgments.
- Frustration is prevented when a difficult task is made achievable.
- Discrimination among alternatives is clarified.
- Organization is assured by the very nature of the strategy.

## Evaluation by Elimination Matrix

Compare each alternative on each criterion. When a criterion receives a negative answer, that alternative is deleted.

| Criteria | Wind | Fossil Fuel |
|---|---|---|
| Environmentally friendly | Yes | No |
| Sustainable | | |
| Sustainable within U.S. | | |
| Safe | | |
| Inexpensive | | |
| Steady supply | | |
| Hazardous | | |

## ⌐ Key 59 is the Evaluation by Addition Matrix

The strategy that we use for Evaluation by Addition Matrix is a simplified version of Multiattribute Utility Theory (MAUT). Like the Evaluation by Elimination Matrix, Baron (1994) noted that MAUT is predicated upon the motto "Divide and conquer." By this, he meant that the alternative solutions are divided into psychologically independent attributes. MAUT is used to make decisions by the U.S. Air Force, as well as in a range of international public decision-making endeavors such as nuclear emergency management, telecommunications policy-making, and environmental planning.

Whereas in the Evaluation by Elimination Matrix each alternative solution is compared to each criterion in an all-or-nothing approach, in the Evaluation by Addition Matrix, each alternative solution is examined and given a weighted rating. In addition, the criteria are not listed in order of importance because an alternative is not eliminated simply by failing to meet a criterion. A solution might fail to meet one or more criteria and still be selected because it scored higher than the other alternatives overall.

The most difficult aspect of this strategy is determining how much weight to accord each alternative. We generally use a simple scheme of 1 to 3; that is, some aspects have possible scores of 0 or 1, some aspects have a possible score of 0, 1, or 2, and other aspects have a possible score of 0, 1, 2, or 3.

We have used this decision-making scheme on the same kinds of topics that we used the Evaluation by Elimination Matrix. Because finer shades of discrimination are possible, this strategy tends to engender more disagreement and excitement among the students. Everyone gets involved. Specifically, we have used the strategy in physics to decide the best location for a nuclear power plant and a nuclear waste facility; we have used it in literature classes to determine the best solution to a character's problem; and we have used it in government to select the best solution to a civic problem.

Like the Evaluation by Elimination Matrix, students tell us that they use the strategy at home and teach it to their family members. One family used it to decide on a family vacation; another used it to decide how to spend a small but unexpected inheritance; and another used it to decide what breed of dog would best fit with their family.

Following is the example that students constructed in their science class after a student had read a selection on alternative energy sources.

The Evaluation by Addition Matrix is a good strategy for including students with special needs because

- 🔓 Motivation is greater when a difficult task is made doable.
- 🔓 Frustration is prevented when a difficult task is made doable.
- 🔓 Attention is captured when students are asked to make judgments.
- 🔓 Discrimination among alternative solutions is clarified.
- 🔓 Organization is assured by the very nature of the strategy.

## Evaluation by Addition Matrix

Compare and rate each alternative on each criterion.

| Criteria | Wind | Fossil Fuel |
|----------|------|-------------|
| Environmentally friendly 0-3 | 3 | 0 |
| Sustainable 0-3 | 3 | 2 |
| Sustainable within U.S. 0-2 | 2 | 1 |
| Safe 0-3 | 3 | 1 |
| Inexpensive 0-2 | 2 | 0 |
| Steady supply 0-2 | 1 | 2 |
| Total | 14 | 6 |

# 9

# Improving the Quality of Expository Writing

## In This Chapter

*Writing is a complex process that involves most of the thinking skills and certainly the analysis, synthesis, and evaluation skills. First, our students must acquire knowledge through reading, listening, viewing, or doing; in addition, they must understand well the knowledge they collect. Then, they must analyze that knowledge to determine what is relevant to the paper they are to write. Often they must also analyze cause and effect, break something down into its parts, or compare and contrast two or more things. Then, they have to synthesize that knowledge. Finally, they must use an evaluation tool to evaluate and edit their written product.*

*Such a complex task is difficult for most students with learning problems, but the skills a student needs in order to write competently can be taught. The job of teaching them falls to us.*

We can only write clearly if we understand clearly, and this is one reason that writing assignments are especially difficult for students with special needs. But understanding clearly is only one prerequisite for being able to write well. Like narrative writing, expository writing is a synthesis level skill, and knowing what kinds of data to collect, collecting those data, clearly and completely understanding those data, organizing them and getting them down on paper can be overwhelming.

Fortunately, however, we can teach our students to be better writers in our content domains. Speaking at a National Center for Learning Disabilities conference, Gersten and Baker (1999) noted that teachers can help students significantly improve their writing through explicit instruction, teacher demonstration, and teacher and/or peer feedback. Speaking at the same conference, Swanson (1999) reported on a meta-analysis of 58 interventions and found that strategy instruction and direct instruction were the most effective approaches for teaching students with learning problems to write well.

Each content area has its own specific genre, so students should be taught genre-specific strategies. The instructional focus is varied depending on the discipline. Wong (2000) wrote that for opinion genre, teachers should focus on students' (1) clarity, (2) organization, and (3) cogency of arguments. For compare and contrast, she recommended that teachers focus students' attention on (1) clarity, (2) aptness of ideas, and (3) organization. Regardless of the genre, she recommended that teachers train students to use the following stages in the writing process: (1) collaborative planning, (2) independent writing, (3) peer and teacher conferencing, (4) independent revision, and (5) touch-up.

The first six keys in this chapter focus on research and planning strategies. The last strategy, Rubrics, assists not only in the planning stage, but also in the other four writing stages as well. The strategies provide explicit instruction that helps students improve their writing in the content areas. The strategies are not only explicit, but they also provide the much-needed structure that helps students with learning problems meet their academic goals. The strategies this chapter addresses are

- ☛ Key 60: Data Retrieval Chart
- ☛ Key 61: Charting
- ☛ Key 62: Semantic Webbing
- ☛ Key 63: Power Notes
- ☛ Key 64: Campfire
- ☛ Key 65: Evaluation Matrices
- ☛ Key 66: Teaching Text Structure
- ☛ Key 67: Rubrics

## ⌐ Key 60 is the Data Retrieval Chart

The social studies scion, Hilda Taba, first discussed the Data Retrieval Chart as part of an inductive learning strategy. However, it is also a powerful tool for helping students with learning problems to improve their writing skills. We use this strategy when we have assigned students to learn from multiple sources and synthesize that information into a report. The strategy is good for inclusion because it explicitly identifies the information which the student seeks, and it provides structure in the form of a graphic organizer (GO). The GO not only provides visual structure, but it creates a structure by which the student approaches the problem of data gathering and synthesis.

First, we have the students construct a matrix. We then help the students identify three or four questions to guide their data search. We have the students write these questions in the boxes in the first column. Second, we help the students identify three or four relevant sources. We might include an encyclopedia, a textbook, a trade book, a Web site, and so forth. Then, we have the students search each source for the answer to the questions they identified.

The students then write the information answering each question in the box at the intersection of the row headed by that question and the column headed by the data source. They can then construct a summary of the information on each row, with that information providing the material for one well-developed paragraph or for several paragraphs in a longer paper. The students then construct both an introductory and a conclusion paragraph based on what they learned in their search.

Many students, both with and without learning problems, have told us how much learning this strategy has helped them improve their writing skills. A high school junior student told us, "I would have made much better grades as a sophomore and freshman if someone had taught me how to do this. I felt blown-away by the idea of having to write a paper. Doing it this way makes it so much easier." In addition, teachers who have used this strategy tell us that their students produce much more well-organized papers.

The Data Retrieval Chart is a powerful strategy for helping students synthesize material into a written report because

- Motivation is enhanced when a daunting task becomes manageable.
- Attention is focused when motivation is enhanced.
- Discrimination between essential and nonessential information is supported because the student is looking for the answers to specific questions.
- Organization is provided by the nature of the strategy itself.

Here is an example of a Data Retrieval Chart for a report in a science class.

### Data Retrieval Chart for Plutonium Report

| | Encyclopedia On-line | Website Llnl.gov | Website Pu.org | Website greenpeace.org | Summary |
|---|---|---|---|---|---|
| What is plutonium? | Transuranium element; traces found naturally, most human made; halflife of 24,360 yrs! | $P^{239}$ made from bombarding $U^{238}$ w/ neutrons | Dull silver, 2X as heavy as lead | | P exists in traces in nature, but most is human made. It is . . . |
| What is plutonium used for? | Nuclear reactors/ weapons/ power equipment on the moon | Satellites/ nuclear weapons | Power plants/ Long range space missions/ smoke detectors | | |
| How dangerous is pluto-nium? | "extremely" | Dose, duration, route, etc. determine danger; in dog experiments, cancer, immune problems, from 1 day exposure | Not very. | 1 minute within 1 m of single, glassified waste brick is fatal! Government doesn't want us to know! | |
| How is waste handled? | | | | Discharged into air, ground, sea, glass bricks to be buried | |

## ⚷ Key 61 is Charting

Like the Data Retrieval Chart, Charting (Stein, 1988) helps students gather information and organize it for the writing task. However, instead of using multiple sources of information, students can use Charting with only one data source. While the Data Retrieval Chart addresses several questions about one general topic, Charting is used to take notes when students are studying a topic that involves a number of interconnected facts. Stein recommended its use as a notetaking device in science when students are learning about a specific type of organism or behavior.

While Stein (1988) did not discuss Charting as a writing tool, we use Charting to help students write. Charting helps students organize their writing when we want them to compare and contrast several items or even when we simply want them to describe items within a class.

Charting uses the principle of explicitness because it explicitly identifies the information that the students should include in their writing; the students do not have to guess what should be included and what should not. While the students can fill in details from the text when they write, the main ideas are laid out on the chart. As a graphic organizer, the tool provides the structure that students with learning problems need to succeed; the students have their writing plans laid out on the paper in front of them.

Ophelia, a junior, told us, "I like this Charting way. I don't really like to write, but this makes it easy. It's like, you know, like a 1-2-3 thing!" That is quite an endorsement.

The Charting strategy is effective in helping students with synthesizing because

- Motivation is enhanced when a frightening task becomes approachable.
- Attention is focused when motivation is heightened.
- Discrimination between essential and nonessential information is supported because the student is searching for and writing about specified information.
- Organization is provided by the essence of the strategy itself.

Here is an example from one of our students in an English class. Her assignment was to write a paper explaining types of evidence.

### Chart for Kinds of Evidence in an Argument

| Kinds of Evidence | Examples |
|---|---|
| Facts | Verifiable statements by observation or research: *No traffic signal is at the intersection of 24th and Martin.* |
| Statistics | Facts expressed in numbers: *48 traffic accidents happened at 24th and Martin last year.* |
| Examples | Specific cases: *I had a traffic accident there.* |
| Expert opinions | Judgments of authorities: *The City Engineer says we need a traffic signal there.* |
| Appeals to readers' beliefs or needs | Asks readers to accept an assumption without evidence because they believe it is true or it coincides with their needs: *We need to keep our city's children safe when they have to cross the street at 24th and Martin.* |

## ✏ Key 62 is using Semantic Webbing to organize writing

After we teach our students a unit or even an individual lesson, we can have them use Semantic Webbing to organize a writing assignment. First, the students either create their own webs, or we cocreate a web by brainstorming as a class and drawing the web on an overhead transparency while the students make a copy in their notebooks. Then, each student can use the web to construct his or her expository piece. The central circle in the web is the topic of the piece; the introductory paragraph explains that the essay is about the topic and lists the main ideas that will be covered.

In the circles attached to the center circle, the first tier of circles, are the topics of each paragraph of the body of the paper. The content of those paragraphs consists of the information in the second tier of circles. Students with special needs may have difficulty ordering the paragraphs if a particular order is indicated. We can help them address this problem by talking about the order that is indicated as we co-construct the web.

This strategy creates an order out of what may seem like an amorphous mass of information to students who have learning problems. Octavio, an eighth grader, wrote the best paper he had ever created using the Semantic Webbing strategy. He said, "Miss, when you said we were going to have to write about geometric shapes, I didn't think I could do it. I mean, you had taught us all about geometric shapes and stuff, but I didn't know how to write about them. They're math, and I never had to write about math before. But the way you went over it with us, using the Web and all, I could write about it real good!"

The strategy uses explicitness and structure, two keys to teaching students with special needs. The information in the web explicitly identifies the information to be included in the paper, and the web itself provides a structure. The structure is different in nature from that provided by the matrices in the two previous strategies, but still provides the assistance students need. Writing in the *Journal of Reading, Writing, and Learning Disabilities International*, Washington (1989) noted that a semantic mapping heuristic provides a strategy for notetaking, recognizing main ideas and important supporting details, and organizing them into a report. This allows students who have learning problems to read independently about a topic and then write a report, establishing a link between reading and writing.

Using a Semantic Webbing strategy is good inclusionary practice because

- Motivation grows when an amorphous assignment crystallizes.
- Attention is heightened when motivation is heightened.
- Discrimination between essential and nonessential information is assured because only the essential information is included in the web.
- Organization is provided by the essence of the strategy itself.

This example resulted from a writing assignment using Semantic Webbing in a mathematics class in which students were writing about triangles.

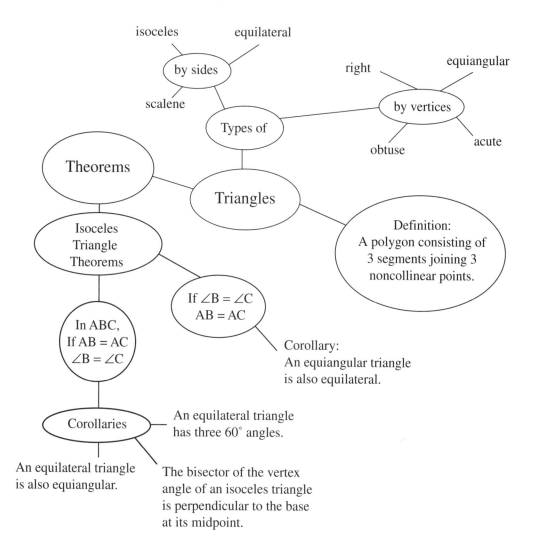

## ⚭ Key 63 is Using Power Notes

Power Notes are one of the CRISS strategies: Content Reading in Secondary Schools. The CRISS strategies were developed by the Kalispell, Montana public schools (Santa et al., 1988). Later repackaged and changed in name to Creating Independence with Student-owned Strategies and available in a video-training program, the CRISS strategies are effective, both for students going on to college and more importantly, for students not going on to college.

Although they were originally developed for and evaluated on secondary school students, Buehl (2001) recommended Power Notes to middle school content area teachers as well; he also stressed that Power Notes are not the sole purview of reading teachers. They were specifically developed for content area teachers to increase their students' independent learning. The strategy is presented as one that promotes effective reading, related literacy skills, and study strategies that help students tackle increasingly complex materials.

When using Power Notes in the study of expository writing, students identify the title of the chapter as a Power 1 idea. Power 2s are usually bold subheadings within chapters, the concepts that support the Power 1. Power 3s are drawn from the text within each subheading; they are the supporting details for the Power 2s. This format not only helps students take comprehensive notes, but it also assists them in writing about the content they have studied.

When we have used Power Notes with students, we have often allowed them to work with partners. We place them in heterogeneous pairs, each student with disabilities paired with a strong student. The students with learning problems have increased their understanding of their reading assignments, as well as increased their understanding of text structure through the structured interaction with the stronger students. When they begin to write, the students with disabilities have a well-organized framework from which to work. First, they clearly understand the text structure and can use that structure in their writing. Second, they clearly understand the material. Thus, their writing improves in both form and content.

Some students have told us that taking Power Notes is like a puzzle; they enjoy finding where the pieces of information fit. A junior student said, "Power Notes help me see how it all fits together. When I write, I feel more like I know what I'm doing."

Power Notes are explicit and structured and are an effective inclusionary practice because

- Motivation is increased when students see an assignment as attainable.
- Attention is increased when motivation is increased.
- Organization is assisted by the very nature of the strategy.

| Power Notes for Tectonic Plate Boundary Motions | |
|---|---|
| **Power 1** | Understanding Tectonic Plate Motions: Plate Movement Causes Changes in the Earth. |
| **Power 2** | Four types of plate boundaries are: Divergent, Convergent, Transform, & Plate Boundary Zones. |
| **Power 3** | Divergent boundaries: new crust is formed as plates move away from each other. Magma pushes up. Mid-Atlantic Ridge best known, spreading at 2.5 cm/yr. Most studied is Iceland, because ridge runs through it. Rifting & volcanic activity. |
| **Power 3** | Convergent boundaries: Two plates come together. One subducts under the other. Very slow collision. 4 types: Oceanic-Continental Convergence, which created Andes & Cascade Mountain range. Earthquakes & volcanoes result. Ring of Fire . . . |

## ⊶ Key 64 is using Campfire to guide cause and effect writing

The cause and effect graphic organizer, Campfire, can be used both to teach content across the curriculum and writing across the curriculum. Ellis (1995), writing in an article on orienting students to organizational devices, noted that graphic organizers are ideally suited for teaching content and then helping students structure their writing about the content they have been taught.

The metaphorical nature of Campfire can also aid students in improving their writing. Fleckenstein (1995) recommended using metaphor as an organizational strategy in helping underprepared two-year college students improve their writing. She also noted that metaphor can help students improve their logical thinking skills; such an improvement should result in improved writing.

When we used Campfire with a high school history class, Flika said, "This (Campfire) makes things much more clear to me than the Timeline did. With the Timeline, I got the idea of all the causal events leading up to the American Revolution, but Campfire makes it all make more sense. This helps me see it better." Flika then suggested that wind fans the flames of a campfire and asked us what might constitute some winds that fanned the flames of the revolution after it had started. We were delighted to see how the strategy helped her think metaphorically. She began to use the Campfire metaphor to structure her writing about cause and effect.

Campfire is a good strategy for making information explicit and structured, thus affording two keys to teaching students with learning problems. Campfire helps students with learning problems improve their writing because

- Motivation is piqued by the interesting nature of the metaphor and ensured by breaking the difficult writing task down into manageable steps.
- Attention is heightened when motivation is heightened.
- Organization is supported by the temporal structure of the strategy.

Here is an example of Campfire that we used in a science class.

**Campfire**

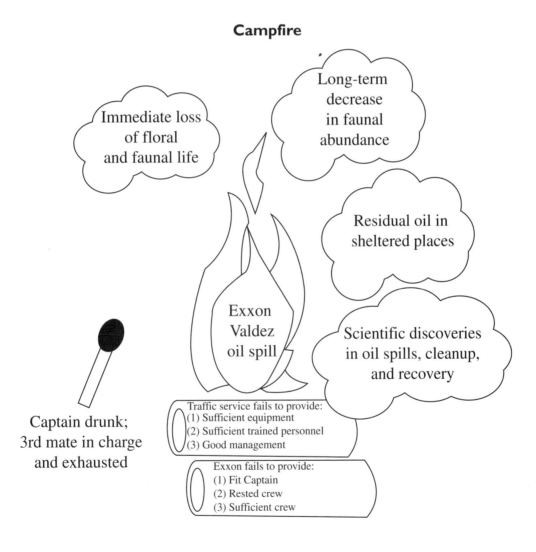

## ⬦ Key 65 is Using Evaluation Matrices

Evaluation Matrices help students improve their ability to justify and defend their decisions, and the tool can assist them in improving their writing about such decisions. Not only does the tool help students develop evaluation skills, but it also provides an organizational structure for writing. Either Evaluation by Elimination or Evaluation by Addition can be used to support evaluative writing.

In a study of first-year teachers' objectives, Sultana and Klecker (1999) found that only 3.2% of lessons involved evaluative thinking. We think more teachers, first-year and otherwise, would engage their students in evaluative thinking if they knew about Evaluation Matrices. This graphic organizer provides the explicitness and structure that students with learning problems need in order to do well, but it also is a powerful tool for students who do not have learning problems. For both groups, it provides a superior framework for constructing a persuasive essay.

Noting that argumentative writing is more cognitively demanding than other types of writing, Crowhurst (1988) argued that such writing can be taught. She further contended that all students, not only older and brighter students, should be taught to write and be expected to write evaluative papers.

In the *NAEP 1992 Writing Report Card* (National Assessment of Educational Progress), Applebee and his colleagues (1994) assessed samples of writing from 30,000 students in Grades 4, 8 and 12. They found that overall, when provided with enough information about a subject, students wrote acceptable narrative and descriptive papers. However, all groups experienced difficulty in writing assignments that required them to present evidence and create an argument. Little writing instruction was dedicated to the persuasive essay; we think that is because teachers do not know what great tools the Evaluation Matrices are in not only teaching students to evaluate, but also helping them write good arguments.

We have been consistently pleased with the results we have received when we have taught students to use the Evaluation Matrices to write persuasive essays. Even college students have told us that the strategy has had a powerful effect on their writing skills.

Evaluation Matrices explicitly identify the evidence for an argument, and they structure the evidence both conceptually and graphically. Evaluation Matrices are excellent tools for inclusion because

- Motivation can result when students see a task in manageable steps.
- Attention results when motivation is engaged.
- Discrimination between essential and nonessential is ensured.
- Frustration is diminished when the cognitive load is eased.
- Organization is supported by the very structure of the tool.
- Reasoning is strengthened when the invisible is made visible and has a structure imposed upon it.
- Production problems are assuaged when a difficult task becomes manageable.

Here is an example of an Evaluation Matrix that a student used to write an argument in science.

## Evaluation Matrix

Compare and rate each alternative on each criterion.

| Criteria | Wind | Fossil Fuel |
|---|---|---|
| Environmentally friendly 0-3 | 3 | 0 |
| Sustainable 0-3 | 3 | 2 |
| Sustainable within U.S. 0-2 | 2 | 1 |
| Safe 0-3 | 3 | 1 |
| Inexpensive 0-2 | 2 | 0 |
| Steady supply 0-2 | 1 | 2 |
| Total | 14 | 6 |

## ⚬━ Key 66 is Teaching Text Structure

Wong (2000) wrote that students with learning disabilities appear not to have any notion of the structure of a paragraph. They do not realize that it consists of a main idea and sentences that support that idea. In addition, they do not appear cognizant of the fact that they need to organize the sentences within a paragraph logically when they write. They consistently have difficulty with organization in their writing.

We know that Teaching Text Structure not only helps students improve their reading comprehension and notetaking ability, but it also helps students with disabilities learn to write in our various disciplines. Our disciplines seek truth in different ways, and they express the truth they find in different writing styles (Wong, 2000). Basic English composition classes teach students to write in a variety of genres, but they cannot be expected to teach students to write in the lexicon and style of every discipline. Colomb (1988) noted that

> A mistake is made when writing is taught as though what students learn in one discipline (usually English) can simply be carried forward unchanged to any number of different writing situations and tasks . . . grammar changes from discipline to discipline. These variations occur at every level of text structure, from syntax through global discourse structure, and they occur in ways that are miscellaneous and unpredictable. The dominant grammatical feature of student-produced texts is that these texts make points, but where and how points can be made, and even what counts as a point worth making, changes from discipline to discipline. (p. 1)

Because students with learning problems have difficulty both ascertaining text structure in their reading and using it in their writing (Englert & Thomas, 1987), they, even more than their peers, need instruction in identifying and using text structure in their writing. Our small time investment in teaching them to do so can help them become more competent writers in our various subject matter areas.

As part of a larger study, Raphael and Kirschner (1985) taught text structure in social studies to 22 middle school students; 23 peers served as a control group. Specifically, the researchers taught the students to select relevant information from multiple social studies texts, add requisite background information, and identify and use appropriate text structure. On the posttest, the trained group outperformed the control group on all measures, including the production of well-organized social studies writing.

Teaching Text Structure is both explicit and structured, so it uses two of the critical keys to special education. It helps students improve their writing and is an excellent strategy because

- ♪ Production is increased when an assignment is seen as achievable.
- ♪ Confusion is avoided when students have a pattern to follow.
- ♪ Frustration is avoided when confusion is circumnavigated.
- ♪ Organization is supported by the pattern structure.

We created and posted the following Text Structure Chart on the walls of one of our classrooms. Students used the chart to structure their writing when using the Evaluative Matrices. We think the improvement that resulted from the chart was commendable.

## Text Structure Chart

| Compare & Contrast Text Structure | Cause & Effect Text Structure |
|---|---|
| In contrast. . . | Because. . . |
| As compared to. . . | Therefore. . . |
| As opposed to. . . | As a result. . . |
| On the other hand. . . | For this reason. . . |
| Different from. . . | In order to. . . |
| But. . . | Thus. . . |
| However. . . | So that. . . |
| Unlike. . . | Causes/is caused by. . . |
| Similarly. . . | Consequently. . . |
| In the same way. . . | Due to. . . |
| Like. . . | So that. . . |
| Both. . . | Contributes to. . . |
| Likewise. . . | |
| In sharp relief to. . . | |
| Any sequence words | Any sequence words |

## ⚷ Key 67 is Using Rubrics

A rubric provides a guide that shows students exactly what they must do in order to do well on an assignment. Andrade (2000) wrote in *Educational Leadership* that rubrics are teacher-friendly and student-friendly, make teacher expectations explicit, provide constructive feedback to students, and support their learning, skill development, understanding, and thinking.

Writing in the ERIC Digest, *Scoring Rubrics Part I: What and When,* Moskal (2000) noted that writing rubrics have been used successfully from kindergarten through college. She also noted that several categories of rubrics exist, beginning with holistic versus analytic rubrics. Writing in *Teaching Exceptional Children,* Schirmer and Bailey (2000) stated that rubrics for writing assignments may be generic or content specific; however, Smagorinsky (2000) and others have argued that every writing assignment should be accompanied by a rubric specific to that assignment because good writing in one context is bad writing in another.

Wong (2000) wrote that a writing checklist rubric provided to students with disabilities fosters self-regulation as they self-monitor and self-check. She recommended that students tape their checklist to a folder for handy reference. The students then tape a pocket on the folder to hold their writing computer disk; in that way, the rubric and the disk are always together.

When we used rubrics to guide students' writing for several consecutive assignments and then failed to provide a rubric for a writing assignment, the students complained. They argued that having the rubric reduced their anxiety about our expectations and that they liked being able to ensure that their work would receive a good grade.

Rubrics provide explicitness through their very nature: the criteria are explicitly identified. They also provide structure by their graphic structure.

Rubrics are good inclusionary strategies because:

- *Motivation* is increased when students understand exactly what to expect and exactly what they must do in order to earn a good grade.
- *Attention* is elevated when motivation is increased.
- *Organization* is supported if the rubric includes organizational information.

Here is a rubric we used in a class on writing about mathematics.

## Rubric for *Issues in the News* Report

| | 20 points | 15 points | 10 points |
|---|---|---|---|
| 1. Relevance of topic to course | Timely and important | Within last 10 years & important | More than 10 years old or not important |
| 2. References used | 5 or more valid references | 4 reference valid | 3 valid references |
| 3. Perspectives presented | 2 or more perspectives presented | | Only 1 perspective presented |
| 4. Evidence presented | 3 or more kinds of evidence presented for each perspective | 2 types of evidence presented for each perspective | 1 type of evidence presented |
| 5. Writing style | Well-organized with well-developed paragraphs with main idea and supporting details | Organization competent with well-developed paragraphs with main idea and supporting details | Organization difficult to follow; paragraphs include main idea and supporting details |

# 10

# Mnemonic Devices

## In This Chapter

*Mnemonics strategies are the single most powerful inclusion strategy (Kavale & Forness, 1999), with an astonishing effect size of 1.62. In addition, the playful nature of Keyword, Pegword, and Musical Mnemonics strategies motivate students and capture their attention.*

*Because students must master discipline-specific Knowledge level information before they can engage in higher-order thinking in that discipline, just as they must gather rough gems before they can process them and create beautiful jewelry, mnemonic devices are valuable tools for working with students with memory problems. The fact that they are fun as well is a delightful bonus.*

As middle and secondary school teachers, we love to teach higher-order thinking skills. But just as we must gather rough gems before we can grade and sort, cut and polish, analyze for use, create and design, and appraise and set a value on our finished products of precious stones, we must teach knowledge level information first. Our students must first know the basic facts of our disciplines. While it is de rigueur in education to scoff at knowledge level teaching, the knowledgeable teacher knows that Bloom's Taxonomy defines Knowledge as a discipline's terminology, specifics, ways and means of dealing with those specifics (conventions, trends and sequences, classifications and categories, criteria, and methodology), and universals and abstractions (principles and generalizations and theories and structures). Knowledge is significant, and Knowledge is prerequisite to higher levels of thinking.

An important key to teaching knowledge to students with disabilities is mnemonic instruction. In fact, mnemonic strategies are the single most powerful key to increasing the achievement of students with learning problems. In a mega-analysis of meta-analyses, Kavale and Forness (1999), fondly known throughout the profession as two of the "greybeards," revealed in their classic monograph, *Efficacy of Special Education and Related Services,* that the single most effective teaching strategy with special education students is mnemonic instruction. The effect size is 1.62. That means

> Students in special education . . . who receive mnemonic instruction would be better off than 98% of students not receiving such instruction and would gain over 1 ½ years of credit on an achievement measure. (p. 81)

In "Mega-Analysis of Meta-Analyses: What Works in Special Education and Related Services," published in *Teaching Exceptional Children,* Forness et al. (1997) explained that a meta-analysis aggregates research findings on a subject by converting the findings to an effect size (ES). The ES is calculated by subtracting the mean of the control group from the mean of the experimental group and dividing the difference by the standard deviation of the control group or a similar measure of variance. When no control group is used, alternate statistical strategies are employed.

In the monograph, Kavale and Forness (1999) noted,

> Mastropieri and Scruggs (1989) synthesized the experimental literature investigating the effectiveness of mnemonic instruction with special education students using meta-analytic procedures. Across 19 studies and 983 subjects, the ES was 1.62, indicating that the average special education students receiving instruction would be better off than 95% of students not receiving such instruction. The expected 45 percentile-rank gain on an outcome assessment means that special education students may almost double their original scores when instructed mnemonically. The associated standard deviation (.79) is also noteworthy because it indicates the presence of no negative effects (i.e., control subjects outperforming experimental subjects). The uniformly positive effects (range = .68 to 3.42) for mnemonic instruction suggest that it represents an effective means for enhancing the academic performance of special education students. (p. 74)

Scruggs and Mastropieri (1990) wrote that the foundations of mnemonic instruction are meaningfulness, concreteness, and elaboration. We more easily learn information that is meaningful to us rather than that which is not meaningful; concreteness, as opposed to abstractness, promotes retention. The more we elaborate on concepts, the more fully we encode them for later retrieval.

The strategies we discuss in this chapter are

- Key 68: Keyword Mnemonics
- Key 69: Pegword Mnemonics
- Key 70: Musical Mnemonics

## ⚷ Key 68 is Keyword Mnemonics

Keyword mnemonic strategies were described by Lorayne and Lucas, popular memory mavens, in 1974. The first scientific investigation of mnemonics as a teaching and learning strategy was conducted by Atkinson (1975) within the context of foreign language classes. A rich corpus of research supports their use with students who have disabilities (Forness et al. 1997).

In the vocabulary chapter, we discussed Keyword Mnemonics in the context of remembering the definition of a word. Here, we discuss the strategy as it is used to learn an association between two words, such as a state and its capital, or a group of related words, such as the names of the presidents. In this context, the Keyword Mnemonics strategy involves finding a word that sounds like each of the target words, creating a story about the keywords that connect them, and making a picture that demonstrates the story. For example, Santa Fe, New Mexico could have Santa Claus and new moccasins as its keywords. The story for such a connection might be: Santa Claus bought some new moccasins. The picture of a beaming Santa Claus in his traditional red suit sporting moccasins instead of the usual high black boots would demonstrate the story. We then would have the student practice saying the keywords and their target words several times. Next, we would have the student look at the picture and practice telling the story several times. Finally, we would ask the student the capital of New Mexico. The student would talk-aloud the story without seeing the picture and tell us the capital.

Brigham (1993) used the Elaborative Keyword method to help 72 middle school students with learning disabilities remember the locations of battles of the American Revolutionary War. He taught such battles as Ticonderoga as a tiger firing a cannon to represent the Battle of Ticonderoga in which the troops captured a cannon that they later used, and the Battle of Paoli as a sleeping soldier dreaming of his paycheck. This battle was lost because the soldiers were caught sleeping. The various pictures were placed in the appropriate locations on a map. The Elaborative Keyword group significantly outscored the control group.

Research shows that for students with disabilities, Keyword Mnemonics instruction has produced remarkable results across the curriculum, in lectures and in prose adaptations (Scruggs & Mastropieri, 1990). We used the strategy to teach the provinces and territories of Canada after a Dear Abby column noted that while Canadian students are expected to know all of the states and capitals of the U.S., few citizens of the United States know any of the Canadian equivalents. In addition to the usual Keyword Mnemonics strategy, we required the students to reproduce the drawings that we had provided.

Our students were six high school students with mild mental retardation. On the pretest, none of the students were able to produce the name of even one province or territory. After Keyword Mnemonics instruction, four of the students were able to identify all of the territories and provinces, and two could identify at least four. One week later, the gains remained strong.

We think that secondary students should know the names and liberal-conservative status of the Justices of the United States Supreme Court so they can better understand court cases in the news. The figure below is part of a Keyword Mnemonics story we used for teaching the material.

The Keyword Mnemonics strategy works for students with special needs because

- Memory is enhanced when material is presented auditorily and visually and because the information requires students to elaborate on material that is made concrete and meaningful.
- Motivation is elevated by the playful nature of the strategies.
- Attention is increased when motivation is elevated.

**Conservative = Convertible**
**Day O'Connor = One Day**
**Rehnquist = Ring Quest**
**Scalia = Scaly**
**Kennedy = Kenny G**
**Thomas = To Mass**

One day I decided to go on a Ring Quest. I got in my Scaly convertible and set off. I asked my friend Kenny G to go with me, but he said he was going To Mass.

## ⚷ Key 69 is Pegword Mnemonics

Pegword Mnemonics, which are often used with Keyword Mnemonics strategies, provide a procedure that is useful when information must be remembered in a given order. In this strategy, the following associations are generally made: 1 is bun, 2 is shoe, 3 is tree, 4 is door, 5 is hive, 6 is sticks, 7 is Heaven, 8 is gate, 9 is line, and 10 is hen. (We like to create our own lists, such as using snore for 4, tricks for 6, and wine for 9, and so forth.)

Regardless of whether we use the traditional list or devise one of our own, once a list is learned, it is crucial to stick with that set of associations in order to avoid confusion.

Tolfa, Scruggs, and Mastropieri (1985) used a Pegword/Keyword Mnemonics strategy to teach 64 junior high students with learning disabilities the attributes of dinosaurs and reasons for extinction, as well as other information about dinosaurs. The control group was taught using other strategies. The mnemonic group not only outperformed the control group on a delayed memory test, but they also performed better than the control group on an application and a vocabulary test.

Scruggs and Mastropieri (1990) used Pegword/Keyword Mnemonics strategies to teach students with learning disabilities the hardness of minerals on the Mohs hardness scale. They provided the example of the mineral hornblende, which is a hardness of 5. Their Keyword was horn, and the Pegword for 5 is hive. Their pictorial representation was a hive in a horn.

A rehearsal-based group rehearsed the names of the minerals and their hardness as they looked at photographs of the minerals for the same amount of time as the experimental group used per mineral. A free-study group used any method they chose to study on their own.

In the assessment, the Pegword/Keyword group significantly outperformed the other two groups, scoring 79% as compared to a mean of 28%. After 24 hours, the comparison groups had essential forgotten what they had learned, while the experimental group actually increased their results slightly.

Pegword Mnemonics is an effective strategy because

- ♪ Memory is enhanced when information is elaborated, given concreteness, and is meaningful, as well as when information is encoded in multiple modalities.
- ♪ Motivation is elevated by the playful nature of the strategies.
- ♪ Attention is increased when motivation is elevated.

Here we used Pegword Mnemonics to teach the five most populous states.

California 1   Collie on a Bun

Texas  2   Shoe   Taxi Wearing Shoes

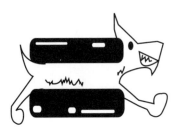

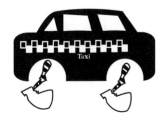

New York  3   Tree   New Fork in Tree

Florida  4  Snore   Flowers Snoring

Pennsylvania  5   Hive   Bees Bring Pens Back to the Hive.

## ➴ Key 70 is Musical Mnemonics

Whenever we are around teenagers who are unsupervised, we hear music. This makes Musical Mnemonics a natural motivator for students who have learning problems.

Cade and Gunter (2002) used Musical Mnemonics with three severely emotionally disturbed boys in mathematics instruction. Using the Semple (1992) mathematics strategy, the students were taught the multiplication family of seven in order to meet IEP objectives of dividing by seven. The strategy involves assigning the fingers 1 through 10 when placed on a table in keyboard position. As the student sings the song for seven, he taps each finger as its fact is sung. The song is:

Seven, fourteen, twenty-one, look at me, I'm having fun!

Twenty-eight and thirty-five, fun-fun-fun, man alive! (Semple, p. 133)

Each student was taught the tapping strategy in a few minutes and then was taught the seven song. He was then given 15 minutes of free time. Afterward, he was tested with a division fact worksheet and told to use the strategy. The strategy was then repeated, with five repetitions on the first day. Thereafter, only a review of the song was provided each day in which no test was administered.

Student A increased from 4% to 96% after one intervention. After the second intervention, he scored 100% and maintained his proficiency for 20 days. Student B increased from 4% to 83% after the first intervention and to 100% after the second, maintaining his proficiency with a final score of 96% on session 20. Student C started at 8% and ended and maintained at 100%.

Green (1992) and others have recommended the use of Musical Mnemonics strategies with students with learning disabilities as well as with students with emotional disorders.

Although no formal research has investigated the use of student-generated music as a mnemonic strategy, we have had success with the Musical Mnemonics strategy in all content areas and from elementary school through graduate school.

Musical Mnemonics is a good memory strategy for students with disabilities because

🎵 Memory is supported when the words are linked together with a melody.

🎵 Motivation is elevated by the playful nature of the strategies.

🎵 Attention is increased when motivation is elevated.

Here are the words to the song we used to teach our students the Big Ideas in science. We used the tune of Jingle Bells

### Mnemonic Device for the Big Ideas in Science, Sung to the Tune of *Jingle Bells*

Systems, models, change and stability,
Evolution and scale, what this means to me is
The Big Ideas in science will help you and me
Make this world, this big blue ball,
A better place to be!

# 11

# Possible Future Keys

The Overview of the No Child Left Behind Act of 2001 (www.nclb.gov) notes that in our schools:

- Reading performance has remained stable for 15 years in spite of dramatically increased funding;
- Fewer than 20 % of our country's high school seniors score proficiently in mathematics on achievements tests; and
- Our seniors rank near the bottom in science and mathematics as compared to the seniors of other industrialized nations.

When Corwin Press received the first draft of this book, they noted the need for a final chapter. They said, "Tell us what you think will come next regarding the development of strategies for the inclusion of students with special needs in secondary content classes." When they asked for such a chapter, the first thing that came to mind was the No Child Left Behind Act of 2001 (www.ed.gov).

The No Child Left Behind Act identifies four priorities, of which two are directly related to the contents of this book: (1) greater accountability for students' academic achievement and (2) an emphasis on research-supported instructional strategies. We cannot think about future directions for the development of new keys for helping students with disabilities access the jewels until we think about these two mandates.

## THE ACCOUNTABILITY MANDATE ■

The accountability proviso requires that states implement statewide accountability systems that will

- Set academic standards in each content area for what students should know and be able to do.
- Gather specific, objective data through tests aligned with those standards.

- Use test data to identify strengths and weaknesses in the system.
- Report school academic achievement to parents and communities.
- Empower parents to take action based on school information.
- Recognize schools that make real progress.
- Direct changes in schools that need help.

## No Child Left Behind Act 2001

Each state will test all of its students and disaggregate their test scores. The disaggregates will identify our students' scores by individual school; the disaggregates will identify the scores of our students with disabilities by individual schools.

That is not all. The data from each of our individual schools will be published so that the public can examine and compare the performance of (1) our and other schools, (2) our content area teachers and those of other schools in our districts, and (3) our content area teachers and those of schools in other districts.

Woe onto us if our scores are lower than the national mean; woe especially to those of us who are secondary teachers whose students do not perform satisfactorily in our specific content areas. Woe to us especially if our students score lower in our content area than in other content classes in our school, or if our students score lower in our content area than the students in other schools in our district.

Because the No Child Left Behind Act directs principals to focus on their schools' academic performance and make whatever changes are necessary to improve it, our failure to ensure that our students with disabilities are making satisfactory progress could result in our termination. Because parents are empowered with control of federal funds, including the authority to transfer their children out of a low-performing school, woe onto us whose students transfer to another school because our scores are low.

That is the first proviso, and it leads us to the second: the mandate that schools use only "scientifically proven" instructional materials and strategies.

## Research-Supported Effective Strategies

The No Child Left Behind Act states that it "only funds curricula and teaching methods that are scientifically proven to work." (No Child Left Behind, 2001). Use of nonsupported strategies could result in loss of federal funds.

This book presents instructional strategies that have empirical support, especially for students who have learning problems. Many of the strategies include brief references to research that supports their effectiveness. If the strategy does not include a reference to a specific study, then it derives support by its foundation in (1) the Master Keys of Explicitness, Structure, and Repetition and (2) Tri-Coding of Information and Paivio's Dual Processing Theory. We have a robust body of research that supports those principles; so strategies that employ them are grounded in research.

Because the No Child Left Behind Act only funds the use of research-supported strategies, it logically follows that strategies that work with students with disabilities who are included in high school content classrooms will receive increasing interest from researchers. After all, research follows the money. In this case, that is good.

*Keys to Successful Learning: A National Summit on Research in Learning Disabilities* was sponsored by the National Center for Learning Disabilities in 1999. The summit included four papers designed to synthesize past research and predict future trends in the education of students with learning problems.

Gersten and Baker (1999) wrote on reading comprehension instruction. Their research led them to recommend that the future focus on teaching students a multiplicity of broadband comprehension and self-monitoring strategies. They suggest that teachers model an array of comprehension strategies such as those described in this book. They pointed out the need for instruction in generalization of strategies because students with learning problems do not generalize/ transfer skills well without structured teaching for generalization. Finally, they recommended the use of peer-mediated learning.

Gersten, Baker, and Edwards (1999) addressed the teaching of writing skills. Their survey of the research led them to recommend explicit instruction. They noted the need for explicit teacher modeling of the writing process with explicitly stated steps and mnemonic strategies or cue cards to remind students of the necessary steps in the process. They recommended the explicit teaching of various types of writing and reminded us of the importance of providing multiple examples, stating that, "The more explicit the examples, the more effectively students learn these writing conventions."

Swanson (1999) provided the article on the future of higher-order thinking skills instruction for students with disabilities. He found that interventions with elements of Direct Instruction and Strategy Instruction provided the keys to effective intervention. He wrote,

> It is important to include the following components when designing material and instruction for adolescents with LD: breaking down the task into smaller steps, using step-by-step prompts, drill-repetition-practice, individual and small group instruction, focusing on isolated processing components and then synthesizing components, and using computer-mediated instruction.

Central to Direct Instruction and Strategy Instruction are the Master Keys presented in Chapter 2 and from which all other keys are derived: Explicitness, Structure, and Repetition. Breaking down the task into smaller steps allows us to create a structure and teach each step explicitly. Using step-by-step prompts provides structure and explicit instruction. Drill-repetition-practice provides for structure, explicit feedback, and prima facie, for repetition.

## Technology

As noted in Key 36, we think the most exciting future direction for the inclusion of students with disabilities into general education content area classes is the development of Universal Learning Environments. When every student, with or without learning problems, has a computer with software that is designed to meet individual needs, we will all benefit. Each student's terminal will remember his or her individual strengths and needs and respond accordingly, providing more representations for the students who need them and fewer for those who do not. Student stimuli attraction will be encoded so that in mathematics or language arts the student who is interested in space travel will have problems based around that theme, the student who is interested in oceanography will have problems based around that theme, and the student who is interested in social justice issues will have those issues around which instruction will revolve.

Other technological advances will benefit all students as well. Writing in *CyberPsychology and Behavior*, Reid (2002) predicted that virtual reality hardware and software will assume a crucial place in the education of students with disabilities. Students could practice safety procedures required for science classes until we determined that the student could safely use realia, or realia might even become unnecessary as students conducted all of their science experiments in virtual reality. We could program the reality to provide a textbook-perfect example of the dissection of a human being, or we could program it to include the diseased lung of a cigarette smoker. A student could conduct the dissection repeatedly until he or she had mastered the targeted objectives.

The possibilities are endless. Students could compare the effects of various chemicals on the growth of plants, and instead of waiting weeks to see the results, they could see them immediately. They could combine any number of dangerous chemicals in the safety of their virtual worlds without serious injury. They could experience physics firsthand as they raced down a virtual roller coaster at various angles. Potentially talented students could view themselves as competent scientists, creating a pool of candidates for the science jobs that go wanting because so many students do not appreciate the thrills of science or see the challenges as within their ability.

The technological advances as described by Hitchcock (2001) and Reid (2002) will allow us to provide highly individualized explicit, structured, and repetitive multisensory, multirepresentational instruction for students who need it.

## IN SUMMARY  ■

So that is what we expect for the future, but in the meantime, what do we do about today and tomorrow morning? Our first task is to use the keys on our key rings. This book has 70 of them. Our second task is to try out new keys that have shown promise through research in the beginning stages. We will keep the keys that work and toss out the rest. That way we will be able to open the locks to the doors that bar our students' way to the jewels inside the stronghold of our disciplines, and they, too, will be able to access the precious gems that we have to offer.

# Resources

Abrams, J. C. (1984). Interaction of neurological and emotional factors in learning disability. *Learning Disabilities: An Interdisciplinary Journal, 3*(3), 27-37.

Adams, R. (1971). A sociological approach to classroom research. In J. Westbury & A. Bellack (Eds.), *Research in classroom processes: Recent developments and next steps* (pp. 101-117). New York: Columbia University, Teachers College Bureau of Publications.

Adelman, H. S., & Taylor, L. (1983a). Classifying students by inferred motivation to learn. *Learning Disability Quarterly, 6,* 201-206.

Adelman, H. S., & Taylor, L. (1983b). Enhancing motivation for overcoming learning and behavior problems. *Journal of Learning Disabilities, 16,* 384-392.

Adelman, H. S., & Taylor, L. (1990). Intrinsic motivation and school misbehavior: Some intervention implications. *Journal of Learning Disabilities, 23,* 541-550.

Alexander, A. A., Schallert, D. L., & Hare, C. H. (1991). Coming to terms: How researchers in learning and literacy talk about knowledge. *Review of Educational Research, 61,* 315–343.

Al-Hilawani, Y. A., & Poteet, J. A. (1995). *Cognitive processing in mild disabilities.* (ERIC Document Reproduction Service No. ED383143)

Allsopp, D. H. (1999). Using modeling, manipulatives, and mnemonics with eighth-grade math students. *Teaching Exceptional Children, 32*(2), 74-81.

Alvermann, D. (1981, April). *The compensatory effect of graphic organizer instruction on text structure.* Paper presented at the Annual Meeting of the American Educational Research Association, Los Angeles, CA. (ERIC Document Reproduction Service No. ED208019)

American Association for the Advancement of Science. (1989). *Science for all Americans.* Retrieved November 21, 2002, from http://www.project2061.org/tools/sfaaol.chap11.htm

Anday-Porter, S., Henne, K., & Horan, S. (2000). *Improving student organizational skills through the use of organizational skills in the curriculum.* M.A. Research Project, Saint Xavier University and SkyLight Professional Development. (ERIC Document Reproduction Service No. ED442139)

Anderson, T. H., & Armbruster, B. B. (1986). *The value of taking notes* (Reading Education Report No. 374). Champaign: University of Illinois at Urbana-Champaign, Center for the Study of Reading. (ERIC Document Reproduction Service No. ED277996)

Andrade, H. G. (2000). Using rubrics to promote thinking and learning. *Educational Leadership, 57*(5), 13-18.

Annis, L. F., & Annis, D. B. (1987, April). *Does practice make perfect? The effects of repetition on student learning.* Paper presented at the Annual Meeting of the American Educational Research Association, Washington, DC. (ERIC Document Reproduction Service No. ED281861)

Applebee, A. N., Langer, J. A., Mullis, I. V. S., Latham, A. S., & Gentile, C. A. (1994). *NAEP 1992 writing report card.* Washington, DC: U.S. Department of Education, Office of Educational Research and Improvement, National Center for Education Statistics. (ERIC Document Reproduction Service No. ED370119)

Armbruster, B. B., & Anderson, T. H. (1988). On selecting "considerate" content area textbooks. *Remedial and Special Education, 9*, 47–52.

Arons, A. B. (1984). Student patterns of thinking and reasoning: Part two of three parts. *Physics Teacher, 22*, 21-26.

Asher, J. (1981). *Learning another language through actions: The complete teacher's guidebook.* Los Gatos, CA: Sky Oaks. (ERIC Document Reproduction Service No. ED191314)

Asher, J. J. (1969). The total physical response technique of learning. *Journal of Special Education, 3*(3), 253-262.

Asher, J. J. (1977). Children learning another language: A developmental hypothesis. *Child Development, 48*, 1040-1048.

Atkinson, R. C. (1975). Mnemotechnics in second language learning. *American Psychologist, 30*, 821-828.

Ausubel, D. P. (1963). Cognitive structure and the facilitation of meaningful verbal learning. *Journal of Teacher Education, 14*, 217-222.

Ausubel, D. P. (1968). *Educational psychology: A cognitive view.* New York: Holt, Rinehart & Winston.

Ayres, R., et al. (1990). Self-concept, attribution, and persistence in learning-disabled students [Abstract]. *Journal of School Psychology, 28*(2), 153-163.

Balajthy, E., & Weisberg, R. (1988, December). *Effects of transfer to real-world subject area materials from training in graphic organizers and summarizing on developmental college readers' comprehension of the compare/contrast text structure in science expository text.* Paper presented at the 38th Annual Meeting of the National Reading Conference, Tucson, AZ. (ERIC Document Reproduction Service No. ED300771)

Barkin, B., Gardner, E., Kass, L., & Polo, M. (1981). *Activities, ideas, definition, strategies (AIDS). Learning disabilities: A book of resources for the classroom teacher.* New Rochelle, NY: City School District of New Rochelle. (ERIC Document Reproduction Service No. ED214358)

Baron, J. (1994). *Thinking and deciding* (2nd ed.). Cambridge, England: Cambridge University.

Barrell, J., & Oxman, W. G. (1984, April). *"Hi heels and walking shadows": Metaphoric thinking in schools.* Paper presented at the annual meeting of the American Educational Research Association, New Orleans, LA.

Barsch, R. H., & Bryant, N. D. (1966, April). *Symposium on the education of children with learning disabilities.* New Brunswick, NJ: Rutgers State University. (ERIC Document Reproduction Service No. ED014176)

Barton, M. L. (1997). Addressing the literacy crisis: Teaching reading in the content areas. *NASSP Bulletin, 81*(587), 22-30.

Batts, G. R. (1999). Learning about color subtraction by role-play. *School Science Review, 80*(292), 99-100.

Bean, T. W., Singer, H., & Cowen, S. (1985). Analogical study guides: Improving comprehension in science. *Journal of Reading, 29,* 246-250.

Beck, I. L., & McKeown, M. (1991). Conditions of vocabulary acquisition. In R. Barr, M. L. Kamil, P. B. Mosenthal, & D. P. Pearson (Eds.), *Handbook of reading research* (Vol. 2, pp. 789-814). Mahwah, NJ: Erlbaum.

Beck, I. L., McKeown, M. G., & Gromoll, E. W. (1989). Learning from social studies texts. *Cognition and Instruction, 6,* 99–158.

Becker, L., & Morrison, G. (1978). *The effects of levels of organization on clustering and recall in normal, learning disabled, and educable mentally retarded children. Final Report.* (ERIC Document Reproduction Service No. ED180147)

Beckman, K. R. (1968, January). *Characteristics of the child with learning disabilities.* Paper presented at the workshop on Learning Disabilities — Identification and Remediation, Chicago, IL. (ERIC Document Reproduction Service No. ED060578)

Belfiore, P. J., Skinner, C. H., & Ferkis, M. A. (1995). Effects of response and trial repetition on sight-word training for students with learning disabilities. *Journal of Applied Behavior Analysis, 28*(3), 347-348.

Bergert, S. (2000). *The warning signs of learning disabilities* (ERIC Digest E603). (ERIC Document Reproduction Service No. ED449633)

Billingsley, B. S., & Wildman, T. M. (1988). The effects of prereading activities on the comprehension monitoring of learning disabled adolescents. *Learning Disabilities Research, 4,* 36-44.

Birnbaum, B. W. (1989). *Increasing organizational skills and homework productivity with ninth grade emotionally handicapped and regular students.* Ed.D. Practicum, Nova University, Fort Lauderdale, FL. (ERIC Document Reproduction Service No. ED321428)

Blabock, J. W. (1982). Persistent auditory language deficits in adults with learning disabilities. *Journal of Learning Disabilities, 15,* 604-609.

Blake, C. R. L., & Garner, P. (2000, April). *"We may give advice but we can never prompt behavior": Lessons from Britain in teaching students whose behavior causes concern.* Paper presented at the Annual Meeting of the American Educational Research Association, New Orleans, LA. (ERIC Document Reproduction Service No. ED442209)

Blankenship, T. (1982). Is anyone listening? *Science Teacher, 49*(9), 40-41.

Bloom, B. S. (Ed.). (1956). *Taxonomy of educational objectives: The classification of educational goals. Handbook 1: Cognitive domain.* New York: McKay.

Blosser, P. E. (1988). *Teaching problem solving — secondary school science* (ERIC/SMEAC Science Education Digest No. 2). (ERIC Document Reproduction Service No. ED309049)

Boden, C., & Brodeur, D. A. (1999). Visual processing of verbal and nonverbal stimuli in adolescents with reading disabilities. *Journal of Learning Disabilities, 32,* 58-71.

Bos, C. S., Anders, P. L., Filip, D., & Jaffe, L. E. (1989). The effects of an interactive instructional strategy for enhancing reading comprehension and content area learning for students with learning disabilities. *Journal of Learning Disabilities, 22*(6), 384-390.

Bos, C. S., & Vaughn, S. (1994). *Strategies for teaching students with learning and behavior problems.* Boston: Allyn & Bacon.

Boudah, D. J., & Weiss, M. P. (2002). *Learning disabilities overview: Update 2002* (ERIC Digest E624). (ERIC Document Reproduction Service No. ED462808)

Bowman, L. A., Carpenter, J., & Paone, R. A. (1998). *Using graphic organizers, cooperative learning groups, and higher order thinking skills to improve reading comprehension.* M. A. Action Research Project, Saint Xavier University. (ERIC Document Reproduction Service No. ED420842)

Boyle, J. (1996). Thinking while notetaking: Teaching college students to use notetaking during lectures. In B. G. Grown (Ed.), *Innovative learning strategies: Twelfth yearbook* (pp. 9-18). Newark, DE: International Reading Association.

Boyle, J. R. (2000). The effects of a Venn diagram strategy on the literal, inferential, and relational comprehension of students with mild disabilities. *Learning Disabilities: A Multidisciplinary Journal, 10*(1), 5-13.

Boyle, J. R., & Weishaar, M. (2001). The effects of strategic notetaking on the recall and comprehension of lecture information for high school students with learning disabilities. *Learning Disabilities: Research & Practice, 16*(3), 133-141.

Boyle, J. R., & Yeager, N. (1997). Blueprints for learning: Using cognitive frameworks for understanding. *Teaching Exceptional Children, 29*(4), 26-31.

Brand, A. G. (1998). *Writing in the majors: A guide for disciplinary faculty.* New York: SUNY College at Brockport. (ERIC Document Reproduction Service No. ED421723)

Brandhorst, A., & Splittgerber, F. (1984, March). *Teaching thinking skills using the concept time.* Paper presented at the National Council for the Social Studies Southeast Regional Conference, New Orleans, LA. (ERIC Document Reproduction Service No. ED247159)

Brenner, M. E., Mayer, R. E., Moseley, B., Brar, T., Duran, R., Reed, B. S., & Webb, D. (1980). Learning by understanding: The role of multiple representations in learning algebra. *American Educational Research Journal, 34*(4), 663-689.

Brigham, F. J. (1993, April). *Places, spaces and memory traces: Showing students with learning disabilities ways to remember locations and events on maps.* Paper presented at the 71st Annual Conference of the Council for Exceptional Children, San Antonio, TX. (ERIC Document Reproduction Service No. ED357558)

Brigham, F. J., & Scruggs, C. (1995). Elaborative maps for enhanced learning of historical information: Uniting spatial, verbal, and imaginal information. *Journal of Special Education, 28*(4), 440-460. Retrieved January 4, 2003, from Academic Search Premier database.

Brock, H. B., & Kowitz, G. T. (October, 1980). *Learned helplessness in exceptional children.* Paper presented at the Annual Conference of the Rocky Mountain Educational Research Association, Holy Cross, NM. (ERIC Document Reproduction Service No. ED060578)

Brophy, J. (1988). Research linking teacher behavior to student achievement: Potential implications for instruction of Chapter 1 students. *Educational Psychologist, 23,* 235-286.

Brown, A. I. (1975). The development of memory: Knowing, knowing about knowing, and knowing how to know. In W. H. Reece (Ed.), *Advances in child development and behavior* (Vol. 10). New York: Academic Press.

Brown, A. I. (1978). Knowing when, where, and how to remember: A problem of metacognition. In R. Glaser (Ed.), *Advances in instructional psychology.* Hillsdale, NJ: Earlbaum.

Brown, A. I. (1979). Metacognitive development and reading. In R. J. Spiro, B. Bruce, & W. F. Brewer (Eds.), *Theoretical issues in reading comprehension.* Hillsdale, NJ: Earlbaum.

Brown, A. L., & Barclay, C. R. (1976). The effects of training specific mnemonics on the metamnemonic efficacy of retarded children. *Child Development, 47,* 71-80.

Brown, A. L., & Palincsar, A. S. (1982). Inducing strategic learning from texts by means of informed self-control training. *Topics in Learning and Learning Disabilities, 2,* 1-17.

Brown-Chidsey, R., & Boscardin, M. L. (1999). *Computers as accessibility tools for students with and without learning disabilities.* (ERIC Document Reproduction Service No. ED433671)

Brunn, M. (2002).The four-square strategy. *Reading Teacher, 55*(6), 522-525.

Buehl, D. (2001). *Classroom strategies for interactive learning* (2nd ed.). Newark, DE: International Reading Association.

Bull, B. L., & Wittrock, M. C. (1973). Imagery in the learning of verbal definitions. *British Journal of Educational Psychology, 43,* 289-293.

Bull, K. S., Montgomery, D., Hyle, A., & Salyer, K. (1991, March). Administrator's perceptions of special education dropouts: A comparison of priorities by school location. In *Reaching our potential: Rural education in the 90s. Conference Proceedings* (pp. 1-12). Nashville, TN: Rural Education Symposium. (ERIC Document Reproduction Service No. ED342550)

Bullock, J. O. (1994). Literacy in the language of mathematics. *American Mathematical Monthly, 101,* 735-743.

Burton, G. M. (1986). Using neurolinguistic programming: Some suggestions for the remedial teacher. *Focus on Learning Problems in Mathematics, 8*(2), 41-49.

Byrne, F. X. (1981). Acquisition of physics principles. *Physics Teacher, 19*(2), 122-123.

Cade, T., & Gunter, P. L. (2002). Teaching students with severe emotional or behavioral disorders to use a musical mnemonic technique to solve basic division calculations. *Behavioral Disorders, 27*(3), 208-214.

Cahnmann, M. (2000). Rhythm and resource: Repetition as a linguistic style in an urban elementary classroom. *Working Papers in Educational Linguistics, 16,* 39-52. (ERIC Document Reproduction Service No. ED446431)

Cajete, G. A. (1999). *Igniting the sparkle: An indigenous science education model.* Skyland, NC: Kivaki.

Calfee, R., & Chambliss, M. (1988). Beyond decoding: Pictures of expository prose. *Annals of Dyslexia, 38,* 243-257.

Calhoun, M. L., & Beattie, J. (1987). School competence needs of mildly handicapped adolescents. *Adolescence, 22,* 555-563.

Canino, F. J. (1981). Learned-helplessness theory: Implications for research in learning disabilities. *Journal of Special Education, 15,* 471-484.

Carlisle, J. (1993). Selecting approaches to vocabulary instruction for the reading disabled. *Learning Disabilities Research & Practice, 8,* 97-105.

Carney, J. J., Anderson, D., Blackburn, C., & Blessing, D. (1984). Preteaching vocabulary and the comprehension of social studies materials by elementary school children. *Social Education, 48,* 195-196.

Carnine, D. (1994). The big accommodation program. *Educational Leadership, 51*(6), 87.

Carnine, D. W. (1994). Introduction to the mini-series: Educational tools for diverse learners. *School Psychology Review, 23,* 341-350.

Carr, E., & Wixson, K. K. (1986). Guidelines for evaluating vocabulary instruction. *Journal of Reading, 29,* 588-595.

Carrier, C. (1983). Notetaking research. *Journal Instructional Development, 6*(3), 19-26.

Carrier, C. A., Williams, M. D., & Dalgaard, B. R. (1988). College students' perceptions of notetaking and their relationship to selected learner characteristics and course achievement. *Research in Higher Education, 28,* 223-239.

Carroll, J. B. (Ed.). (1956). *Language, thought, and reality: Selected writings of Benjamin Lee Whorf.* New York: Technology Press of Massachusetts Institute of Technology, John Wiley.

Cass, M., Cates, D., Jackson, C. W., & Smith, M. (2002, March). Facilitating adolescents with disabilities understanding of area and perimeter concepts via manipulative instruction. In *No child left behind: The vital role of rural schools.* 22nd Annual National Conference Proceedings of the American Council on Rural Special Education, Reno, NV. (ERIC Document Reproduction Service No. ED463113)

Chalfant, J. C., & Scheffelin, M. A. (1969). *Central processing dysfunctions in children: A review of research.* (ERIC Document Reproduction Service No. ED040546)

Chall, J. S. (1987). Two vocabularies for reading: Recognition and meaning. In M. G. McKeown & M. E. Curtis (Eds.), *The nature of vocabulary acquisition* (pp. 7-17). Hillsdale, NJ: Erlbaum.

Chalmers, L. (1995). Mediating content area learning through the use of flip-flop study guides. *LD Forum, 20*(4), 37-38.

Chang, K.-E., Sung, Y.-T., & Chen, I.-D. (2002). Effect of concept mapping to enhance text comprehension and summarization. *Journal of Experimental Education, 71*(1), 5-26.

ChanLin, L.-J., & Chan, K.-C. (1996, February). *Computer graphics and metaphorical elaboration for learning science concepts.* Paper presented at the Annual Meeting of the Association for Educational Communication and Technology, Indianapolis, IN. (ERIC Document Reproduction Service No. ED392390)

Charuhas, M. S. (1983). *A curriculum for logical thinking* (NAAESC Occasional Papers, 1(4)). (ERIC Document Reproduction Service No. ED256908)

Cherkes-Julkowski, M., & Stolzenberg, J. (1991, October). *Reading comprehension, extended processing and attention dysfunction.* Paper presented at the meeting of the National Council on Learning Disabilities, Minneapolis, MN. (ERIC Document Reproduction Service No. ED340194)

Chiu, M. M. (1994, April). *Metaphorical reasoning in mathematics: Experts and novices solving negative number problems.* Paper presented at the Annual

Meeting of the American Educational Research Association, New Orleans, LA. (ERIC Document Reproduction Service No. ED374988)

Christidou, V., Koulaidis, V., & Christidis, T. (1997). Children's use of metaphors in relation to their mental models: The case of the ozone layer and its depletion. *Research in Science Education, 27,* 541-552.

Chyczij, M. A. (1993). Self-report measures of perceived difficulty and strategies used in dichotic listening. *Canadian Journal of Special Education, 9,* 160-170.

Ciardiello, A. V. (1998). Did you ask a good question today? Alternative cognitive and metacognitive strategies. *Journal of Adolescent & Adult Literacy, 42*(3). Retrieved December 19, 2002, from Academic Search Premier database.

Ciardiello, A. V. (2002). Helping adolescents understand cause/effect text structure in social studies. *Social Studies, 93*(1). Retrieved January 14, 2003, from Academic Search Premier database.

Clark, J. M., & Paivio, A. (1991). Dual coding theory and education. *Educational Psychology Review, 3*(3), 149-210.

Cohen, L., Spruill, J., & Herns, V. (1982, April). *The relationship between language disorders, learning disabilities, verbal and performance IQ discrepancies and measures of language abilities.* Paper presented at the Annual International Convention of the Council for Exceptional Children, Houston, TX. (ERIC Document Reproduction Service No. ED223011)

Cohen, M. P., & Carpenter, J. (1980). The effects of nonexamples in geometrical concept acquisition. *International Journal of Mathematical Education in Science and Technology, 11,* 259-263.

Cohen, M. W. (1986). Intrinsic motivation in the special education classroom. *Journal of Learning Disabilities, 19,* 258-261.

Cole, C. L., Gardner, W. I., & Karan, O. C. (1983). *Self-management training of mentally retarded adults with chronic conduct difficulties.* A part of the series in Rehabilitation of the Developmentally Disabled: Issues, Research and Practices. (ERIC Document Reproduction Service No. ED271937)

Cole, M. (1979, April). *Language training for the nonverbal or language delayed child.* Paper presented at the 57th Annual International Convention of the Council for Exceptional Children, Dallas, TX. (ERIC Document Reproduction Service No. ED171022)

Collea, F. P. (1981). *Intellectual development of college science students.* California State University at Fullerton, Development of Reasoning in Science Project. (ERIC Document Reproduction Service No. ED226620)

Colomb, G. G. (1988, March). *Where should students start writing in the disciplines?* Paper presented at the 39th Annual Meeting of the Conference on College Composition and Communication, St. Louis, MO.

Cook, G. (1994). Repetition and learning by heart: An aspect of intimate discourse, and its implications. *ELT Journal, (48),* 133-141.

Cook, R. E. (1983). Why Jimmy doesn't try. *Academic Therapy, 19,* 155-163.

Cooney, J. B., & Swanson, H. L. (1987). Memory and learning disabilities: An overview. In H. L. Swanson (Ed.), *Advances in learning and behavioral disabilities: Memory and learning disabilities* (pp. 1-40). Greenwich, CT: JAI.

Corson, D. (1983). Social dialect, the semantic barrier, and access to curricular knowledge. *Language in Society, 12*(2), 213-222.

Coull, J. T. (1998). Neural correlates of attention and arousal: Insights from electrophysiology, functional neuroimaging and psychopharmacology. *Progress in Neurobiology, 55,* 343-361.

Courson, F. H., & Heward, W. L. (1988). Increasing active student response through the effective use of paraprofessionals. *Pointer, 33,* 27-31.

Coyne, M. D., Kame'enui, E. J., & Simmons, D. C. (2001). Prevention and intervention in beginning reading: Two complex systems. *Learning Disabilities Research & Practice, 16*(2). Retrieved December 24, 2002, from Academic Search Premier database.

Craik, F., & Lockhart, R. (1972). Levels of processing: A framework for memory research. *Journal of Verbal Learning and Verbal Behavior, 11,* 671-684.

Crank, J. N., & Bulgren, J. A. (1993). Visual depictions as information organizers for enhancing achievement of students with learning disabilities. *Learning Disabilities Research and Practice, 8,* 140-147.

Crowhurst, M. (1988). *Research review: Patterns of development in writing persuasive/ argumentative discourse.* (ERIC Document Reproduction Service No. ED299596)

Cruickshank, W. M. (1977). Myths and realities in learning disabilities. *Journal of Learning Disabilities, 10,* 51-58.

Curtain, H., & Haas, M. (1995). *Integrating foreign language and content instruction in grades K-8* (ERIC Digest). (ERIC Document Reproduction Service No. 381018)

Darch, C., & Eaves, R. (1986). Visual displays to increase comprehension of high school learning disabled students. *Exceptional Children, 20,* 309-318.

David, P., & Pierson, M. M. (1998). Public affairs decision-making in the U.S. Air Force: An application of multiattribute utility theory. *Journalism & Mass Communication Quarterly, 75,* 606-627.

Desberg, P., et al. (1981, September). *The effect of humor on retention of lecture material* [Abstract]. Paper presented at the Annual Meeting of the American Psychological Association, Montreal, Quebec, Canada. (ERIC Document Reproduction Service No. ED223118)

Dev, P. C. (1998). Intrinsic motivation and the student with learning disabilities. *Journal of Research and Development in Education, 31*(2), 98-108.

DeWispelaere, C., & Kossack, J. (1996). *Improving student higher order thinking skills through the use of graphic organizers.* Master's Thesis, Saint Xavier University. (ERIC Document Reproduction Service No. ED400684)

DiCecco, V. M., & Gleason, M. M. (2002). Using graphic organizers to attain relational knowledge from expository text. *Journal of Learning Disabilities, 35*(4). Retrieved December 31, 2002, from Academic Search Premier database.

DiGennaro, M., & Picciarelli, V. (1992). Incidental science knowledge in fifth grade children. *Research in Science & Technological Education, 10*(1), 117. Retrieved January 1, 2003, from Academic Search Premier database.

DiLella, C. A. (1992, March). *Popcorn story frames.* Paper presented at the 5th Annual Midwest Regional Reading and Study Skills Conference, Kansas City, MO. (ERIC Document Reproduction Service No. ED344184)

DiVesta, F., & Gray, G. S. (1972). Listening and note taking. *Journal of Educational Psychology, 63*(1), 8-14.

DiVesta, F. J., & Smith, D. A. (1979). The pausing principle: Increasing the efficiency of memory for ongoing events. *Contemporary Educational Psychology, 4,* 288-296.

Downing, J. (1970, December). *Specific cognitive factors in the reading process.* Paper presented at the National Reading Conference, St. Petersburg, FL. (ERIC Document Reproduction Service No. ED046639)

Downing, J. A., Bakken, J. P., & Whedon, C. K. (2002). Teaching text structure to improve reading comprehension. *Intervention in School & Clinic, 37*(4). Retrieved December 16, 2002, from Academic Search Premier database.

Dreyer, L. J. (1974, November). *Yes! Individualized instruction for international students is possible in the conventional classroom — It is a formula for holding power.* Paper presented at the 64th Annual Meeting of the National Council of Teachers of English, New Orleans, LA. (ERIC Document Reproduction Service No. ED101369)

Duffelmeyer, D. A., Baum, D. D., & Merkley, D. J. (1987). Maximizing reader-text confrontation with an extended anticipation guide. *Journal of Reading, 31,* 146-150.

Duffelmeyer, F. A. (1980). The influence of experience-based vocabulary instruction on learning word meanings. *Journal of Reading, 24,* 35-40.

Duit, R. (1991). On the role of analogies and metaphors in learning science. *Science Education, 75,* 649-672.

Dunston, P. J. (1992). A critique of graphic organizer research. *Reading Research and Instruction, 31*(2), 57-65.

Dye, G. A. (2002). Graphic organizers to the rescue: Helping students link — and remember — information. In K. L. Freiberg, (Ed.), *Annual editions: Educating exceptional children. 2002/2003.* Guilford, NJ: McGraw/Hill-Dushkin.

Eaton, M. D., & Hansen, C. L. (1978). Classroom organization and management. In N. G. Haring, T. C. Lovitt, M. D. Eaton, & C. L. Hansen (Eds.), *The fourth R: Research in the classroom* (pp. 191-217). Upper Saddle River, NJ: Merrill/Prentice Hall.

Ediger, M. (1998). *Grammar revisited in the English curriculum.* (ERIC Document Reproduction Service No. ED421713)

Egan, M. (1999). Reflections on effective use of graphic organizers. *Journal of Adolescent & Adult Literacy, 42*(8), 641-645.

Eisenman, G, & Payne, B. D. (1997). Effects of the higher order thinking skills program on at-risk young adolescents' self-concept, reading achievement, and thinking skills. *Research in Middle Level Education Quarterly, 20*(3), 1-25.

Ellis, E. S. (1992). *LINCS: A starter strategy for vocabulary learning.* Lawrence, KS: Edge Enterprises.

Englert, C. S., & Thomas, C. C. (1987). Sensitivity to text structure in reading and writing: A comparison between learning disabled and non-learning disabled students. *Learning Disability Quarterly, 10*(2), 93-105.

Erven, J. L. (1991). *Increasing the social studies performance of middle school special education students using multisensory strategies.* Unpublished master's thesis, Nova University.

Espin, C. A., & Deno, S. L. (1993). Content-specific and general reading disabilities: Identification and educational relevance. *The Journal of Special Education, 27*, 321–337.

Espin, C. A., & Deno, S. L. (2000). Introduction to the special issue of *Learning Disabilities Research & Practice:* Research to practice: Views from researchers and practitioners. *Learning Disabilities Research & Practice, 15*(2), 67-69. Retrieved December 26, 2002, from Academic Search Premier database.

Espin, C. A., & Foegen, A. (1996). Validity of general outcome measures for predicting secondary students' performance on content-area tasks. *Exceptional Children, 62*, 497–514.

Faber, J. E., Morris, J. D., & Lieberman, M. G. (2000). The effects of notetaking on ninth grade students' comprehension. *Reading Psychology, 21*, 257-270.

Fahmy, J. J., & Bilton, L. (1990a, April). *Lecture comprehension and note-taking for L2 students.* Paper presented at the 9th World Congress of Applied Linguistics sponsored by the International Association of Applied Linguistics, Thessaloniki, Greece. (ERIC Document Reproduction Service No. ED323785)

Fahmy, J. J., & Bilton, L. (1990b). Listening and notetaking in higher education. In A. Sarinee (Ed.), *Language teaching methodology for the nineties* (Anthology Series 24). Selected papers from the Southeast Asian Ministers of Education Organization (SEAMEO) Regional Language Centre Seminar. (ERIC Document Reproduction Service No. ED366189)

Felton, R. H. (2001). Students with three types of severe reading disabilities: Introduction to the case studies. *Journal of Special Education, 35*, 122-124.

Fisher, J. B., Schumaker, J. B., & Deshler, D. D. (1995). Searching for validated inclusive practices: A review of the literature. *Focus on Exceptional Children, 28*(4), 1-20.

Flavell, J. H. (1971). What is memory development the development of? *Human Development, 14,* 272-278.

Flavell, J. H. (1979). Metacognitive and cognitive monitoring: A new area of cognitive-developmental inquiry. *American Psychologist, 34,* 906-911.

Flavell, J. H. (1999). Cognitive development: Children's knowledge about the mind. *Annual review of psychology, 50,* 21-45.

Fleckenstein, K. S. (1995). Writing and the strategic use of metaphor. *Teaching English in the two-year college, 22*(2), 110-115.

Flynn, L. L., Dagostino, L., & Carifio, J. (1995). Learning new concepts independently through metaphor. *Reading Improvement, 32*(4), 200-219.

Foil, C. R., & Alber, S. R. (2002). Fun and effective ways to build your students' vocabulary. *Intervention in School & Clinic, 37*(3). Retrieved February 1, 2003, from Academic Search Premier database.

Forness, S. R., Kavale, K. A., Blum, I. A., & Lloyd, J. W. (1997). Mega-analysis of meta-analyses: What works in special education and related services. *Teaching Exceptional Children, 29*(6), 4-9.

Foss, J. M. (2001). *Nonverbal learning disability: How to recognize it and minimize its effects* (ERIC Digest E619). (ERIC Document Reproduction Service No. ED461238)

Frank, G. (1984). *Alleviating auditory figure-ground disability in kindergarten and first-grade children using rehabilitative and nonrehabilitative techniques.* Ed.D. Practicum Report, Nova University, Fort Lauderdale, FL. (ERIC Document Reproduction Service No. ED256096)

Frayer, D. A., Frederick, W. C., & Klausmeier, H. J. (1969). *A schema for testing the level of concept mastery* (Working Paper No. 16). Madison: University of Wisconsin, Wisconsin Research and Development Center for Cognitive Learning.

Freedman, G., & Reynolds, E. G. (1980). Enriching basal reader lessons with semantic webbing. *Reading Teacher, 33,* 677-684.

Frostig, M., & Maslow, P. (1969). Reading, developmental abilities, and the problem of the match. *Journal of Learning Disabilities, 2,* 572-574.

Fulk, B. M., Brigham, F. J., & Lohman, D. A. (1998). Motivation and self-regulation: A comparison of students with learning and behavior problems. *Remedial and Special Education, 19,* 300-309.

Fulk, B. M., & Stormont-Spurgin, M. (1995). Fourteen spelling strategies for students with learning disabilities. *Intervention in School and Clinic, 31*(1), 16-20.

Gallagher, J. J., & Aschner, M. J. (1963). A preliminary report on analyses of classroom interaction. *Merrill-Palmer Quarterly, 9,* 183-194.

Ganguly, I. (1995, October). *Scientific thinking is in the mind's eye. Eyes on the future: Converging images, ideas, and instruction.* Selected readings from the 27th Annual Conference of the International Visual Literacy Association, Chicago, IL. (ERIC Document Reproduction Service No. ED391504)

Garner, R., & Taylor, N. (1982). Monitoring of understanding: An investigation of attentional assistance needs at different grades and reading proficiency levels. *Reading Psychology, 3,* 1-6.

Gasser, J. (2000). Logic and metaphor. *History and Philosophy of Logic, 20,* 227-238.

Gates, R. W. (1970). *An analysis of student outcomes using audiotapes to supplement reading in the Level One Course of the Intermediate Science Curriculum Study.* Doctoral dissertation, University of Iowa. (ERIC Document Reproduction Service No. ED091149)

Gazzaniga, M. (1998). *The mind's past.* Berkeley, CA: University of California Press.

Gellevij, M., Van Der Meij, H., De Jong, T., & Pieters, J. (2002). Multimodal versus unimodal instruction in a complex learning context. *Journal of Experimental Education, 70*(3), 215-240.

Gersten, R., & Baker, S. (1999). *Teaching expressive writing to students with learning disabilities.* A paper presented at Two Decades of Research in Learning Disabilities: Reading Comprehension, Expressive Writing, Problem-Solving, Self-Concept. Keys to Successful Learning: A National Summit on Research in Learning Disabilities. (ERIC Document Reproduction Service No. ED430365)

Gersten, R., Baker, S., & Edwards, L. (1999). *Teaching expressive writing to students with learning disabilities* (ERIC/OSEP Digest E590). Retrieved February 1, 2003 from http://www.ldonline.org

Gersten, R., Baker, S. K., & Marks, S. U. (1998). Strategies for teaching English-language learners. In K. R. Harris, S. Graham, & D. Deshler (Eds.), *Teaching every child every day: Learning in diverse schools and classrooms* (Advances in teaching and learning series). Cambridge, MA: Brookline Books.

Gilhool, M., Byer, J., Parmer, L., Howe, M., Dana, M., & Cliburn, A. (1996). *A qualitative study: The effect of modeling nonfiction text strategies on third and fourth grade students' nonfiction writing.* University of Southern Mississippi, Hattiesburg. (ERIC Document Reproduction Service No. ED403589)

Gilles, D. C. (1972). *An exploration of perceptual and cognitive processes involved in piano study with implications for learning disabled children.* (ERIC Document Reproduction Service No. ED119435)

Gleason, M. M. (1988). Study skills. *Teaching Exceptional Children, 20*(3), 52-57.

Glen, M. L., & Miller, K. (1977, February). *Inservice diffusion of reading into technical areas.* Paper presented at the Annual Meeting of the Midwest Regional Conference on English in the Two-Year College, Dayton, OH. (ERIC Document Reproduction Service No. ED141747)

Goldberg, R. L., & Zern, D. S. (1982). *Learning styles, learning abilities and learning problems in college: An exploration of learning disabilities in college students. Final Report.* (ERIC Document Reproduction Service No. ED247682)

Goldenberg, E. P., & Kliman, M. (1988). *Metaphors for understanding graphs: What you see is what you see.* (ERIC Document Reproduction Service No. ED303369)

Good, T. L., & Brophy, J. E. (1984). *Looking in classrooms* (3rd ed.). New York: Harper & Row.

Gottesman, R. L. (1994). The adult with learning disabilities: An overview. *Learning Disabilities: A Multidisciplinary Journal, 5,* 1-14.

Graham, S., MacArthur, C., Schwartz, S., & Page-Voth, V. (1992). Improving the compositions of students with learning disabilities using a strategy involving product and process goal setting. *Exceptional Children, 58,* 322-334. Retrieved March 4, 2003, from Health and Wellness Resource Center database.

Graves, A., Semmel, M., & Gerber, M. L. (1994). The effects of story prompts on the narrative production of students with and without learning disabilities. *Learning Disability Quarterly, 17,* 154-164.

Graves, M. F. (1984). Selecting vocabulary to teach in the intermediate and secondary grades. In J. Flood (Ed.), *Promoting reading comprehension.* Newark, DE: International Reading Association.

Graves, M. F. (1985). *A word is a word . . . Or is it?* New York: Scholastic.

Graves, M. F., & Penn, M. C. (1986). Costs and benefits of various methods of teaching vocabulary. *Journal of Reading, 29,* 596-609.

Gray, T. (2000). *Documents related to Churchill and FDR. The Constitution community: The Great Depression and World War II (1929-1945).* Washington, DC: National Archives and Records Administration. (ERIC Document Reproduction Service No. ED463208)

Greene, G. (1992). Multiplication facts: Memorization made easy. *Intervention in School and Clinic, 27*(3), 150-154.

Greenwood, S. C. (2002). Making words matter: Vocabulary study in the content areas. *Clearing House, 75,* 258-263.

Grobecker, B. (1997). Partitioning and unitizing in children with learning differences [Abstract]. *Learning Disability Quarterly, 20,* 317-337.

Grobecker, B. (1998, April). *The evolution of proportional structures in children with and without learning differences.* Paper presented at the Annual Meeting of the American Educational Research Association, San Diego, CA. (ERIC Document Reproduction Service No. ED421820)

Grobecker, B. (1999). The evolution of proportional structures in children with and without learning differences [Abstract]. *Learning Disability Quarterly, 22,* 192-211.

Grobecker, B., & Lawrence, F. (2000). Associativity and understanding of the operation of addition in children with learning differences [Abstract]. *Learning Disability Quarterly, 23,* 300-313.

Grossen, B., Caros, J., Carnine, D., Davis, B., Deshler, D., Schumaker, J., Bulgren, J., Lenz, K., Adams, G., Jantzen, J.-E., & Marquis, J. (2002). OSEP Research Institutes: Bridging research and practice. Big ideas (plus a little effort) produce big results. *Teaching Exceptional Children, 34*(4), 70-73.

Grossen, B. J. (2002). The BIG accommodation model: The direct instruction model for secondary schools. *Journal of Education for Students Placed at Risk, 7,* 241-264.

Guastello, E. F. (2000). Concept mapping effects on science content comprehension of low-achieving inner-city seventh graders. *Remedial & Special Education, 21*(6), 356. Retrieved January 23, 2003, from Academic Search Premier database.

Guha, S. (2000). *Temperate facts in fictitious time.* (ERIC Document Reproduction Service No. ED437290)

Guyer, B. P., & Sabatino, D. (1989). The effectiveness of a multisensory alphabetic phonetic approach with college students who are learning disabled. *Journal of Learning Disabilities, 22*(7), 430-434.

Guyton, G. (1968, February). *Individual programming for children with learning disabilities as determined by screening, identification, and differential diagnosis.* Paper presented at the Association for Children with Learning Disabilities, Boston, MA. (ERIC Document Reproduction Service No. ED029756)

Hakerem, G., et al. (1993, April). *The effect of interactive, three-dimensional, high speed simulations on high school science students' conceptions of the molecular structure of water.* Paper presented at the Annual Meeting of the National Association for Research in Science Teaching, Atlanta, GA. (ERIC Document Reproduction Service No. ED362390)

Hämäläinen, R. P., Lindstedt, M. R. K., & Sinkko, K. (2000). Multiattribute risk analysis in nuclear emergency management. *Risk Analysis: An Official Publication of the Society for Risk Analysis, 20,* 455-469.

Hamburg, D. A., & Takanishi, R. (1989). Preparing for life: The critical transition of adolescence. *American Psychologist, 44,* 825-827.

Hardy, B. W., McIntyre, C. W., Brown, A. S., & North, A. J. (1989). Visual and auditory coding confusability in students with and without learning disabilities. *Journal of Learning Disabilities, 22,* 646-651.

Harris, B., Kohlmeier, K., & Kiel, R. D. (1999). *Crime scene investigation.* Englewood, CO: Teacher Ideas Press.

Harris, C., Miller, P., & Mercer, C. D. (1995). Teaching initial multiplication skills to students with disabilities in general education classrooms. *Learning Disabilities Research and Practice, 10,* 180-195.

Harris, K. R., & Graham, S. (1992). *Helping young writers master the craft strategy instruction and self-regulation in the writing process.* Cambridge, MA: Brookline Books.

Harste, J. C. (1980, October). *Semantic mapping: A text perspective.* Paper presented at the annual meeting of the Mid-western Educational Research Association, Toledo, OH. (ERIC Document Reproduction Service No. ED195959)

Hartman, K. A., & Stewart, T. C. (2001). It's a wrap: Writing, reading, and art projects for developmental college students. *Research and Teaching in Developmental Education, 18*(1), 79-83.

Hawkey, R. (1998). Have you heard the one about . . . science? *School Science Review, 80*(290), 29-36.

Hawkins, J., & Brady, M. (1994). The effects of independent and peer guided practice during instructional pauses on the academic performance of students with mild handicaps. *Education and Treatment of Children, 17,* 1-28.

Hayes, D. A. (1986, April). *Readers' use of analogic and visual aids for understanding and remembering complex prose.* Paper presented at the 67th Annual Meeting of the American Educational Research Association, San Francisco, CA. (ERIC Document Reproduction Service No. ED271735)

Hebb, D. (1949). *The organization of behavior.* New York: Wiley.

Heimlich, J. E., & Pittelman, S. D. (1986). *Semantic mapping: Classroom applications* (Reading Aids Series, IRA Service Bulletin). Newark, DE: International Reading Association.

Hemmerich, H., Lim, W., & Neel, A. (1994). *Prime time: Strategies for life-long learning in mathematics and science in the middle and high school grades.* Portsmouth, NH: Heinemann.

Hendricks, K. (1995). Research using higher order thinking skills to improve reading comprehension. *Middle Level Education Quarterly, 20*(3), 1-25.

Hendricks, K., Newman, L., & Stropnik, D. (1995). *Using higher order thinking skills to improve reading comprehension. Action research project.* Chicago, IL: Saint Xavier University. (ERIC Document Reproduction Service No. ED398538)

Hennings, D. G. (2000). Contextually relevant word study: Adolescent vocabulary development across the curriculum. *Journal of Adolescent & Adult Literacy, 44,* 268-279.

Herbel-Eisenmann, B. A. (2002). Using student contributions and multiple representations to develop mathematical language. *Mathematics Teaching in the Middle School, 8*(20). Retrieved May 23, 2003, from Professional Development database.

Herber, H. L. (1970). *Teaching reading in the content areas.* Englewood Cliffs, NJ: Prentice Hall.

Heward, W. L., Gardner, R., III, & Barbetta, P. M. (1996). Everyone participates in this class. *Teaching Exceptional Children, 28*(2), 4.

Higgins, K., & Boone, R. (1990). Hypertext computer study guides and the social studies achievement of students with learning disabilities, remedial students, and regular education students. *Journal of Learning Disabilities, 23*(9), 529-540. Retrieved January 4, 2003, from Academic Search Premier database.

Highsmith, V. (1988). *Remediating handwriting skills for learning disabled students.* (ERIC Document Reproduction Service No. ED299783)

Hisama, T. (1976). Achievement motivation and the locus of control of children with learning disabilities and behavior disorders. *Journal of Learning Disabilities, 9,* 387-392.

Hitchcock, C. (2001). Balanced instructional support and challenge in universally designed learning environments. *Journal of Special Education Technology, 16*(4), 23-30.

Hodges, D. L. (1982). *Findings from cognitive psychology and their applications to teaching.* (ERIC Document Reproduction Service No. ED220154)

Hollingsworth, M., & Woodward, J. (1993). Integrated learning: Explicit strategies and their role in problem-solving instruction for students with learning disabilities. *Exceptional Children, 59*(5), 444-456.

Holt, G. M. (1995). *Teaching low-level adult ESL learners* (ERIC Digest). (ERIC Document Reproduction Service No. ED379965)

Hoone, C. J. (1989). Teaching timelines to fourth, fifth, and sixth graders. *Social Studies and the Young Learner, 2*(2), 13-15.

Horn, L., & Berktold, J. (1999). *Students with disabilities in postsecondary education: A profile of preparation, participation, and outcomes* (Postsecondary Education Descriptive Analysis Reports, Statistical Analysis Report). National Center for Education Statistics. (ERIC Document Reproduction Service No. ED431268) Retrieved November 24, 2002, from http://nces.ed.gov/pubsearch/index.asp

Horton, S. V., & Lovitt, T. C. (1989). Using study guides with three classifications of secondary students. *Journal of Special Education, 22*(4), 447-462.

Horton, S. V., Lovitt, T. C., & Bergerud, D. (1990). The effectiveness of graphic organizers for three classifications of secondary students in content area classes. *Journal of Learning Disabilities, 23*(1), 12-22. Retrieved January 12, 2003, from Academic Search Premier database.

Horton, S. V., Lovitt, T. C., Givens, A., & Nelson, R. (1989). Teaching social studies to high school students with academic handicaps in a mainstreamed setting: Effects of a computerized study guide. *Journal of Learning Disabilities, 22*(10), 2-107.

Horton, S. V., Lovitt, T. C., & Slocum, T. (1988). Teaching geography to high school students with academic deficits: Effects of a computerized map tutorial. *Learning Disability Quarterly, 11,* 371-379.

Hudson, P. J., et al. (1988). Successfully employed adults with handicaps: Characteristics and transition strategies [Abstract]. *Career Development for Exceptional Individuals, 11,* 7-14.

Hughes, C. A. (1991). Studying for and taking tests: Self-reported difficulties and strategies of university students with learning disabilities. *Learning Disabilities, 2,* 65-71.

Hughes, C. A., Hendrickson, J. M., & Hudson, P. J. (1986). The pause procedure: Improving factual recall from lectures by low and high achieving middle school students. *International Journal of Instructional Media, 13,* 217-226.

Hughes, C. A., & Smith, J. O. (1990). Cognitive and academic performance of college students with learning disabilities: A synthesis of the literature. *Learning Disability Quarterly, 13,* 66-79.

Hughes, C. A., & Suritsky, S. K. (1993). Notetaking skills and strategies for students with learning disabilities. *Preventing School Failure, 38*(1), 7-12. Retrieved February 2, 2003, from Academic Search Premier database.

Hughes, C. A., & Suritsky, S. K. (1994). Notetaking skills of university students with and without learning disabilities. *Journal of Learning Disabilities, 27*(1), 20-25. Retrieved February 2, 2003, from Academic Search Premier database.

Hulland, C., & Munby, H. (1994). Science, stories, and sense-making: A comparison of qualitative data from a wetlands unit. *Science Education, 78,* 117-136.

Hurford, D. P., & Shedelbower, A. (1993). The relationship between discrimination and memory ability in children with reading disabilities. *Contemporary Educational Psychology, 18,* 101-113.

Hurst, D., & Smerdon, B. (Eds.). (2000). Postsecondary students with disabilities: Enrollment, services, and persistence. *Education Statistics Quarterly, 2*(3), 55-58.

Irvin, J. L. (1990). *Vocabulary knowledge: Guidelines for instruction.* Washington, DC: National Education Association.

Ivie, S. D. (1998). Ausubel's learning theory: An approach to teaching higher order thinking skills. *High School Journal, 82*(1), 35-43.

Jackson, L. (2000). *Increasing critical thinking skills to improve problem-solving ability in mathematics.* Master of Arts Action Research Project, Saint Xavier University and Skylight Professional Development. (ERIC Document Reproduction Service No. ED446995)

James, D. L. (2001). *Split a gut and learn: Theory and research.* (ERIC Document Reproduction Service No. ED458671)

Jitendra, A. K., Nolet, V., Xin, Y. P., Gomez, O., Renouf, K., Iskold, L., & DaCosta, J. (2001). An analysis of middle school geography textbooks: Implications for students with learning problems. *Reading and Writing Quarterly: Overcoming Learning Difficulties, 17*(2), 151-173.

Johnson, D., Cantrell, R. J., Willis, K. L., & Josel, C. A. (1997). Open to Suggestion. *Journal of Adolescent & Adult Literacy, 40,* 390-395.

Johnson, D., & Myklebust, H. R. (1967). *Learning disabilities: Educational principles and practices.* New York: Grune and Stratton.

Johnson, G. (1999). Kidney role-plays. *School Science Review, 80*(292), 93-97.

Johnson, S. D., & Thomas, R. (1992). Technology education and the cognitive revolution. *Technology Teacher, 51*(4), 7-12.

Jones, E. D., & Wilson, R. (1997). Mathematics instruction for secondary students with learning disabilities. *Journal of Learning Disabilities, 30*(2), 151-164. Retrieved January 4, 2003, from Academic Search Premier database.

Jones, R. W. (1975, January). *The target groups: Description of learning disabled and normal subjects participating in prototype evaluation studies.* Paper presented at the 2nd Conference of the International Scientific Federation of Learning Disabilities, Brussels, Belgium. (ERIC Document Reproduction Service No. ED113859)

Jordan, D. R. (2000). Understanding and managing learning disabilities in adults. *Professional Practices in Adult Education and Human Resource Development Series.* Melbourne, FL: Krieger.

Jordan, L., Miller, M. D., & Mercer, C. D. (1999). The effects of concrete to semiconcrete to abstract instruction in the acquisition and retention of fraction concepts and skills. *Learning Disabilities: A Multidisciplinary Journal, 9*(3), 115-122.

Jordan, M. K. (1983, June). *Developing the listening speaking component in English for academic purposes.* Paper presented at the Second Language Acquisition and Second Language Teaching Conference, Tampa, FL. (ERIC Document Reproduction Service No. ED236927)

Kagan, S. (1992). *Cooperative learning* (7th ed.). San Juan Capistrano, CA: Resources for Teachers.

Kalispell School District #5, MT. (1987). *CRISS: Content reading in secondary schools. National Diffusion Network Programs.* (ERIC Document Reproduction Service No. ED377455)

Kame'enui, E. J., & Carnine, D. W. (1998). *Effective teaching strategies that accommodate diverse learners.* Columbus, OH: Merrill, Prentice Hall.

Kameenui, E. J., & Simmons, D. C. (1990). *Designing instructional strategies: The prevention of academic learning problems.* Columbus, OH: Merrill.

Karlin, R. (1964). *Teaching reading in high school.* New York: Bobbs-Merrill.

Katims, D. S., & Harmon, J. M. (2000). Strategic instruction in middle school social studies: Enhancing academic and literacy outcomes for at-risk students. *Intervention in School & Clinic, 35*(5). Retrieved January 4, 2003, from Academic Search Premier database.

Kavale, K. A. (1982). Meta-analysis of the relationship between visual perceptual skills and reading achievement. *Journal of Learning Disabilities, 15*(1), 42-51.

Kavale, K. A. (1993). How many learning disabilities are there? A commentary on Stanovich's "Dysrationalia: A new specific learning disability." *Journal of Learning Disabilities, 26,* 520-523.

Kavale, K. A., & Forness, S. R. (1999). *Efficacy of special education and related services* (Monograph of the American Association on Mental Retardation). Washington, DC: American Association on Mental Retardation.

Keel, M. C., Dangel, H. L., & Owens, S. H. (1999). Selecting instructional interventions for students with mild disabilities in inclusive classrooms. *Focus on Exceptional Children, 31*(8), 1-16.

Kelly, G. J., Chen, C., & Prothero, W. (2000). The epistemological framing of a discipline: Writing science in university oceanography. *Journal of Research in Science Teaching, 37*(7), 691-718.

Kerber, J. E. (Ed.). (1980). Vocabulary development. *Ohio Reading Teacher, 14*(2), 1-32. (ERIC Document Reproduction Service No. ED181413)

Kerka, S. (1992). *Higher order thinking skills in vocational education* (ERIC Digest No. 127). (ERIC Document Reproduction Service No. ED350487)

Kidd, J. W. (1970). The discriminatory repertoire — The basis of all learning. *Journal of Learning Disabilities, 3,* 530-533.

Kiewra, K. A. (1985). Learning from a lecture: An investigation of notetaking, review, and attendance at a lecture. *Human Learning, 44,* 73-77.

Kinder, D., & Bursuck, W. (1991). The search for a unified social studies curriculum: Does history really repeat itself? *Journal of Learning Disabilities, 24*(5), 270-275, 320.

King, A. (1992). Facilitating elaborative learning through guided student generated questioning. *Educational Psychologist, 27,* 111-126.

King, C. (2002). Teaching through explanatory stories: "The dynamic Earth's crust." *School Science Review, 83*(304), 63-72.

King, K. D. (2001). Conceptually-oriented mathematics teacher development: Improvisation as a metaphor. *For the Learning of Mathematics, 21*(3), 9-15.

King-Sears, M. E., Mercer, C. D., & Sindelar, P. T. (1992). Toward independence with keyword mnemonics: A strategy for science vocabulary instruction. *Remedial and Special Education, 13,* 22-33.

Kintsch, W., & van Dijk, T. A. (1978). *Toward a model of text comprehension and production.* Unpublished manuscript, University of Colorado, Boulder, Department of Psychology.

Klein, M. L. (1988). *Teaching reading comprehension and vocabulary.* Englewood Cliffs, NJ: Prentice Hall.

Kline, C. (1986). *Effects of guided notes on academic achievement of learning disabled high school students.* Unpublished master's thesis, Ohio State University.

Klorman, R. (1991). Cognitive event-related potentials in attention deficit disorder. *Journal of Learning Disabilities, 24*(3), 130-140.

Kops, C., & Belmont, I. (1985). Planning and organizing skills of poor school achievers. *Journal of Learning Disabilities, 18,* 8-14.

Kornblum, R. B. (1982). *A perceptuo-cognitive-motor approach to the special child.* (ERIC Document Reproduction Service No. ED223016)

Kotulak, R. (1996). *Inside the brain: Revolutionary discoveries of how the mind works.* Kansas City, KS: McMeel.

Kronick, D. (1978). An examination of psychosocial aspects of learning disabled adolescents. *Learning Disability Quarterly, 1*(4), 86-93.

Kruger, R. J., Kruger, J. J., Hugo, R., & Campbell, N. G. (2001). Relationship patterns between central auditory processing disorders and language disorders, learning disabilities, and sensory integration dysfunction. *Communication Disorders Quarterly, 22*(2), 87-98.

Kubina, R. M., Jr., & Cooper, J. O. (2000). Changing learning channels: An efficient strategy to facilitate instruction and learning. *Intervention in School and Clinic, 35*(3), 161-166.

Kumar, D., & Wilson, C. L. (1997). Computer technology, science education, and students with learning disabilities. *Journal of Science Education and Technology, 6,* 155-160.

Ladas, H. (1980). Summarizing research: A case study. *Review of Educational Research, 50*(4), 597-624.

Lai, S. K., & Hopkins, L. D. (1995). Can decisionmakers express multiattribute preferences using AHP and MUT? An experiment. *Environment & Planning B: Planning & Design, 22*(1), 21-35.

Lancaster, S., Mellard, D., & Hoffman, L. (2001). *Experiences of students with disabilities in selected community and technical colleges. The individual accommodations model: Accommodating students with disabilities in post-secondary settings.* (ERIC Document Reproduction Service No. ED452617) Retrieved February 3, 2003, from University of Kansas, Center for Research on Learning Web site: http://das.kucrl.org/iam/reports.html

Langan-Fox, J., Waycott, J. L., & Albert, K. (2000). Linear and graphic advance organizers: Properties and processing. *International Journal of Cognitive Ergonomics, 4*(1), 19-35.

Lapp, D., Fisher, D., & Flood, J. (1999). Integrating the language arts and content areas: Effective research-based strategies. *California Reader, 32*(4), 35-38.

Larson, K. A., & Gerber, M. M. (1987). Effects of social metacognitive training for enhancing overt behavior in learning disabled and low achieving delinquents. *Exceptional Children, 54,* 201-211.

Lazarus, B. D. (1988). Using guided notes to aid learning-disabled adolescents in secondary mainstream settings. *Pointer, 33*(1), 32-35.

Lazarus, B. D. (1991). Guided notes, review, and achievement of secondary students with learning disabilities in mainstream content courses. *Education and Treatment of Children, 14*(2), 112-127.

Lazarus, B. D. (1996). Guided notes: Effects with secondary and post secondary students with mild disabilities. *Education and Treatment of Children, 16*(3), 272-289. Retrieved December 17, 2002, from Professional Development Collection database.

Lebzelter, S., & Nowacek, E. J. (1999). Reading strategies for secondary students with mild disabilities. *Intervention in School & Clinic, 34*(4), 212-219.

Lenz, B. K., & Alley, G. R. (1983). *The effect of advance organizers on the learning and retention of learning disabled adolescents within the context of a cooperative planning model. Final Report.* (ERIC Document Reproduction Service No. ED257247)

Lenz, B. K., Alley, G. R., & Schumaker, J. B. (1987). Activating the inactive learner: Advance organizers in the secondary content classroom. *Learning Disability Quarterly, 10*(1), 53-67.

Lenz, B. K., Ehren, B. J., & Smiley, L. R. (1991). A goal attainment approach to improve completion of project type assignments by adolescents with learning disabilities. *Learning Disabilities Research and Practice, 6,* 166-176.

Lenz, K. (1998). How SIM addresses what is unique about teaching students with LD. *Stratenotes, 6*(7), 1-8.

Levin, J. R. (1988). Elaboration-based learning strategies: Powerful theory = powerful application. *Contemporary Educational Psychology, 13,* 191-205.

Levine, M. G. (1994). Effective ways to involve limited English students in the study of history. *Social Studies Review, 33*(2), 16-22.

Lloyd, J., et al. (1981). Predictable generalization in academic learning as a result of preskills and strategy training [Abstract]. *Learning Disability Quarterly, 4,* 4203-4216.

Lomika, L. L. (1998). "To gloss or not to gloss": An investigation of reading comprehension online. *Language Learning & Technology, 1*(2), 41-50.

Lorayne, H., & Lucas, J. (1974). *The memory book.* New York: Stein and Day.

Lowry, C. M. (1990). *Teaching adults with learning disabilities* (ERIC Digest No. 99). Retrieved January 1, 2003, from ERIC database.

Maccini, P., & Hughes, C. A. (2000). Effects of a problem-solving strategy on the introductory algebra performance of secondary students with learning disabilities. *Learning Disabilities Research and Practice, 15*(1), 10-21.

Maccini, P., McNaughton, D., & Ruhl, K. L. (1999). Algebra instruction for students with learning disabilities: Implications from a research review. *Learning Disability Quarterly, 22*(2), 113-126.

Maccini, P., & Ruhl, K. L. (2000). Effects of a graduated instructional sequence on the algebraic subtraction of integers by secondary students with learning disabilities. *Education & Treatment of Children, 23*(40), 465-490.

Malcolm, C. B., Polatajko, H. J., & Simons, J. (1990). A descriptive study of adults with suspected learning disabilities. *Journal of Learning Disabilities, 23,* 518-520.

Maley, A. (1993). Repetition revisited. *Guidelines, 15*(1), 1-11.

Marder, C., & D'Amico, R. (1992). *How well are youth with disabilities really doing? A comparison of youth with disabilities and youth in general. A report from the National Longitudinal Transition Study of Special Education Students.* (ERIC Document Reproduction Service No. ED369233) Marshall, K. J., Lussie, R., & Stradley, M. (1989). Social studies. In G. A. Robinson, J. R. Patton, E. A. Polloway, & L. R. Sargent (Eds.), *Best practices in mild mental disabilities* (pp. 155-178). Reston, VA: The Division on Mental Retardation of the Council for Exceptional Children.

Marshall, R. M., & Hynd, G. W. (1997). Academic achievement in ADHD subtypes. *Journal of Learning Disabilities, 30,* 635.

Martin, D. C., & Blanc, R. A. (1994). VSI: A pathway to mastery and persistence. *New Directions for Teaching and Learning, 60,* 83-91.

Mastropieri, M. A., & Scruggs, T. E. (1989). Constructing more meaningful relations: Mnemonic instruction for special populations. *Educational Psychology Review, 1*(2), 83-111.

Mastropieri, M. A., Emerick, K., & Scruggs, T. E. (1988). Mnemonic instruction of science concepts. *Behavioral Disorders, 14,* 48-56.

Mastropieri, M. A., & Scruggs, T. E. (1991). *Teaching students ways to remember: Strategies for learning mnemonically.* Cambridge, MA: Brookline Books.

Mastropieri, M. A., & Scruggs, T. E. (1994). Applications of mnemonic strategies with students with mild disabilities. *Remedial & Special Education, 15*(1). Retrieved December 29, 2002, from Academic Search Premier database.

Mastropieri, M. A., Scruggs, T. E., & Butcher, K. (1997). How effective is inquiry learning for students with mild disabilities? *Journal of Special Education, 31*(2), 199-211. Retrieved December 29, 2002, from Academic Search Premier database.

Mastropieri, M. A., Scruggs, T. E., & Mushinski, B. J. T. (1990). Teaching abstract vocabulary with the keyword method: Effects on recall and comprehension. *Journal of Learning Disabilities, 23*(2), 92-96,107.

Mays, F., & Imel, S. (1982). *Adult learning disabilities. Overview* (ERIC Fact Sheet No. 9). (ERIC Document Reproduction Service No. ED237797)

McDermott, P. C., & Rothenberg, J. J. (1999, April). *Teaching in high poverty, urban schools — Learning from practitioners and students.* Paper presented at the Annual Meeting of the American Educational Research Association,

Montreal, Quebec, Canada. (ERIC Document Reproduction Service No. ED431058)

McDorman, M. B. E. (1976). *The effects of directionality and complexity on learning disabled and normal subjects' learning sentence sequence, comprehending sentences and recognizing sentence relationships* [Abstract]. Doctoral dissertation, University of Georgia. (ERIC Document Reproduction Service No. ED140220)

McGinty, R. L., & Van Beynen, J. G. (1985). Activities: Deductive and analytical thinking. *Mathematics Teacher, 78*(3), 188-194.

McGrady, H. J., & Olson, D. A. (1967). *Visual and auditory learning processes in normal children and children with specific learning disabilities. Final report* [Abstract]. (ERIC Document Reproduction Service No. ED025894)

McKay, E. (1999). Exploring the effect of graphical metaphors on the performance of learning computer programming concepts in adult learners: A pilot study. *Educational Psychology, 19,* 471-488.

McLeod, J. (1966). Psychological and psycholinguistic aspects of severe reading disability in children: Some experimental studies. Proceedings of the Third Annual International Conference of the ACLD, Tulsa, OK. In S. Kirk & J. M. McCarthy (Eds.), *Learning disabilities: Selected papers* (pp. 286-305). Boston: Houghton Mifflin.

McLeskey, J. (1977, December). *Learning set acquisition by reading disabled and normal children.* Paper presented at the 27th Annual Meeting of the National Reading Conference, New Orleans, LA. (ERIC Document Reproduction Service No. ED151754)

McMillen, M. M., Kaufman, P., & Klein, S. (1997). *Dropout rates in the United States: 1995.* Washington, DC: U.S. Government Printing Office. (ERIC Document Reproduction Service No. ED410370)

McMurray, N. E. (1974). *The effects of four instructional strategies on the learning of a geometric concept by elementary and middle school EMR students.* Doctoral dissertation, University of Wisconsin, Madison. (ERIC Document Reproduction Service No. ED110334)

McNamara, J. K. (1999). *Social information processing in students with and without learning disabilities.* (ERIC Document Reproduction Service No. ED436867)

Mellard, D. F., & Alley, G. R. (1981). *Production deficiency vs. processing dysfunction: An experimental assessment of LD adolescents.* (ERIC Document Reproduction Service No. ED217650)

Meyer, V., & Keefe, D. (1998). Supporting volunteer tutors: Five strategies. *Adult Basic Education, 8*(2), 59-67.

Meyrowitz, J. (1980, November). *Analyzing media: Metaphors as methodologies.* Paper presented at the New England Conference on Teaching Students to Think, Amherst, MA. (ERIC Document Reproduction Service No. ED206030)

Michalak, L. (2000). *The story of Joseph from the Koran. Lessons from ORIAS Institute on history through literature in the 6th grade/7th grade core classrooms, 1998-2000.* (ERIC Document Reproduction Service No. ED463195)

Miles, C. (1981). The 4th "R" revisited. *Journal of Developmental & Remedial Education, 5*(1), 2-4.

Miller, D. L. (1993). Making the connection with language. *Arithmetic Teacher, 40,* 311-316.

Miller, G. A. (1956). The magical number seven, plus or minus two: Some limits on our capacity for processing information. *Psychological Review, 63,* 81-97.

Miller, S. P., & Mercer, C. D. (1993). Using data to learn about concrete-semiconcrete-abstract instruction for students with math disabilities. *Learning Disabilities Research and Practice, 8*(2), 89-96.

Mitchell, M. (Ed.). (1996). *School completion rates for children with disabilities: The role of economic and demographic factors. A Project ALIGN issue brief.* Richmond, VA: Donald Oswald, Commonwealth Institute for Child and Family Studies. (ERIC Document Reproduction Service No. ED408771)

Moffatt, C. W., et al. (1995, March). Discrimination of emotion, affective perspective- taking and empathy in individuals with mental retardation. *Education and Training in Mental Retardation and Developmental Disabilities, 30*(1), 76-85.

Molino, J. (1979). Metaphores, modeles et analogies dans les sciences (Metaphors, models, and analogies in the sciences). *Languages, 54,* 83-102.

Monroe, E. E. (1997). *Using graphic organizers to teach vocabulary: How does available research inform mathematics instruction?* (ERIC Document Reproduction Service No. ED414256)

Monroe, E. E., & Orme, M. P. (2002). Developing mathematical vocabulary. *Preventing School Failure, 46*(3), 139-142.

Monroe, E. E., & Pendergrass, M. R. (1997). *Effects of mathematical vocabulary instruction on fourth grade students.* Paper presented at the 1997 BYU Public School Partnership Symposium on Education. (ERIC Document Reproduction Service No. ED414182)

Montague, M. (1992). The effects of cognitive and metacognitive strategy instruction on the mathematical problem solving of middle school students with learning disabilities. *Journal of Learning Disabilities, 25*(4), 230-248.

Moon, K. (1992). Flowing through the American Revolution. *Social Studies Texan, 8*(1), 37.

Moore, D. W., & Readence, J. E. (1984). A quantitative and qualitative review of graphic organizer research. *Journal of Educational Research, 78,* 11-17.

Moore, D. W., Readence, J. E., & Rickelman, R. J. (1989). *Prereading activities for content area reading and learning* (2nd ed.). Newark, DE: International Reading Association.

Moran, M. (1980). *An investigation of the demands on oral language skills of learning disabled students in secondary classrooms* (Report No. 1). Lawrence, KS: University of Kansas, Institute for Research in Learning Disabilities.

Moreno, V., & DiVesta, F. J. (1994). Analogies (adages) as aids for comprehending structural relations in text. *Contemporary Educational Psychology, 19*(2), 179-198.

Morin, V. A., & Miller, S. P. (1998). Teaching multiplication to middle school students with mental retardation. *Education and Treatment of Children, 21*(1), 22-36.

Moseley, B., & Brenner, M. E. (1997). *Using multiple representations for conceptual change in pre-algebra: A comparison of variable usage with graphic and text based problems.* (ERIC Document Reproduction Service No. ED413184)

Mosher, D. J. (1999). *Improving vocabulary knowledge and reading attitudes in 4th grade students through direct vocabulary instruction.* Master's Action Research Project, Saint Xavier University. Chicago, IL: IRI/Skylight.

Moskal, B. M. (2000). *Scoring rubrics part I: What and when* (ERIC/AE Digest). (ERIC Document Reproduction Service No. ED446110)

Most, T., & Greenbank, A. (2000). Auditory, visual, and auditory-visual perception of emotions by adolescents with and without learning disabilities and their relationship to social skills. *Learning Disabilities: Research & Practice, 15*, 171-178.

Murray, J., & Whittenberger, D. (1983). The aggressively, severely behavior disordered child. *Journal of Learning Disabilities, 16*, 76-80.

Muscari, P. G. (1988). The metaphor in science and in the science classroom. *Science Education, 72*, 423-431.

Myer, B. J., & Ganschow, L. (1988). Profiles of frustration: Second language learners with specific learning disabilities. In J. F. Lalande II (Ed.), *Shaping the future of language education: FLES, articulation, and proficiency.* Report of Central States Conference on the Teaching of Foreign Language. (ERIC Document Reproduction Service No. ED292335)

Myrah, G. E., & Erlauer, L. (1999). The benefits of brain research: One district's story. *High School Magazine, 7*(1), 34-40.

National Center to Improve the Tools of Educators. (1998). NCITE's principles for evaluating and adapting curricula. *Teaching Exceptional Children, 31*(1), 84.

National Center to Improve the Tools of Educators, National Council of Teachers of Mathematics Standards. (1995). *Vocabulary acquisition: Curricular and instructional implications for diverse learners* (Technical Report No. 14). Retrieved November 25, 2002, from http://www.idea.uoregon.edu/~ncite/documents/techrep/reading.html

National Information Center for Children and Youth with Disabilities. (2000). *Reading and learning disabilities. Briefing paper 17 (FS17)* (3rd ed.). Available from http://www.nichcy.org

Neumark, V. (2001, March 23). Forging confident connections [Issue 4421, TES Curriculum Special]. *Times Educational Supplement*, p. 9.

No Child Left Behind Act, Pub. L. No. 107-110 (2001). Retrieved November 10, 2002 from http://www.nclb.gov

Noice, H., Noice, T., & Kennedy, C. (2000). Effects of enactment by professional actors at encoding and retrieval. *Memory, 8*(6), 353-363.

Novemsky, L., & Gautreau, R. (1997, October). Perception in the invisible world of physics. In *VisionQuest: Journeys toward visual literacy.* Selected readings from the Annual Conference of the International Visual Literacy Association, Cheyenne, WY. (ERIC Document Reproduction Service No. ED408978)

Oakhill, J., & Patel, S. (1991). Can imagery training help children who have comprehension problems? *Journal of Research in Reading, 14,* 106-115.

Oetting, J. B., & Rice, M. L. (1995). Quick incidental learning (QUIL) of words by school-age children with and without SLI. *Journal of Speech & Hearing Research, 38*(2), 434. Retrieved January 4, 2003, from Academic Search Premier database.

Ogle, D. M. (1986). K-W-L: A teaching model that develops active reading of expository text. *Reading Teacher, 39,* 564-570.

Oja, L. A. (1996). Using story frames to develop reading comprehension. *Journal of Adolescent & Adult Literacy, 40,* 129-130.

Okolo, C. M., & Bahr, C. M. (1995). Increasing achievement motivation of elementary school students with mild disabilities. *Intervention in School and Clinic, 30*(5), 279-286, 312. Retrieved December 21, 2002, from Professional Development Collection database.

Ollmann, H. E. (1989). Cause and effect in the real world. *Journal of Reading, 33,* 224-225.

Olson, M. W. (1980, January). *Pattern guides: An alternative for content teachers.* Paper presented at the 89th Annual Meeting of the Southwest Regional Conference of the International Reading Association, Albuquerque, NM. (ERIC Document Reproduction Service No. ED185580)

Orlow, M. (1974). Low tolerance for frustration: Target group for reading disabilities. *Reading Teacher, 27,* 669-674.

Paivio, A. (1990). *Mental representations: A dual coding approach.* New York: Oxford University Press.

Paivio, A., & Walsh, M. (1994). Concreteness effects on memory: When and why? *Journal of Experimental Psychology/Learning, Memory & Cognition, 20*(5), 1196-1205.

Pauk, W. (1978). A notetaking format: Magical but not automatic. *Reading World, 18*(1), 96-97.

Peters, C. (1974). A comparison between the Frayer model of concept attainment and the textbook approach to concept attainment. *Reading Research Quarterly, 10,* 252-254.

Peterson, S. K., Mercer, C. D., Tragash, J., & O'Shea, L. (1987). *Comparing the concrete to abstract teaching sequence to abstract instruction for initial place value skills* (Monograph #19). Gainesville, FL: University of Florida, Shands Teaching Hospital. (ERIC Document Reproduction Service No. ED301777)

Pimm, D. (1981). Metaphor and analogy in mathematics. *For the Learning of Mathematics, 1*(3), 47-50.

Pimm, D. (1988). Mathematical metaphor. *For the Learning of Mathematics, 8*(1), 30-34.

Pittelman, S. D., Heimlich, J. E., Berglund, R. L., & French, M. P. (1991). *Semantic feature analysis: Classroom applications.* Newark, DE: International Reading Association.

Pollio, H. R. (1990). *Remembrances of lectures past: Notes and note-taking in the college classroom. Teaching/Learning Issues.* Knoxville, TN: University of Tennessee, Learning Research Center. (ERIC Document Reproduction Service No. ED364179)

Polloway, E. A., Patton, J. R., Epstein, M. H., Aquah, T., Decker, T. W., & Carse, C. (1991). *Characteristics and services in learning disabilities: A report on elementary programs.* (ERIC Document Production Service No. ED342158)

Polloway, E. A., Patton, J. R., & Serna, L. (2001). *Strategies for teaching learners with special needs.* Upper Saddle River, NJ: Merrill/Prentice Hall.

Porter, A. C., & Brophy, J. (1988). Synthesis of research on good teaching: Insights from the work of the Institute for Research on Teaching. *Educational Leadership, 45*(8), 74-85.

Porter, P. (1993). Activities for social math. Pull-out feature. *Social Studies and the Young Learner, 6*(1), 1-4.

Potts, B. (1993). *Improving the quality of student notes* (ERIC/AE Digest). (ERIC Document Reproduction Service No. ED366645)

Powell, M. B., & Thomson, D. M. (1996). Children's memory of an occurrence of a repeated event: Effects of age, repetition, and retention interval across three question types. *Child Development, 67*(5), 1988-2004.

Powers, M. H. (1984). A computer assisted problem solving method for beginning chemistry students. *Journal of Computers in Mathematics and Science Teaching, 4*(1), 13-19.

Prawat, R. S. (1989). Promoting access to knowledge, strategy, and disposition in students: A research synthesis. *Review of Educational Research, 59*(1), 1-41.

Pressley, M., & Harris, K. R. (1990). What we really know about strategy instruction. *Educational Leadership, 48*(1), 31-34.

Putnam, M. L. (1992a). Characteristics of questions on tests administered by mainstream secondary classroom teachers. *Learning Disabilities Research & Practice, 7*, 129-136.

Putnam, M. L. (1992b). The testing practices of mainstream secondary classroom teachers. *Remedial and Special Education, 13*(3), 11-21.

Putnam, M. L., Deshler, D. D., & Schumaker, J. B. (1993). The investigation of setting demands: A missing link in learning strategy instruction. In L. S. Meltzer (Ed.), *Strategy assessment and instruction for students with learning disabilities* (pp. 325-354). Austin, TX: PRO-ED.

Raphael, T. E., & Kirschner, B. M. (1985). *The effects of instruction in compare/ contrast text structure on sixth-grade students' reading comprehension and writing products* (Research Series No. 161). (ERIC Document Reproduction Service No. ED264537)

Rauschenbach, J. (1994). Checking for student understanding — Four techniques. *Journal of Physical Education, Recreation and Dance, 64*(4), 60-63.

Reid, D. (2002). Virtual reality and the person — environment experience. *CyberPsychology & Behavior, 5,* 559-565.

Reis, S. M., Neu, T. W., & McGuire, J. M. (1995). *Talents in two places: Case studies of high ability students with learning disabilities who have achieved* (Research Monograph 95114). (ERIC Document Reproduction Service No. ED388021)

Rekrut, M. D. (1996). Effective vocabulary instruction. *High School Journal, 80*(1), 66-75.

Resnick, M., & Wilensky, U. (1998). Diving into complexity: Developing probabilistic decentralized thinking through role-playing activities. *Journal of the Learning Sciences, 7*(2), 153-172.

Renick, M. J. (1985, April). *Assessing learning disabled children's motivational orientations in the classroom.* Paper presented at the Biennial Meeting of the Society for Research in Child Development, Toronto, Canada. (ERIC Document Reproduction Service No. ED260568)

Rice, M. L., & Buhr, J. A. (1992). Specific-language-impaired children's quick incidental learning of words: The effect of a pause. *Journal of Speech & Hearing Research, 35*(5), 1040. Retrieved December 18, 2002, from Academic Search Premier database.

Rice, M. L., & Oetting, J. B. (1994). Frequency of input effects on word comprehension of children with specific language impairment. *Journal of Speech & Hearing Research, 37*(1), 106-123. Retrieved December 18, 2002, from Academic Search Premier database.

Richards, G. P., Samuels, J., Ternure, J. E., & Ysseldyke, J. E. (1990). Sustained and selective attention in children with learning disabilities. *Journal of Learning Disabilities, 23,* 129-136. Retrieved January 14, 2003, from Academic Search Premier database.

Ritger, S. D., & Cummins, R. H. (1991). Using student-created metaphors to comprehend geologic time. *Journal of Geological Education, 39*(1), 9-11.

Robb, L. (1999). Identify, preteach, connect. *Instructor, 108*(8), 6.

Robb, L. (2002). Tackling tough words. *Instructor, 110* (3), 35-36, 38.

Rosen, C. L. (1968). An investigation of perceptual training and reading achievement in first grade [Abstract]. *American Journal of Optometry, 45,* 322-332. (ERIC Document Reproduction Service No. ED025400)

Rowe, M. B. (1976). The pausing principle: Two invitations to inquiry. *Research on College Science Teaching, 5,* 258-259.

Rowe, M. B. (1980). Pausing principles and their effects on reasoning in science. *New Directions in Community College, 31,* 27-34.

Rowe, M. B. (1983). Getting chemistry off the killer course list. *Journal of Chemical Education, 60,* 954-956.

Rowell, R. M. (1975, March). *Children's concepts of natural phenomena: Use of a cognitive mapping approach to describe these concepts.* Paper presented at the 48th Annual Meeting of the National Association for Research in Science Teaching, Los Angeles, CA. (ERIC Document Reproduction Service No. ED106117)

Rubenstein, R. N. (2000). Word origins: Building communication connections. *Mathematics Teaching in the Middle School, 5*(8), 493. Retrieved January 1, 2003, from Academic Search Premier database.

Rubman, C. N., & Waters, H. S. (2000). A, B seeing: The role of constructive processes in children's comprehension monitoring. *Journal of Educational Psychology, 92,* 503-514.

Ruhl, K. L., Hughes, C. A., & Gajar, A. H. (1990). Efficacy of the pause procedure for enhancing learning disabled and nondisabled college students' long- and short-term recall of facts presented through lecture. *Learning Disability Quarterly, 13,* 55-64.

Ryan, M., Miller, D., & Witt, J. C. (1984). A comparison of the use of orthographic structure in word discrimination by learning disabled and normal children. *Journal of Learning Disabilities, 17,* 38-40.

Saenz, L. M., & Fuchs, L. S. (2002). Examining the reading difficulty of secondary students with learning disabilities: Expository versus narrative text. *Remedial and Special Education, 23*(1), 31-42.

Salend, S. J., & Gajria, M. (1995). Increasing the homework completion states of students with mild disabilities. *Remedial and Special Education, 16,* 271-278. Retrieved January 4, 2003, from Academic Search Premier database.

Salyer, B. K., Curran, C., & Thyfault, A. (2002, March). What can I use tomorrow? Strategies for accessible math and science curriculum for diverse learners in rural schools. In *No child left behind: The vital role of rural schools.* 22nd Annual National Conference Proceedings of the American Council on Rural Special Education (ACRES), Reno, NV. (ERIC Document Reproduction Service No. ED463109)

Santa, C. M., et al. (1988). *Content reading including study systems: Reading, writing and studying across the curriculum* [Abstract]. Dubuque, IA: Kendall/Hunt. (ERIC Document Reproduction Service No. ED372363)

Sanza, J. (1982). *Category priming in the lexical decision task and evidence of repetition effects.* Paper presented at the 28th Annual Meeting of the Southeastern Psychological Association, New Orleans, LA. (ERIC Document Reproduction Service No. ED215337)

Satcher, J. (1990). *Accommodating workers with learning disabilities.* (ERIC Document Reproduction Service No. ED320099)

Scerbo, M. W., Warm, J. S., & Dember, W. N. (1992). The role of time and cuing in a college lecture. *Contemporary Educational Psychology, 17*(4), 312-328.

Schiff, M. M., Kaufman, A. S., & Kaufman, N. L. (1981). Scatter analysis of WISC-R profiles for learning disabled children with superior intelligence. *Journal of Learning Disabilities, 14*(7), 400-404. Retrieved January 1, 2003, from the Professional Development Collection database.

Schiff, P. (2000). Shakespeare answering machines: A popular culture and creative dramatics exercise. *Exercise Exchange, 45*(2), 6-7.

Schirmer, B. R., & Bailey, J. (2000). Writing assessment rubric: An instructional approach with struggling writers. *Teaching Exceptional Children, 33*(1), 52-58.

Scholes, C. (1998). General science: A diagnostic teaching unit. *Intervention in School and Clinic, 34,* 107-114. Retrieved January 4, 2003, from Academic Search Premier database.

Schur, J. B. (1980). EJ workshop: Helping students to visualize what they read. *English Journal, 69*(2), 64-65.

Schwartz, R. M., & Raphael, T. E. (1985). Concept of definition: A key to improving students' vocabulary. *Reading Teacher, 39,* 198-205.

Schwarz, R., & Burt, M. (1995). *ESL instruction for learning disabled adults* (ERIC Digest). (ERIC Document Reproduction Service No. ED379966)

Schweitzer, K., Zimmermann, P., & Koch, W. (2000). Sustained attention, intelligence, and the crucial role of perceptual processes. *Learning and Individual Differences, 12*(3), 271-287. Retrieved February 13, 2003, from the Professional Development Collection database.

Scott, K. S. (1993). Multisensory mathematics for children with mild disabilities. *Exceptionality, 4*(2), 97-111.

Scott, T. M., & Nelson, C. M. (1998). Confusion and failure in facilitating generalized social responding in the school setting: Sometimes 2 + 2 = 5. *Behavioral Disorders, 23,* 264-275.

Scruggs, T. E., & Mastropieri, M. A. (1989). Reconstructive elaborations: A model for content area learning. *American Educational Research Journal, 26,* 311-327.

Scruggs, T. E., & Mastropieri, M. A. (1990a). The case for mnemonic instruction: From laboratory research to classroom applications. *Journal of Special Education, 24*(1), 7-33. Retrieved January 4, 2003, from Professional Development Collection database.

Scruggs, T. E., & Mastropieri, M. A. (1990b). Mnemonic instruction for students with LD: What it is and what it does. *Learning Disability Quarterly, 19,* 271-280.

Seitz, S., & Scheerer, J. (1983). *Learning feasibilities: Introduction and strategies for college teaching.* (ERIC Document Reproduction Service No. ED235864)

Seligman, M. E. P. (1975). *Helplessness: On depression, development, and death.* San Francisco: W. H. Freeman.

Semple, J. L. (1992). Semple math: A basic mathematics program for beginning, high-risk and/or remedial students. Attleboro, MA: Stevenson Learning Skills, Inc.

Seung-Hoon, Y., Jun-Sang, K., & Tai-Yoo, K. (2001). Value-focused thinking about strategic management of radio spectrum for mobile communications. *Telecommunications Policy, 25*(10/11), 703-719.

Sexton, T. G., & Poling, D. R. (1973). *Can intelligence be taught?* Bloomington, IN: Phi Delta Kappa Educational Foundation.

Shields, J. M., & Heron, T. E. (1989). Teaching organizational skills to students with learning disabilities. *Teaching Exceptional Children, 21*(2), 8-13.

Siegel, D. J. (1999). *The developing mind: Toward a neurobiology of interpersonal experience.* New York: Guilford.

Siegler, R. S. (1998). *Children's thinking* (3rd ed.). Upper Saddle River, NJ: Erlbaum.

Silbert, J., Carnine, D., & Stein, M. (1990). *Direct instruction mathematics* (2nd ed.). Columbus, OH: Merrill.

Simpson, S. B. (1992). The impact of an intensive multisensory reading program on a population of learning-disabled delinquents. *Annals of Dyslexia, 42,* 54-66.

Simpson, T. J. (1997). Tri-Coding of Information. In *VisionQuest: Journeys toward visual literacy.* Selected readings from the 28th Annual Conference of the International Visual Literacy Association, Cheyenne, WY. (ERIC Document Reproduction Service No. ED408953)

Singer, H., & Donlan, D. (1980). *Reading and learning from text.* Boston, MA: Little Brown.

Sisterhen, D. H., & Gerber, P. J. (1989). Auditory, visual, and multisensory non-verbal social perception in adolescents with and without learning disabilities. *Journal of Learning Disabilities, 22,* 245-249, 257. Retrieved January 25, 2003, from Academic Search Premier database.

Skrtic, T. M. (1980). *Formal reasoning abilities for learning disabled adolescents: Implications for mathematics instruction.* (ERIC Document Reproduction Service No. ED217624)

Smagorinsky, P. (2000). *What English educators have to say to assessment specialists.* (ERIC Document Reproduction Service No. ED446050)

Smith, D. D. (1981). *Teaching the learning disabled.* Englewood Cliffs, NJ: Prentice Hall.

Smith, P. L. (1986, January). *The effects of organizational cues on learners' processing of instructional prose.* Paper presented at the Annual Convention of the Association for Educational Communications and Technology, Las Vegas, NV.

Smith, P. L., & Friend, M. (1986). Training learning disabled adolescents in a strategy for using text structure to aid recall of instructional prose. *Learning Disabilities Research, 2*(1), 38-44.

Smith, S. W. (1992). Effects of a metacognitive strategy on aggressive acts and anger behavior of elementary and secondary-aged students. *Florida Educational Research Council Research Bulletin, 24,* 1-2. (ERIC Document Reproduction Service No. ED355687)

Soles, D. (2001, March). *Sharing scoring guides.* Paper presented at the 52nd Annual Meeting of the Conference on College Composition and Communication, Denver, CO. (ERIC Document Reproduction Service No. ED450379)

Sparks, R. L., & Ganschow, L. (1993). The effects of multisensory structured language instruction on native language and foreign language aptitude skills of at-risk high school foreign language learners: A replication and follow-up study. *Annals of Dyslexia, 43,* 194-216.

Stanovich, K. E. (1993). Dysrationalia: A new specific learning disability. *Journal of Learning Disabilities, 26,* 501-515.

Stein, H. (1988). On that note . . . *Science and Children, 26*(3), 16-18.

Stencel, J., & Barkoff, A. (1993). Protein synthesis: Role playing in the classroom. *American Biology Teacher, 55*(2), 102-103.

Sternberg, R. J. (1993). Would you rather take orders from Kirk or Spock? The relation between rational thinking and intelligence. *Journal of Learning Disabilities, 26,* 516-519. Retrieved December 23, 2002, from Academic Search Premier database.

Sternberg, R. J. (1994). What if the construct of dysrationalia were an example of itself? *Educational Researcher, 23*(4), 22-23.

Stevenson, H. W., Hofe, B. K., & Randall, B. (1999). *Middle childhood: Education and schooling.* Unpublished manuscript, University of Michigan, Ann Arbor, Department of Psychology.

Stone, C. A., Forman, E. A., Anderson, C. J., Matthews, F., Rupert, J., & Fyfe, B. (1984). *Assessment and remediation of complex reasoning in specific subgroups of learning disabled adolescents. Final Report.* (ERIC Document Reproduction Service No. ED261505)

Stratford, B., & Metcalfe, J. A. (1982). Recognition, reproduction and recall in children with Down's Syndrome. *Australia and New Zealand Journal of Developmental Disabilities, 8*(3), 125-132.

Stratford, B., & Mills, K. (1984). Colour discrimination in mentally handicapped children with particular reference to Down's Syndrome. *Australia and New Zealand Journal of Developmental Disabilities, 10*(3), 151-55.

Sturm, W., & Zimmermann, P. (2000). Aufmerksamkeitsstorungen (Attention deficits). In W. Sturm, M. Herrmann, & C. W. Wallesch (Eds.), *Lehrbuch der klinischen Neuropsychologie* (pp. 345-365). Lisse: Swets and Zeitlinger.

Sultana, Q., & Klecker, B. M. (1999a, November). *Evaluation of First-Year Teachers' Lesson Objectives by Bloom's Taxonomy*. Paper presented at the Annual Meeting of the Mid-South Educational Research Association, Point Clear, AL. (ERIC Document Reproduction Service No. ED436524)

Sultana, Q., & Klecker, B. M. (1999b). *Two decades of research in learning disabilities: Reading comprehension, expressive writing, problem solving, self-concept.* Paper presented at Keys to Successful Learning: A National Summit on Research in Learning Disabilities, Washington, DC. (ERIC Document Reproduction Service No. ED430365) Available from National Center for Learning Disabilities Web site, http://www.ncld.org

Suritsky, S. K. (1992). Notetaking difficulties and approaches reported by university students with learning disabilities. *Journal of Postsecondary Education and Disability, 10*, 3-10.

Suritsky, S. K., & Hughes, C. A. (1991). Benefits of notetaking: Implications for secondary and post-secondary students with learning disabilities. *Learning Disability Quarterly, 14*, 7-18.

Swanson, H. L. (1994). Short-term memory and working memory: Do both contribute to our understanding of academic achievement in children and adults with learning disabilities? *Journal of Learning Disabilities, 27*, 34-50. Retrieved December 31, 2002, from Academic Search Premier database.

Swanson, H. L. (1999, May). *Intervention research for adolescents with learning disabilities: A meta-analysis of outcomes related to higher-order processing.* A paper presented at Keys to Successful Learning: A National Summit on Research in Learning Disabilities, Washington, DC. (ERIC Document Reproduction Service No. ED430365) Retrieved November 10, 2002, from National Center for Learning Disabilities Web site: http://www.ncld.org

Swanson, H. L. (2001). Research on interventions for adolescents with learning disabilities: A meta-analysis of outcomes related to higher order processing. *Elementary School Journal, 101*, 331-349.

Swanson, H. L., & Hoskyn, M. (2001). Instructing adolescents with learning disabilities: A component and composite analysis. *Learning Disabilities Research and Practice, 16*(2), 109-120.

Swanson, J. E. (1972). *The effects of number of positive and negative instances, concept definition, and emphasis of relevant attributes on the attainment of three environmental concepts by sixth-grade children: Report from the Conditions of Learning and Instruction Component of Program 1* (Technical Report No. 244). (ERIC Document Reproduction Service No. ED073412)

Tam, B. K. Y., & Scott, M. L. (1996). Three group instructional strategies for students with limited English proficiency in vocational education. *Journal for Vocational Special Needs Education, 19*(1), 31-36.

Tarquin, P., & Walker, S. (1997). *Creating success in the classroom: Visual organizers and how to use them.* Englewood, CO: Teacher Ideas Press.

Teachers' Curriculum Institute. (1999). *History alive! Engaging all learners in the diverse classroom* (2nd ed.). Mountain View, CA: Author.

Terepocki, M., Kruk, R. S., & Willows, D. M. (2002). The incidence and nature of letter orientation errors in reading disability. *Journal of Learning Disabilities, 35*, 214-233. Retrieved December 18, 2002, from the Academic Search Premier database.

Thomas, R. G. (1992). *Cognitive theory-based teaching and learning in vocational education* (Information Series No. 349). (ERIC Document Reproduction Service No. ED345109)

Titsworth, B., & Kiewra, K. (1998, April). *By the numbers: The effect of organizational lecture cues on notetaking and achievement.* Paper presented at the American Educational Research Association Convention, San Diego, CA.

Titsworth, B. S. (2001). The effects of teacher immediacy, use of organizational lecture cues, and students' notetaking on cognitive learning. *Communication Education, 50*, 283-297.

Tobin, K. (1990). *Metaphors and images in teaching. What research says to the science and mathematics teacher* (No. 5). (ERIC Document Reproduction Service No. ED370786)

Tolfa, D., Scruggs, T. E., & Mastropieri, M. A. (1985). *Extended mnemonic instruction with learning disabled students.* (ERIC Document Reproduction Service No. ED267544)

Tominey, M. F. (1996). *Attributional style as a predictor of academic success for students with learning disabilities and/or Attention Deficit Disorder in postsecondary education* [Abstract]. (ERIC Document Reproduction Service No. ED407815)

Torgesen, J. K. (1982). The learning disabled child as an inactive learner: Educational implications. *Topics in Learning and Learning Disabilities, 2*, 45-52.

Torgesen, J. K. (1988). Studies of children with learning disabilities who perform poorly on memory span tasks. *Journal of Learning Disabilities, 21*, 605-612. Retrieved December 30, 2002, from the Academic Search Premier database.

Toro, P. A., Weissberg, R. P., Guare, J., & Libenstein, N. L. (1990). A comparison of children with and without learning disabilities on social problem-solving skill, school behavior, and family background. *Journal of Learning Disabilities, 23*, 115-120. Retrieved December 28, 2002, from Academic Search Premier database.

Tversky, A. (1969). Intransitivity of preferences. *Psychological Review, 76*, 31-48.

Tversky, A. (1972). Elimination by aspects: A theory of choice. *Psychological Review, 79*, 281-299.

Tyas, T., & Cabot, J. (1999). A role-play to illustrate the energy changes occurring in an exothermic reaction. *School Science Review, 80*(293), 113-114.

Utzinger, J. (1982). *Logic for everyone. Alternative techniques for teaching logic to learning disabled students in the university. A part of the HELDS Project (Higher Education for Learning Disabled Students).* (ERIC Document Reproduction Service No. ED234549)

Vacca, R. T., & Vacca, A. L. (1996). *Content area reading* (5th ed.). New York: Harper Collins/College.

Valas, H. (2001). Learned helplessness and psychological adjustment II: Effects of learning disabilities and low achievement. *Scandinavian Journal of Educational Research, 45*(2), 101-114. Retrieved December 23, 2002, from Professional Development Collection database.

Van Dyke, F. (1995). Activities: A visual approach to deductive reasoning. *Mathematics Teacher, 88,* 481-486, 492-494.

van Someren, M. W., Reimann, P., Boshuizen, H. P. A., & de Jong, T. (Eds.). (1998). *Learning with multiple representations* (Advances in learning and instruction series). (ERIC Document Reproduction Service No. ED437929)

Vine, F. L. (1999). *Self-esteem within children, adolescents, and adults diagnosed with Attention-Deficit Hyperactivity Disorder: A review of the literature.* Doctoral Research Paper, Biola University, La Mirada, CA. (ERIC Document Reproduction Service No. ED437768)

Vygotsky, L. S. (1962). *Thought and language* (E. Hanfmann & G. Vakar, Eds. & Trans.). Cambridge, MA: M. I. T. Press.

Waber, D. P., Weiler, M. D., Wolff, P. H., Bellinger, D., Marcus, D. J., Ariel, R., Forebes, P., & Wypig, D. (2001). Processing of rapid auditory stimuli in school-age children referred for evaluation of learning disorders. *Child Development, 72*(1), 37-49.

Walton, S., & Hoblitt, R. (1989). Using story frames in content-area classes. *Social Studies, 80*(3), 103-106.

Wang, M. C. (1987). Toward achieving educational excellence for all students: Program design and instructional outcomes. *Remedial and Special Education, 8*(3), 25-34.

Wang, M. C., Haertel, G. D., & Walberg, H. J. (1993/1994). What helps students learn? *Educational Leadership, 51*(4), 74-79.

Ward-Lonergan, J. M., Liles, B. Z., & Anderson, A. M. (1998). Listening comprehension and recall abilities in adolescents with language-learning disabilities and without disabilities for social studies lectures. *Journal of Communication Disorders, 31*(1), 1-32.

Washington, V. M. (1989). Semantic mapping: A heuristic for helping learning disabled students write reports. *Journal of Reading, Writing, and Learning Disabilities International, 4*(1), 17-25.

Watson, B. U. (1991). Some relationships between intelligence and auditory discrimination. *Journal of Speech and Hearing Research, 3,* 621-627.

Webb, N. (1995). The textbook business: Education's big dirty secret. *Harvard Education Letter, 11*(4), 1-3.

Webster, R. E., Hall, C. W., Brown, M. B., & Bolen, L. M. (1996). Memory modality differences in children with attention deficit hyperactive disorder with and without learning disabilities. *Psychology in the Schools, 33,* 193-201.

Weiler, M. D., Harris, N. S., Marcus, D. J., Bellinger, D., Kosslyn, S. M., & Waber, D. P. (2000). Speed of information processing in children referred for learning problems: Performance on a visual filtering test. *Journal of Learning Disabilities, 33,* 538-550. Retrieved January 1, 2003, from Academic Search Premier database.

Weisberg, R., & Balajthy, E. (1989). *Effects of topic familiarity and training in generative learning activities on poor readers' comprehension of comparison/contrast expository text structure: Transfer to real-world materials.* Paper presented at the 34th Annual Meeting of the International Reading Association, New Orleans, LA. (ERIC Document Reproduction Service No. ED305618)

Welch, M. (1992). The PLEASE strategy: A metacognitive learning strategy for improving the paragraph writing of students with mild learning disabilities. *Learning Disability Quarterly, 15,* 119-128.

Werker, J. F., Bryson, S. E., & Wassonberg, K. (1985, April). *Consonant errors of severely disabled readers.* Paper presented at the Meeting of the Society for Research in Child Development, Toronto, Ontario, Canada. (ERIC Document Reproduction Service No. ED259318)

Westendorf, D. K., Cape, E. L., & Skrtic, T. M. (1982). *A naturalistic study of post-secondary setting demands.* Unpublished manuscript, University of Kansas. Retrieved February 2, 2003, from Academic Search Premier database.

Whitin, P., & Whitin, D. J. (2000). *Math is language too: Talking and writing in the mathematics classroom.* Urbana, IL: National Council of Teachers of English.

Whitman, N. A. (1982). *There is no gene for good teaching: A handbook on lecturing for medical teachers.* (ERIC Document Reproduction Service No. ED233624)

Wiens, J. W. (1983). Metacognition and the adolescent passive learner. *Journal of Learning Disabilities, 16,* 144-149.

Williams, M. L. (1995). The conundrum of Federalism: Can there be strong state governments and a strong national government? Teaching Strategy. *Update on Law-Related Education, 19*(3), 9-11.

Wilson, D. R., & David, W. J. (1994). Academic intrinsic motivation and attitudes toward school and learning of learning disabled students. *Learning Disabilities Research and Practice, 9*(3), 148-156.

Wilson, E. K. (1997). A trip to historic Philadelphia on the web. *Social Education, 61,* 170-175.

Wing, H. (1980). Age, sex, and repetition effects with an abilities test battery. *Applied Psychological Measurement, 4*(2), 141-155.

Witzel, B., Smith, S. W., & Brownell, M. T. (2001). How can I help students with learning disabilities in algebra? *Intervention in School and Clinic, 37*(2), 101-105.

Wixson, K. K. (1986). Vocabulary instruction and children's comprehension of basal stories. *Reading Research Quarterly, 21,* 317-329.

Wolfe, D. E., & Jones, G. (1982). Integrating total physical response strategy in a Level I Spanish class. *Foreign Language Annals, 15*(4), 273-280.

Wolfe, P. (2001). *Brain matters: Translating research into classroom practice.* Alexandria, VA: Association for Supervision and Curriculum Development.

Wong, B. Y. L. (1985). Metacognition and learning disabilities. In T. J. Waller, D. Forrest-Pressley, & E. MacKinnon (Eds.), *Metacognition, cognition, and human performance* (pp. 137-180). New York: Academic Press.

Wong, B. Y. L. (1986). Metacognition and special education: A review of a view. *Journal of Special Education, 20*(1), 9-29.

Wong, B. Y. L. (2000). Writing strategies instruction for expository essays for adolescents with and without learning disabilities. *Topics in Language Disorders, 20*(4), 29-44.

Wong, B. Y. L., & Jones, W. (1982). Increasing metacomprehension in learning-disabled and normally-achieving students through self-questioning training. *Learning Disability Quarterly, 5,* 228-240.

Wood, D. D. (1988). Guiding students through informational text. *Reading Teacher, 41*(9), 912-920.

Wood, K. D. (1989, November). *The study guide: A strategy review.* Paper presented at the 33rd Annual Meeting of the College Reading Association, Philadelphia, PA. (ERIC Document Reproduction Service No. ED322472)

Wood, K. D., Lapp, D., & Flood, J. (1992). *Guiding readers through text: A review of study guides.* Newark, DE: International Reading Association.

Wood, S. (1995). Developing an understanding of time-sequencing issues. *Teaching History, 79,* 11-15.

Woods, J., Young, P. L., & Judd, P. A. (1985). *The expanded placement process. Work center staff training programs.* (ERIC Document Reproduction Service No. ED269949)

Woodward, A., & Elliott, D. L. (1990). Textbook use and teacher professionalism. In D. L. Elliott & A. Woodward (Eds.), *Textbooks and schooling in the U.S.* (89th Yearbook of the National Society for the Study of Education, Part 1, pp. 178-193). Chicago: National Society for the Study of Education.

Worsley, D. (1988). Visualization and objective observation. *Teachers and Writers Magazine, 19*(5), 1-3.

Wu, H.-K., Krajcik, J. S., & Soloway, E. (2001). Promoting understanding of chemical representations: Students' use of a visualization tool in the classroom. *Journal of Research in Science Teaching, 38*, 821-842.

Wyatt, M., & Hayes, D. A. (1991). *Analogies as sources of interference to learning from texts with study guides.* (ERIC Document Reproduction Service No. ED351669)

Yoho, R. F. (1985, March-April). *Effectiveness of four concept teaching strategies on social studies concept acquisition and retention.* A paper presented at the annual meeting of the American Educational Research Association, Chicago, IL. (ERIC Document Reproduction Service No. ED260993)

Yopp, H. K., & Yopp, R. H. (1996). *Literature-based reading activities* (2nd ed.). Des Moines, IA: Allyn and Bacon.

Young, B. N., Whitley, M. E., & Helton, C. (1998, November). *Students' perceptions of characteristics of effective teachers.* Paper presented at the Annual Meeting of the Mid-South Educational Research Association, New Orleans, LA. (ERIC Document Reproduction Service No. ED426962)

Zeaman, D., & House, B. J. (1961). *Role of attention in retardate discrimination learning. Progress Report No. 3.* (ERIC Document Reproduction Service No. ED130607)

Zera, D. A., & Lucian, D. G. (2001). Self-organization and learning disabilities: A theoretical perspective for the interpretation and understanding of dysfunction. *Learning Disability Quarterly, 24*, 107-118.

Zetts, R. A., Horvat, M. A., & Langone, J. (1995). Effects of a community-based progressive resistance training program on the work productivity of adolescents with moderate to severe intellectual disabilities. *Education and Training in Mental Retardation and Developmental Disabilities, 30*(2), 166-178.

Zurcher, R. (1995). Memory and learning assessment: Missing from the learning disabilities identification process for too long. *LD Forum, 21*, 27-30.

# Index

**CORWIN PRESS**

The Corwin Press logo—a raven striding across an open book—represents the happy union of courage and learning. We are a professional-level publisher of books and journals for K-12 educators, and we are committed to creating and providing resources that embody these qualities. Corwin's motto is "Success for All Learners."